SPEEDWAY

IN THE NORTH-WEST

SPEEDWAY

IN THE NORTH-WEST

ADRIAN PAVEY

ASSISTED BY TONY JACKSON

TEMPUS

Front cover: *Kauko Nieminen in action at Derwent Park in 2002.* (From the author's collection.)

Back Cover: *Sam Marsland, Roland Stobbart and Maurice Stobbart at Lonsdale Park, Workington, 1937.*

First published 2004

Tempus Publishing Ltd
The Mill, Brimscombe Port
Stroud, Gloucestershire GL5 2QG

© Adrian Pavey, 2004

British Library Cataloguing in Publication Data.
A catalogue record for this book is available from the British Library.

ISBN 0 7524 3192 7

Typesetting and origination by Tempus Publishing.
Printed in Great Britain by Midway Colour Print, Wiltshire

CONTENTS

ACKNOWLEDGEMENTS

There are so many people to thank for their help in writing and illustrating this book, I don't really know where to start.

Firstly, I must thank Tony Jackson, the unofficial Workington Historian, who virtually researched and wrote the Workington chapters on his own. Tony also provided the background information on the Northside track and donated most of the Workington photographs and illustrations too. What this man doesn't know about speedway in Workington isn't worth knowing and this book would not have been possible without him.

Special thanks must also go to Trevor James, Ian Somerville and Barry Stephenson, who have supplied no end of material (sometimes without me even asking!).

Riders and officials (and their families and friends) have been especially forthcoming. It has been my pleasure to either meet or correspond with David Alderson, Cliff Allison, Shaun Bickley, Derek Bridgett, Ken Brown (Aus), George Burgess, Roy Chiswell, Derek Close, Jack & Stan Cordingley, Martin Crooks, Neil Ctercteko (Aus), Bernard Crabtree & Christine Moore, Mark Dickinson, Alan Dobson, Percy Duff, Jean Fisher, Ann Gibson, Ray Harker, Jason Handley, David Harrison, Tom Hayton, Cliff Hindle, Harry Holme, the late Claris Hudson, Eileen Kitchen & Angela Atkinson, Bob McLaughlin, Ken Mellor, John Pepper, the late Maurice Stobbart, the late Eddie Thornborrow, the late George Vingoe, the late Cliff Walmsley, Peter White (Aus), Frank Whiteway, Tom Wightman, Julie & Sheila Wood, and Graham Wood.

Enthusiasts and collectors the world over have come up with some real treasures and nuggets of wisdom, too, and I am eternally grateful to Robert Bamford, Dixon Barron, Cliff Bone, John Chaplin, Mike Craven, Graham Fraser, Colin Greenwell, Jim Henry, Alistair Herd, Maurice Irving, John Jarvis, Peter Lipscomb, Maurice Newsham, John Ogden, Colin Parker, Peter Rance and Darren Riley for sharing their knowledge and pointing me in the right direction.

Libraries, archives, magazines and newspapers have been an invaluable source of information and I am indebted to Cumbrian Newspapers, Cumbria County Records Offices at Whitehaven, Barrow and Carlisle, Workington Library, Burnley Library, Lancashire County Archive Services, East Lancashire Newspapers Ltd, *The Nelson Leader*, *Off Road Review*, *Track Racing Review*, *Vintage Speedway Magazine*, Jim Henry and Graham Fraser of the *Speedway Researcher*, Mortons Motorcycle Media and the National Motor Museum for all their help.

Without photographs, any non-fiction work would be just a lot of hot air, so first of all I would like to pay tribute to the late great C.F Wallace and Wright Wood for being there in the first place and to Wright Wood's daughters, Margaret Harrop and Kay Randle, for allowing me to reproduce these fine photographs. I must also thank Richard Nicholson for allowing me to use photographs taken by the late R. Spencer Oliver, Bill Snelling at FoTTofinders, for digging out some rare pictures from the Keigs collection, and Percy Duff for allowing me access his late wife's incredible photographic collection. I have made every effort to identify the source of every illustration used in the book, but if there are any that I have failed to acknowledge, please accept my humble apologies. I promise to do better next time.

Adrian Pavey – October 2003

INTRODUCTION

Imagine the scene... four modern-day motorcycling gladiators... pumped up with adrenaline and ready for 'battle'. They all have one aim – to race hard and to be the first across that finishing line. The tapes fly up and the riders hurl their powerful racing motorcycles around a quarter-mile oval circuit. The spindly bikes have no gears, no brakes and virtually no suspension, but the riders show no fear as they broadside their bucking 500cc machines around the shale covered bends and turn on the power as they hit the short straight. They do battle for four laps and in the blink of an eye it's all over. This is no ordinary motorcycle race... this is a 60-second rush of methanol-fuelled action... this is Speedway!

I don't think the argument as to where and when speedway racing began will ever really be settled. All over the world, primitive forms of racing on dirt and grass have taken place, but it is in North America and Australia that we find the true origins of the sport we all love.

As early as 1902, American pioneers were racing motorcycles around neglected horse trotting circuits. The tracks were usually about half a mile long and surfaced with compacted dirt – hence the original title of 'dirt-track racing', a term that was used extensively in the UK until the Australian term of 'speedway' was adopted in the early 1930s. Dirt-track racing was immensely popular in North America during the early 1920s, and, as bikes became faster and more powerful, a new style of cornering developed. Maldwyn Jones was the first to master the art of broadsiding in 1916. He would ride his 1000cc Harley-Davidson or Excelsior into the corners with his left leg trailing behind him and the rear wheel performing a controlled power slide. The broadsiding technique was soon adopted by 500cc riders like Eddie Brinck, and by the mid-1920s, every rider on the circuit was riding in the new style.

Another popular theory is that speedway was born out of grass-track racing. Motorcycle races on grass were definitely held in Australia as early as 1911 and properly organised grass-track races had become popular attractions by 1920. Very often the grass would get worn away to such an extent that the track literally became a 'dirt track'. Johnnie Hoskins always maintained that he was the real father of the sport, organising the first speedway meeting in December 1923, at West Maitland, but another Australian, A.J. Hunting, made a counter claim that he invented the sport at Sydney in 1924. Hunting had been organising grass-track races for quite some time, but on this particular day, heavy rain had made the track too dangerous for racing. Rather than disappoint the crowd, Hunting asked the riders if they would like to race on the cinder

Frank and Jack Chiswell enjoy a break in the Lake District, c.1930.

cycling track that ran around the outside of the grass circuit. The result was a resounding success as the riders made the most of the loose surface, sliding around the corners at each end of the oval.

It has always been claimed that Britain's first true speedway meeting was held at High Beech on 19 February 1928. The track was actually an old running track at the back of the Kings Oak Hotel in the Epping Forest. Certainly, this was the one that received the most publicity and caught the public's imagination, but motorcycle enthusiasts in the north-west can argue that the very first dirt-track race meeting was actually held at Droylsden in June 1927. Prior to this, there had been cinder-path races at Parbold, Charnock Richard and in Manchester's Belle Vue Gardens.

Throughout the twentieth century (and into the twenty-first), speedway and grass-track racing has played a major part in the history of a region better known for its lakes, fells, mountains and dales. From Preston up to Carlisle, just about every major town has a part to play and a story to tell. There has been activity somewhere in the region in every decade since the sport began. Even during the Second World War, quite a few of our speedway and grass-track riders trained to be dispatch riders and instructors at the Driver and Maintenance School near Keswick. The instructors included TT stars Freddie Frith and John 'Crasher' White, and trials riders Bob McGregor and Karl Pugh, but so far I have failed to identify the names of the speedway riders who were stationed there.

There is still a lot of work to be done, which is why I have restrained myself from calling this book a 'history'. It has been almost impossible to unearth any information on the Blackpool tracks in 1929 and 1930, and the same can be said for many of the pre-war grass tracks.

In effect, this book is part one of an ongoing project, and only tracks which fall within the current boundaries of Cumbria and Lancashire have been included; other tracks in the north-west may be included in a second book in the future. The history of *Speedway in Manchester* has already been covered by my good friends Barry Stephenson and Trevor James, but there is still a lot of ground to cover.

For now though, the time has come to immerse yourself in a dose of pure nostalgia. Sit back and imagine the scene, the aroma of 'Castrol R' and methanol, the sound of roaring 500cc engines and the cheers of the crowd.

Adrian Pavey – October 2003

1

BLACKPOOL

The new attraction for the 1928 summer season at Blackpool was not another fairground ride, nor a star-studded production at the Winter Gardens; for that particular season it was something very different – motorcycle dirt-track racing on the Highfield Road sports ground, South Shore.

Blackpool Trotting and Sports Ground Ltd announced that they were willing to loan their trotting track on Highfield Road to any motorcycle club in the North-Western Centre of the ACU for regular motorcycle dirt-track races during the summer. North Manchester Motor Club (in conjunction with the Blackpool & Fylde Motor & Aero Club) jumped at the chance, and organised what they claimed to be 'Britain's first genuine dirt-track race meeting'.

No expense was spared in preparing the track for motorcycle racing. The grandstand and fences were given a fresh coat of white paint and the five-acre paddock was converted into one of the best pits in the country. Unlike many of the other dirt tracks that opened in the UK that year, the Blackpool venture had more in common with American dirt tracks than Australian-style speedway. The circuit was a big one, measuring over half a mile to the lap and over 50ft wide on the bends. It was almost

Programme cover from the first dirt-track race meeting at the Highfield Road sports ground, 21 April 1928.

oval in shape with slight banking on the bends, and, unlike most conventional speedway tracks of the time, the surface contained no ash or cinders. The Blackpool circuit was made up with a special composition of sand bound together with earth, which was claimed to be 'safer and more conducive to broadsiding'. Another unique feature of the first meeting at Highfield Road was that all races were run in clockwise direction over six laps, three miles in total!

Wilf McClure, the secretary of the organising club, had spent many days conducting trials and practising at Highfield Road, so his superior knowledge of the track paid dividends in the inaugural meeting on 21 April. Riding a 500cc Scott, he won two out of the four available classes, the Melbourne Cup for 500cc machines and the Adelaide Cup for 750cc machines. Wilf was also awarded the Canberra Cup for setting the fastest time of the day (3 minutes 53 seconds!) and as the track-record holder he took possession of the 'Ace of Clubs' Golden Helmet until such time as his record was broken.

The Sydney Cup, for 350cc machines, produced some of the best racing of the day. In the first heat, one rider crashed right through the fence. Luckily he escaped serious injury, but his bike was wrecked. C. Needham of Blackpool, riding a Rex Acme with spiked tyres, led the first heat for five laps before his engine failed, allowing H. Shelton of Stockport through to take his place in the final. Two heats later, another rider was thrown from his machine when he tried put his bike into a slide on one of the sweeping bends. The oldest competitor of the day was sixty-five-year-old Pa Cowley, the legendary

TT rider from Manchester. Unfortunately, his 348cc DOT broke down on the fourth lap of his first heat and he took no further part in the meeting. The final of the Sydney Cup was won by Harold 'Ginger' Lees of Bury on a 346cc New Imperial.

The final event of the day was the Brisbane Cup for unlimited capacity machines. Several TT riders and notable northern grass-track riders took part in this event, including Tommy Price of Liverpool and Syd Jackson of Coventry. Eric and Oliver Langton of Leeds were also competing, having their first taste of dirt-track racing. Eric, riding a 346cc New Hudson, had already gained two silver plaques for third place in the Sydney Cup and Melbourne Cup, while brother Oliver, riding a 500cc Scott, had a silver trophy for second place in the Adelaide Cup.

Chris Tattersall, a garage owner from St Annes, was the best of the local riders, finishing second in his heat riding a 498cc Sunbeam. But in the final it was Oliver Langton who took the first prize, ahead of Huddersfield's A. Mitchell and Birmingham's G. Baxter.

There was no doubt that the opening meeting was a huge success. Over 7,000 spectators had crammed into the sports ground and the roads near to the stadium were packed full of parked cars and bikes. Originally, Blackpool Trotting and Sports Ground Ltd had said that there would be dirt-track racing on every Saturday afternoon during the summer, but it was another two months before the bikes came back to Highfield Road again.

Blackpool & Fylde Motor & Aero Club arranged a series of twelve open dirt-track meetings, starting in June and running through to the end of October. The first of these was held on Saturday 23 June, but owing to Blackpool's many other attractions, the crowd was nowhere as high as at the first meeting. Nevertheless, a field of twenty-seven riders produced some top-class racing. Races were still held over six laps, but the new promoters had reverted to the conventional way of dirt-track racing, solo races ran 'left-hand in', i.e. anti-clockwise, and only the sidecar outfits ran in a clockwise direction.

Opposite: *Chris Tattersall, a garage mechanic from St Annes, made his dirt-track debut at Highfield Road and later rode for the Preston Speedway team. He is pictured on his own CTS (Chris Tattersall Special) at the 1934 Isle of Man TT. (FoTTofinders)*

Right: *Programme cover from 28 June 1928.*

The first event was for motorcycles up to 350cc. Once again, local rider Needham delighted the crowd with an exciting last to first ride in his first heat, but once again, engine failure robbed him of victory in the final after he had led for four laps. Former sand-racing champion George Reynard, of Easingwold, near York, took full advantage of his mishap to register his first major victory on the dirt tracks ahead of J.A. Smith of Bradford.

In the 500cc event, another local rider, J. Gregson reached the semi-final, but crashed when the forks on his 346cc Ivy snapped clean in half. Gregson was carried from the track on a stretcher with a dislocated shoulder. Other riders who made an impression in the early stages of this event were Len Myerscough of Great Crosby and Frank Charles from Barrow-in-Furness. The eventual winner of the 500cc final was Arthur Wilcock, the eldest of three racing brothers from Nelson in East Lancashire. The sidecar event was won by H. Hutchinson of Littleborough, ahead of local drivers H. Buckley and Harold Stephenson.

Eric Langton set a new track record of 3 minutes, 49.8 seconds during the heats of the 500cc class on 30 June, equivalent to an average speed of 47mph. Eric went on to win the final too, in the second fastest time of the day. Local riders were victorious in the other two classes, R. Sumner of St Annes winning the 350cc final and N.H. Buckley taking the honours in the sidecar class.

Crowd levels began to rise steadily, and over 3,000 spectators turned up for the third open dirt-track meeting on 14 July. The meeting was memorable for the amount of incidents, but luckily none of the riders suffered any serious injuries. In the final of the 350cc event, Needham was the only finisher. Two of his opponents had fallen and the only other rider had to pull up with engine problems. It was a good day all round for

Eric Langton set a new track record at Blackpool on 23 June, equivalent to an average speed of 47mph.

the young rider from Blackpool. Not only did he win the 350cc final by default, but he beat Frank Charles and Eric Langton in the final of the 500cc event. He also won the inaugural 'Golden Ace' Helmet, a new trophy for riders living within a ten-mile radius of Blackpool Town Hall. At the end of the meeting the club announced that Needham, Langton and Charles were prepared to challenge any Australian rider on the Blackpool track for a wager of £10.

The 'Golden Ace' battle proved to be a heart-stopping race for the 3,000 spectators at the next meeting on 21 July. All four riders were hurtling around the course on the second lap, when the leading rider, Norman Nelson, hit the fence and ended up in a heap in the middle of the track. Second-placed Needham narrowly avoided the fallen rider, but third-placed P. Starkey of Fleetwood wasn't so lucky. With his view obscured by the dust, he collided with Nelson's machine and was flung into the air, crashing down on the circuit head first. The race was abandoned with both riders taken to hospital. Nelson had severe injuries to his hands and fingers while Starkey escaped with a badly swollen knee, his helmet having saved him from serious injury.

Up until that point, the meeting had passed without incident. Needham had an easy victory in the final of the 350cc race ahead of another impressive local rider, R. Sumner. The final of the 500cc race produced the best racing of the afternoon, though. Frank Charles made a flying start and was being chased hard by Needham. On the second lap, Needham rode a brilliant line to overtake Charles on the sweeping bend, but Charles turned on the power to reclaim the lead on the next lap. Despite a fearlessly close battle, Charles held on to win the final, with Needham breathing hard on his back wheel. Norman Nelson finished third with Cyril Wilcock bringing up the rear.

The sidecar race provided the crowd with an amusing incident. Norman Buckley's outfit came to a halt when the sidecar wheel shed its tyre. Unperturbed, his passenger threw the tyre onto the centre green and Buckley continued the race, ploughing up the track surface with a bare steel wheel rim to finish in second place behind Harold Jackson, the famous sand racer from Barrow-in-Furness.

The Mayor of Blackpool, Councillor T. Lumb, was a special guest at this meeting and remarked how 'daring and thrilling' the racing was. It was hoped that the Mayor's visit would be taken as a civic recognition of dirt-track racing in the seaside town, and help to bring in more spectators. It must have done the trick. Over 6,000 spectators turned up on 4 August, for the club's most successful meeting to date.

Needham was an easy winner of the 350cc class again, while Charles reigned supreme in the 500cc class, beating Arthur and Cyril Wilcock in the final. As an added attraction, the promoters had organised a special Lancashire *v.* Yorkshire inter-county duel. Arthur Atkinson and A. Mitchell, representing Leeds and Yorkshire, won the first heat, but from then on the Lancashire riders took control, culminating with a magnificent victory in the final race for Frank Charles and Cyril Wilcock.

The sidecar race proved to be a disaster for local pairing Harold Warburton and S. Hampshire. Their Norton outfit overturned at high speed and both riders ended up in hospital. Warburton escaped lightly with injuries to his hands, but his passenger was kept in with internal injuries and shock. Undeterred by his rivals' accident, Harold Stephenson raced to victory in the rerun, setting a new sidecar track record in the process.

Arthur Atkinson, who led a Yorkshire team at Blackpool on 21 July 1928.

The meeting on 11 August featured car racing for the first time, an experiment that went badly wrong and could have ended in a catastrophe. Four members of the Huddersfield Motor Club had been allowed to give the crowd a 'demonstration' of car racing, as they had done on previous occasions in Yorkshire. Two heats were run featuring two cars in each, the winners meeting each other in a final. The dangers were obvious from the outset, as one of the cars hit the railings and finished with large lumps of wood sticking out of its radiator and springs. In the second heat a near certain crash was only avoided when one car pulled up with engine problems. The final race brought disaster though. Sidney Canney's Jowett shed a tyre as it came out of one of the bends and somersaulted down the track in a cloud of dust. The passenger, George Drew, was thrown from the car and landed some yards away. When the dust settled, the bodywork of the car was completely smashed and the unconscious driver was pinned to his seat by the steering wheel. Both men were very lucky to survive the crash and were taken to the Victoria Hospital with concussion and severe bruising. Arthur Hindley, the secretary of the organising club, stated there and then that 'there would be no further car races on the Highfield Road track'.

There had already been a series of spills during the afternoon. C.B. Hands crashed in the opening heat and was taken to hospital with concussion and a badly cut eye, R. Sumner had taken a bad fall in the 350cc race and Frank Charles had crashed right through the barriers into the crowd during the final of the 500cc race. Another rider was unable to avoid Charles's bike and used the back wheel as a ramp, luckily landing safely in one piece a few yards later. Charles was very lucky to escape with only a sprained ankle, but it did mean that he could not take part in a challenge race against the Australian riders at the White City track in Manchester later that week.

With Sumner injured, there was a new name on the 350cc trophy, Arthur Wilcock taking victory ahead of Norman Nelson. Needham could only manage third place due to engine problems. Nelson had his revenge in the 500cc final, though, beating Wilcock into second place with Chris Tattersall, the TT rider from St Annes, in third place. A new event for novices was introduced at this meeting, the final being won by Eric Airey from Lancaster ahead of another rider destined to have a long and distinguished career on the dirt tracks, Joe Abbott of Burnley. Another competitor, Stanley Bryden, a pupil at West Leeds High School, was reputed to have been only fourteen years old when he made his debut in the novice races at Highfield Road.

A meeting originally planned for 18 August does not appear to have taken place, but Eric Langton's track record was finally broken by Norman Nelson on Saturday 25 August. It was definitely a meeting for records to fall. During the heats of the sidecar event, Norman Buckley broke his own track record only to see Harold Jackson smash the record again in the final. In the solo races, Nelson was invincible, winning both the 500cc handicap final and the 500cc scratch final. Admittedly, Frank Charles was still suffering with his ankle injury and Needham was away racing in the Isle of Man, but nonetheless, Nelson's two victories were well deserved and his new track record shaved a full 3 seconds off Langton's previous time.

The next meeting, scheduled for Saturday 8 September, does not appear to have taken place either. It was certainly advertised in the local newspapers, but a possible explanation could be that a new dirt-track had been constructed, just down the road at the South Shore Greyhound Stadium on St Anne's Road.

Greyhound racing had first been staged at the St Anne's Road Stadium on 30 July 1927 and just over twelve months later, a speedway track was laid inside the greyhound course. The British Dirt-Track Racing Association (BDTRA) were behind the venture and planned to hold meetings every Tuesday and Thursday afternoon, starting on Tuesday 11 September.

All of the riders in the opening meeting were regulars at the White City track in Manchester, including Arthur Franklyn, Mark Sheldon, Arthur Jervis and 'Smoky' Stratton. Clem Beckett of Oldham beat New Zealander 'Stewie' St George in a series of three-match races, setting a track record of 95.2 seconds. The Lancashire rider also won the open senior race ahead of 'Ginger' Lees, Dick Hayman and 'Skid' Skinner, who had lost the lead when he fell. The race for the Golden Gauntlet was won by 'Ginger' Lees and the junior race was won by R. Chadwick.

Prior to the open senior final there had been a sidecar race between H. Hughes of Liverpool and Dot Cowley ('Pa' Cowley's seventeen-year-old daughter). The young Manchester girl made the most of her 8-second advantage and held the lead right until the final bend, when Hughes nipped through and won the race right on the line.

BDTRA held another meeting at the Greyhound Stadium two days later with the full co-operation of the Blackpool & Fylde Motor & Aero Club, the promoters from the nearby Highfield Road circuit. The Golden Armlet event featured a young Irish girl named Fay Taylor, who beat Ted Egerton in her heat to finish third behind Arthur Franklyn and 'Smoky' Stratton. Needham, the Blackpool rider who had ridden with such success at the Highfield Road circuit, made little impression on his first

Left: *Dot Cowley, the teenage daughter of veteran racer Pa Cowley, narrowly lost a sidecar race at the Greyhound Stadium on 11 September 1928. Dot was also an accomplished sand racer on the Lancashire coast.*

Below: *Fay Taylor, the Irish girl who beat Ted Egerton in the Golden Armlet event on 11 September.*

appearance at the new track, falling twice and retiring from the open senior race with engine failure. Frank Charles didn't take long to adapt to the smaller circuit, though. He won his heat in the open senior event eventually finishing fourth in the final. 'Ginger' Lees beat Arthur Franklyn and Sid Ball in the final of the Golden Armlet and Ham Burrill of Rainford beat Les 'Smiler' Wotton in the junior race.

A crowd of around 2,000 saw 'Skid' Skinner win the Golden Armlet on 18 September. Arthur Jervis of Coventry was runner-up with 'Ginger' Lees in third place. In the final of the open senior race, the positions were reversed, Jervis taking the chequered flag ahead of Skinner. Needham rode in both events too, but was still unable to master the tiny circuit and fell in both his heats, taking out Geoff Taylor of Huddersfield in one heat.

Arthur Franklyn won the race for the Golden Armlet and the open senior race on the following Thursday, finishing yards ahead of the second-placed rider in both events. Ham Burrill raced to another easy victory in the junior race and Geoff Taylor made an unsuccessful attempt on the track record when he fell on the second lap. In a special challenge race, Norman 'Broadside' Dawson, a White City exponent, had a comfortable 2-0 victory against the rapidly improving Frank Charles from Barrow-in-Furness.

Two days later, on Saturday 22 September, dirt-track racing returned to the Highfield Road circuit where Cyril Wilcock won the 500cc scratch final and the 500cc handicap final. Needham had been favourite for the handicap event, but his run of bad luck continued when he fell off in his heat. He actually made a lightning start in the scratch final, but Wilcock gradually ebbed away at his lead and finally passed him on the third lap. Frank Charles had a poor meeting by his standards. He was disqualified from the semi-final of the handicap race for jumping the start and failed to even make the start in his heat of the scratch event. Needham finally came good in the 350cc race, winning

'Skid' Skinner, winner of the Golden Armlet on 18 September and the Golden Gauntlet on 25 September. Skinner also set the track record at the St Anne's Road circuit. (C.F. Wallace).

his heat and beating Arthur Wilcock in the final. During the afternoon Needham also made a successful attempt on Norman Nelson's track record from a rolling start. The feat was all the more creditable as Needham did it on a 348cc Rex Acme. Three competitors took part in the sidecar race, which was won comfortably by Harold Stephenson.

BDTRA held two further meetings at St Anne's Road in September 1928. 'Skid' Skinner equalled the track record of 91 seconds in the final of the Golden Gauntlet on Tuesday 25 September, beating Larry Boulton, Les Wotton and Frank Charles. It was a good day for Boulton, the Manchester-based rider who was making his first appearance at the Blackpool track. After easily winning the junior final, he was involved in another great duel with Skinner in the final of the open senior race, winning by less than a wheel's length.

The final meeting at St Anne's Road was held on Saturday 29 September, in front of the lowest crowd of the season. Fewer than 1,500 spectators turned up to watch Frank Charles make a clean sweep of the senior trophies on only his third appearance at the track. Charles was so dominant that he finished yards ahead of the second-placed rider in every race he entered. Eric Airey was runner-up in the open senior final and Ham Burrill finished second in the Golden Armlet. Needham never managed to reproduce his Highfield Road form at the greyhound track and once again he failed to complete a race at St Anne's Road. There was a host of crashes in the junior event, all four riders falling in one heat, the junior final eventually being won by Sid Ball of Manchester.

Frank Charles was excluded for looking over his shoulder in his first meeting at Highfield Road, but went on to become one of the few riders to master both of the Blackpool circuits.

The final meeting at Highfield Road took place on 6 October. Once again, Frank Charles stole the limelight, setting a new track record from a standing start. Both of the senior events, the 500cc handicap and the 500cc scratch, were won by Charles too, although at one point, it looked like he wasn't going to make the handicap final. Charles failed to make his customary lightning start in his heat and was left at the gate, but he went after his opponents at amazing speed and eventually passed all of them, including Needham, who was on a 4-second advantage. Needham continued his domination of the 350cc class with another easy victory in the final and Harold Warburton celebrated his return from injury with a victory in the sidecar event.

A further meeting at Highfield Road had been planned for 20 October, but never took place. More meetings were definitely held at Highfield Road, but the local newspapers stopped reporting on them after the 1928 season had finished. I do not know for certain how many open meetings were held in 1929, but there is evidence of at least one meeting, which took place on 31 May. It was also announced in May 1929 that the Northern Dirt-Track Owners Association, were proposing a Second Division for the northern-based English Dirt-Track League. An application from Blackpool was adjourned for one month pending an inspection of the track, but, as history proves, the Second Division never materialised and Blackpool never did enter a team into the English Dirt-Track League.

The 1930 Blackpool dirt-track racing season opened at Highfield Road on 12 April, with a meeting organised by the Blackpool Motor Cycle & Light Car Club. Norman Nelson, riding a 500cc DT Douglas, made a successful attempt on the lap record with a time of 33.8 seconds. Nelson also won the senior final, ahead of Needham and E. Hollingworth. Even after three years, Needham continued to dominate the lighter 350cc class, beating R. Sumner in the final. Two further meetings were held at Highfield Road in April 1930, the final meeting being held on 21 April when Needham was victorious again, taking victory in the Golden Helmet event. Highfield Road never staged motorcycle or horse racing after this date and was reported to be lying idle by the end of the year.

It has also been claimed that dirt-track racing took place at St Anne's Road in 1929 and 1930, but no evidence has been found. The BDTRA would certainly not have been happy with crowd levels at the Greyhound Stadium and many of the star riders did not appear at the later meetings. All things considered, I don't think there was any more racing at St Anne's Road, but I would love to be proved wrong.

The St Anne's Road Stadium continued to host greyhound racing right up until 30 October 1964. In the meantime, it had also been the home of Blackpool Borough Rugby League Club from 1954 until they moved into their new home at Borough Park in 1963. The stadium was finally demolished to make way for housing and the only reminder of the old track is a road named Stadium Avenue.

Numerous attempts have been made to bring speedway back to Blackpool. During the early 1950s, Joseph Waxman and James Wolfenden (who was the original Competitors Manager at St Anne's Road back in 1928) wanted to transfer their Fleetwood operation to Blackpool. They tried to bring racing back to the former St Anne's Road venue, but the stadium owners were not interested, neither were the owners of the Borough Park ground. Then they pestered Blackpool Town Council to set aside an area of land where they could build their own track, but some members of the council were set against the idea from the outset. Eventually, they agreed on a piece of land in Marton, but a combination of local opposition and poor business planning eventually put paid to the whole idea. Ambitious promoter Mike Parker made a further attempt to reintroduce speedway to Blackpool in the mid-1960s. Don Potter (the former Wigan and Fleetwood rider) and Dick Fisher (the Belle Vue rider from Galgate) were rumoured to be involved with the venture too. It was always presumed that Dick would leave Belle Vue at the end of the 1965 season to join the new Blackpool team as rider/manager. Once again, the plans never materialised; Mike Parker moved his attention to Nelson in East Lancashire and Dick stayed at Belle Vue for the remainder of his career.

2

CARLISLE

Carlisle has produced some brilliant motorcycle sportsmen over the years, so it comes as something of a surprise to learn that neither speedway nor grass-track racing has ever captured the imagination in the Border city. There have been a number of attempts to introduce the sport to the city, but due to a combination of poor attendance and sheer bad luck, none of the ventures has succeeded.

The Carlisle & Cumberland Greyhound Racing & Sports Company built a brand new sports stadium at Harraby in 1928, primarily for greyhound racing but also as the home of Carlisle City Rugby League Club. During construction, representatives of the Cumberland County Motor Cycle Club had approached the stadium owners with a proposal to hold dirt-track racing, motorcycle football and motorcycle gymkhanas at Harraby Park. This proposal was declined, but the stadium owners did let the Cumberland County MCC build a makeshift dirt track on land adjacent to the stadium. Research has not revealed how often this facility was used, but there is evidence that club members did practice here during 1928.

Members of the Cumberland County Motor Cycle Club in 1928. 'Gilly' Allison is second in from the left wearing white leathers, Frank Allison is on the bike to Allison's right and Norman Pickersgill is on the next bike in line. Bob Wearmouth is on the bike second from the right, wearing a white scarf. (Cliff Allison)

The first greyhound meeting took place on 9 June 1928 and shortly afterwards, the stadium owners announced that they were going to introduce motorcycle dirt-track racing, starting on Saturday 21 July. Over the next few weeks it was reported that entries were flooding in from all over the country. The *Carlisle Journal* stated that the number of entries had exceeded all expectations and that it may prove impossible to complete all of the heats and finals in one day… all part of the hype, no doubt! An advertisement in the *Cumberland News* for Friday 20 July proclaimed: 'Spend the most hectic afternoon of your life at Harraby Park!' .

On 21 July, Carlisle played host to its first 'Motorcycle Grass-Track Races'. Unfortunately, the attendance was nowhere near as high as expected, a fact that was later blamed on the 'unprecedented number of counter attractions taking place in the area on the same day'. Another disappointment was that five of the original twenty-nine confirmed entries didn't appear and neither did any of the promised top dirt-track stars. Ironically, most of the competitors were members of the Cumberland County MCC.

The first event was the 'Lowther Stakes' for solo motorcycles up to 250cc. The honour of winning the first race went to R.W.N. Holmes on an Excelsior. Heat two provided the first real tussle of the afternoon, W.P. Saunders taking the chequered flag right on the line after a last gasp ride around L. Parker on the last bend. The final of the 250cc event saw a terrific race between Saunders and Holmes, victory eventually falling to Holmes after Saunders' bike packed up with a blocked oilway.

Event two was the 'Petteril Stakes' for solo motorcycles up to 350cc. Eleven competitors competed over five heats for this event with the four fastest heat winners going through to the final. The final was a really close race, eventually won by Cumberland trials star 'Gilly' Allison mounted on an AJS. In second place was Ernie Greenop on a 350 Velocette and in third place was Gilly's brother Frank Allison on a Cotton.

The third event in the programme was the one that really got the crowd on their feet: the 'Harraby Stakes' for sidecars. Only four pairs had entered this event, but they produced some of the best racing of the afternoon. T. Troughear, riding a 490cc Norton, led from the start with his opponent hanging onto his every move for three laps. On the final lap, the second-placed rider skilfully manoeuvred his outfit onto the outside of his opponent and, with a quick burst of speed coming out of the final bend, he squeezed past Troughear to snatch victory right on the line. There is some confusion as to who the winner actually was, though. According to the report in the *Carlisle Journal*, the race was won by a Mr Leck on a Norton outfit, whereas the *Cumberland Evening News* report gives the winner as R. Dent on an AJS outfit! As no programmes appear to survive from this meeting, I'll leave the choice up to you.

The final event of the day was the 'Lonsdale Stakes' for solo motorcycles up to 600cc. Thirteen competitors entered this event, every one of them competing for £10 prize money and the Golden Helmet. The track surface had begun to cut up by this time and made life difficult for some of the riders. Ernie Greenop lost control of his Velocette while leading his heat and was thrown against the fence. Luckily, he was unhurt and picked himself up off the track, dusted himself down and walked back to the pit area. Five heats were run, with the four fastest winners going forward to the final. The heat

Frank Allison leading Bob Wearmouth. (Cliff Allison)

winners were: Frank Allison (Cotton), Gilly Allison (AJS), E.L. Sewell (New Imperial), J.L. Stoddart (Rudge) and Bob Wearmouth (BSA). Stoddart crashed out of the final while engaged in a tussle for third place, but it was Gilly Allison who led all the way from the start to take his second win of the day.

The promoters were hoping to lay a proper cinder circuit in time for the next event on Saturday 28 July. They were also planning to erect floodlights for evening meetings in later months. A few days later, a report appeared in the *Carlisle Journal* explaining that the British Dirt-Track Racing Association were organising a national championship, open to all amateur and professional motorcyclists. The preliminary rounds would be taking place all over the country, with one round definitely taking place in Carlisle. Another announcement in the *Carlisle Journal* of 27 July 1928 declared that, 'a team of Australian riders will be arriving at the circuit in a week or two', but as was so often the case during the early years of the sport in this country, things just didn't work out.

Another advert in the *Carlisle Journal* announced that, 'motorcycle races at Harraby Park Stadium have been postponed until the new dirt track has been completed'. This same advertisement continued to be displayed in the local newspapers until mid-September 1928, but the promised Australians never arrived and the dirt track never did get completed.

It wasn't only the speedway that was having problems either. A poor turnout of around 2,000 watched the first Carlisle City Rugby League fixture at Harraby Park on Saturday 25 August 1928, and less than 400 were at their very last game eight weeks later. After only 10 matches, Carlisle City officially resigned from the league on 8 November 1928.

Insufficient crowds had turned the whole venture into a financial disaster for the Carlisle & Cumberland Greyhound Racing & Sports Company. They had no option but to suspend activities and put the stadium up for sale. Months passed by without a buyer and the company was officially wound up in March 1929.

The grandstand was eventually bought by Gateshead Football Club and the vacant site was purchased by Cowans Sheldon, the crane-makers on London Road. Eventually, the grounds passed into the ownership of the London, Midland and Scottish Railways (LMS). Harraby Park remained as an open field until Gillford Park, the current home of Carlisle Centurions Rugby Club, was built in 1987.

*Roland Stobbart of Aspatria, one of
the promoters at Moorville Speedway.*

The next attempt to bring speedway racing to Carlisle was nine years later in 1937. J. Fraser Crichton and Roland Stobbart had already introduced speedway racing to Lonsdale Park in Workington and Dam Park in Ayr, but their next venture was to construct a brand new speedway track at Carlisle with a view to entering a team into the Provincial League for 1938. Plans were also being made to stage midget-car racing with the co-operation of Harry Skirrow, the former bike racer from Ambleside, who was running speedway cars at Lea Bridge in London.

The chosen site was just north of the city centre in a rural area known as Kingmoor, but the developers hit problems right from the outset. The track was built on Joe Earl's farm land, very near to Robbie Bell's brick yard. Even though it was situated well away from any housing and about 500 yards off the main Kingstown Road, the local residents did not want any interruptions to their peaceful way of life, especially noisy motorcycles, large crowds and traffic. There were also objections to the proposed entrance, which would have meant removing the old horse trough. Amidst heavy local opposition, Crichton and Stobbart pressed ahead with their plans, resited the entrance and finally gained permission from the planning committee, much to the disapproval of the Kingmoor residents.

Robbie Bell's brick yard proved to be a handy source of material for the construction of the new track. It is said that the employees at the yard would take barrow loads of waste brick dust over to the site of the new track and that the base of the track was built using Robbie Earl's finest products too. The 440-yard track, known as Moorville Park, was completed in late August 1937 and finished off with a 4ft-high, white board safety fence. Unusually, the riders' paddock was situated on the centre green.

What turned out to be the first and only speedway meeting at Moorville Park took place on Saturday 18 September 1937. It seems that the people of Carlisle were just not interested in speedway and less than 700 people turned up to watch the racing. Stobbart blamed the wet start to the day for the poor turn out, but the weather had cleared up by the time racing started.

It was an individual meeting featuring regular competitors from the Workington track and several members of the Belle Vue 'Merseysiders' team. The two main events were a scratch race and a handicap trophy, supported by a series of match races and novice races. Roland Stobbart was unable to ride as he was still recovering from a broken collarbone sustained while riding for Bristol, but he still took an active part in the meeting as clerk of the course and announcer. His mechanic, Jack Saul, was machine examiner and pit marshal for the day.

The first event was the scratch races. Heat one was won by Eric Butler ahead of West Ham novice Ken Tidbury. Maurice Stobbart had held the lead for three laps, but misread the marshal's flag and pulled up during the final lap. Alan Butler won heat two ahead of another novice from the West Ham track, Denny 'Crusty' Pye. Sam Marsland had made a late challenge on Butler in this heat by diving down the inside, but lost control and fell. Surprisingly, this was the only fall of the day. Former Preston rider Tommy Price beat Norman Hargreaves in heat three, with Scotsman Dennis Dennie trailing well behind.

The first semi-final produced a good race between brothers Alan and Eric Butler. Eric finally won the heat ahead of Alan and Ken Tidbury. The second semi-final was won by Tommy Price, who passed his opponents in spectacular style. Crusty had made the gate, but he was passed first by Price and then Hargreaves. The scratch final was the closest race of the day, with winner Tommy Price setting the track record of 87.6 seconds. Norman Hargreaves and Eric Butler were neck and neck for two laps before Hargreaves finally gained the advantage and held on for second place.

The second event was a handicap competition. Heat one saw Price and Hargreaves starting from scratch, with Ken Tidbury having a 1-second advantage. Hargreaves passed Tidbury on the last lap, but Price surprisingly missed out. Heat two was won by Sam Marsland, after a terrific four-lap battle with Alan Butler. Marsland got the verdict on the line by the narrowest of margins. Maurice Stobbart won the third heat in spectacular style, with Eric Butler following him home in second place. Dennis Dennie had started with a full 3-second advantage, but was passed by both riders on the third lap.

It only took one lap for Norman Hargreaves to make up Ken Tidbury's 1-second advantage in the first semi-final, but Sam Marsland went round both of them on the third lap in a spectacular manoeuvre. Alan Butler won the second semi-final.

After the wild excitement of the heats and semi-finals, the final was something of an anti-climax. Alan Butler had an easy victory, after Maurice Stobbart, Norman Hargreaves and Sam Marsland all suffered engine problems.

Three rolling start 'two-lap-dash' match races were held during the afternoon. Maurice Stobbart beat Alan Butler in the first, Tommy Price beat Sam Marsland in the second and Norman Hargreaves beat Charlie Oates in the third race.

Following the Carlisle meeting, all of the riders made the relatively short journey to Lonsdale Park in Workington for a challenge match between Workington 'Reds' and the Belle Vue 'Merseysiders'.

Sadly, the Carlisle project was a financial disaster. Stobbart openly admitted that his '...efforts at promoting were not exactly prosperous'. After one solitary meeting,

Left: *Former Preston and Liverpool rider, Tommy Price, winner of the scratch race final at Moorville and holder of the track record.*

Middle: *Alan Butler had an easy victory in the final of the Moorville handicap.*

Right: *Norman Hargreaves had made his speedway debut at Workington earlier in the year and was one of the most spectacular riders in the Carlisle meeting.*

Moorville Park lay idle and slowly fell into dereliction. The track remained visible up until the 1960s, and the site is now buried behind the Aldi store on Kingstown Road.

It seems that speedway is destined never to succeed in Carlisle. Ian Thomas and Jeff Brownhut took a look at Brunton Park, the home of Carlisle United FC, as a possible speedway venue in 1969, but decided that Derwent Park in Workington was a better option. Then, in 1970, Allied Presentations, a consortium of five First Division promoters, Len Silver, Reg Fearman, Maurice Littlechild, Danny Dunton and Ron Wilson, came to the city looking for somewhere to build a speedway track. Allied had recently taken over the promoting rights at First Division Newcastle. The rumour at the time was that they were looking for a new home for the Newcastle team and were thinking of transferring the team across the country to Carlisle. Their search began in May and they spent most of the summer looking at possible sites. They did begin talks with the owners of at least one stadium, but nothing concrete ever came of the proposals and when Newcastle did close down at the end of the 1970 season, their racing licence was transferred to Reading in Berkshire.

3

PRESTON

'Like riding a billiard table with peas on it!' That's how one rider described the Preston Speedway track and Dusty Haigh declared that he would 'never set foot on the track again until the bumps were removed'. The 440-yard circuit at Farringdon Park came in for a lot of criticism during its comparatively short run and three riders lost their lives there. But let's not dwell on this sad statistic for the moment; the chequered history of Preston Speedway has plenty of high spots too.

The Farringdon Park circuit was just one corner of the much larger Preston Pleasure Gardens, laid out in the grounds of Farringdon Hall, off New Hall Lane. Sporting events had been held in the gardens since the latter part of the nineteenth century and in 1878 a cinder cycling track had been laid around the perimeter of the football pitch. During the First World War the gardens became neglected and overgrown, but, in 1925, some order of semblance was restored when Preston Grasshoppers Rugby Club took a lease on the old football ground. Four years later, the rugby club was approached by a syndicate who wanted to reinstate the old cinder track for motorcycle dirt-track racing. The rugby club agreed and the newly formed Preston Speedways Ltd made plans for their opening meeting at Easter.

Programme cover from the grand opening meeting at Preston, 29 March 1929.

Norman Jackman was appointed as the track manager and given the task of finding riders for the new Preston Speedway team. Frank and Jack Chiswell from Essex were amongst the first recruits and Claude Rye and his brother Percy came to Preston from the White City track in London. Dozens of local motorcyclists turned up for trials too, but a demonstration of broadsiding by Paddy Dean had an adverse effect and put a lot of the novices off!

Preston Speedway opened to the public on Good Friday 29 March 1929, when Arthur Jervis became the first winner of the Preston Golden Helmet. Another individual meeting was held on the Easter Monday, 1 April followed by four more meetings in quick succession.

A team representing Preston was entered into the English Dirt-Track League (EDTL) and they made their debut on Saturday 27 April, with a 35-27 victory against Leeds in front of 10,000 ecstatic supporters. Leeds started the match quite strongly, but the home side soon got into their stride and provided the heat winner in each of the last five races. Representing Preston on that historic occasion were Ian Ritchings (captain), Tommy Price, Ham Burrill and Douglas 'Crazy' Hutchins, with the Chiswell brothers at reserve. In the supporting races, Ham Burrill beat Tommy Price, Oliver Langton and Finlay McNab in the final of the Golden Gauntlet and local rider, J. Milsom won the junior scratch final.

Ritchings was dropped in May, and the captaincy was handed to Ham Burrill. Hailing from Rainford, near St Helens, Ham (short for Hamlet) had been the youngest competitor in the 1922 Senior TT, but pulled out with a puncture on Bray Hill. He returned to the Isle of Man in 1926 as a member of the HRD team, but crashed in practice and was replaced by another famous name from the speedway scene, Syd Jackson. Prior to joining Preston, Ham had ridden speedway at Manchester's White City, Liverpool and Belle Vue. At 6ft 3in tall, he was one of the biggest riders in the sport.

Opposite: *The 1929 Preston team (left to right): Ian Ritchings, Tommy Price, Ham Burrill, Frank Chiswell, Jack Chiswell, (unidentified), Claude Rye.*

Above: *Ham Burrill. His full name was Hamlet and he had a brother named Horatio. Apparently, his mother was a great fan of Shakespeare's plays! (FoTTofinders)*

Right: *Jack and Frank Chiswell. Jack is sitting on a bike he built himself using an experimental 500cc JAP engine.*

Riding in the pouring rain at Belle Vue on 4 May, Preston suffered more than their fair share of bad luck. Nearly all of the bikes developed mechanical problems and two riders refused to ride in the treacherous conditions. Tommy Price rode in three consecutive heats and Ham Burrill was forced to take an extra ride to make up the numbers. Not surprisingly, Preston were soundly beaten 40-21. Despite losing their first away fixture, Preston made a strong start to their league campaign. On 11 May they beat Salford 38-24, and on 18 May Warrington were soundly thrashed 47-14. 'Crazy' Hutchins crashed and injured his hand during the win over Salford and aggravated the injury when he fell again in the match against Warrington. His withdrawal meant that Claude Rye was able to make his league debut and Billy Anderton was also called up when Len Myerscough crashed out of the match.

Joe Abbott of Burnley won the Golden Gauntlet on 13 June, and was immediately signed on loan while his own track was temporarily closed. Burnley reopened later that month and Abbott had to return, but within a few weeks Burnley closed for good and Abbott was back at Preston along with two other former Burnley riders, Frank Charles and Jack Lund. Abbott and Charles were an instant hit at Farringdon Park, picking up dozens of individual honours and forming a potent spearhead for the new-look Preston team.

During the summer of 1929, meetings were generally held twice a week, mixing league and cup matches with open and individual events. A succession of riders passed through the Preston ranks during that first season, including Cecil 'Winks' Rice, Norman Evans and north-eastern star Charlie Barrett, who only stayed at Farringdon Park for a few weeks before moving south to join Wembley.

With such a talented squad to call on, Preston completed the league season with only one home defeat, against White City (Manchester) on 13 July, and three away victories at Liverpool, Newcastle and Warrington. They finished the season in second place behind Leeds, but in all honesty, the 1929 English Dirt-Track League was a complete farce. White City (Manchester) had won 19 of their first 21 matches and their points tally was already enough to have given them the league title, but they sensationally resigned before the end of the season. Belle Vue, Burnley and Hanley had also dropped out of the league mid-season, Bolton only completed one fixture (beating Preston 35-24) and Warrington were expelled in September. Dozens of results had to be deleted from the records and a few fixtures were never completed.

The inaugural English Dirt-Track Knockout Cup competition was much more successful, though, and Preston had a fabulous run all the way to the final. Liverpool were easily dispensed of in the first rounds, Sheffield were well beaten in the second round after a near walkover (52 –11) in the home leg and a similar fate befell Leicester in the semi-final. The final saw Preston take on Halifax. Inspired by a Frank Chiswell

This medal was awarded to Frank Chiswell after Preston won the 1929 English Dirt-Track Knock Out Cup. Frank had ridden magnificently in the final and became the first rider to beat 'Squib' Burton on his home track.

Ham Burrill with George Formby's 'Penny Farthing' bicycle.

maximum, Preston made light work of the first round, beating the Yorkshire side 48-11. The second leg was actually ridden at Sheffield, because Halifax's home track at Thrum Hall cricket ground was not considered good enough for such a prestigious event! Once again, Frank Chiswell was on invincible form, and inspired his team mates to a 39-24 victory, bringing the first ever English Dirt-Track Knockout Cup back to Preston.

Forty-eight confirmed speedway meetings had taken place at Farringdon Park when the season ended on 7 October. Popular entertainer George Formby had been a regular visitor and donated his own trophy. He even competed in a couple of novelty match races against Ham Burrill and Frank Chiswell. Formby had beaten Chiswell on 18 April, but he did have the advantage of a one-lap start. Later in the season, Burrill gave Formby a three-lap start! But this time Formby was on a Safety Bicycle (a Penny Farthing to you and me) and Burrill was on his Douglas!

The 1929 season was tinged with sadness too. As I mentioned in the opening paragraph, three riders were killed on the Preston track, two of them during the first season. John Stockdale was killed during the second half of the meeting on 11 May and Jack Smith was involved in a fatal crash on 10 August. Jack was taken to hospital, but died eight days later without ever regaining consciousness.

Shortly after the end of the season, Ham Burrill led Frank Charles, Joe Abbott, Tommy Price, Len Myerscough and the Chiswell brothers on a European tour organised by United Speedways Ltd. They visited Hamburg, Stuttgart, Munich, Prague and Copenhagen, where Burrill won the main event.

During the winter of 1929/1930, the Farringdon Park track was dug up and the infamous bumps were removed. The relaid and reshaped track was actually 27 yards shorter, measuring 413 yards to the lap. Norman Jackman had moved to Liverpool, taking Tommy Price with him. Frank Charles had also moved on after accepting a lucrative deal to sign for White City (Manchester) but, much to the relief of the fans, Joe Abbott decided to make his move to Preston a permanent one. Mr P.N. Goman was appointed as the new team manager, and immediately signed George Reynard and Frank Smith from Halifax, and Fred Proctor from Rochdale. George Reynard was from Easingwold, near York, and like Burrill had ridden in the TT races, finishing in fourth place in 1927. In addition to the new signings, the novice races had produced some promising young talent, notably Jimmie Carnie, Bert Nowell, 'Crasher' Myhill and Jack Tye.

A carpenter by trade, Jack Tye had originally been Ham Burrill's mechanic and used to test ride his bikes prior to every match. On one occasion, though, Tye had crashed Burrill's best bike and the two parted company. William Jones, of New Cock Yard Garage in Preston, took young Jack under his wing and bought him a bike of his own. Tye made rapid progress in the supporting races and showed that he had very little fear of rough tracks.

The new season opened on 18 April with a challenge match between two teams led by Ham Burrill and Joe Abbott. Three days later, Frank Varey dominated an individual event at Farringdon Park.

The English Dirt-Track League had been replaced by the Northern League for 1930, and Preston's season began with a victory at Rochdale. The return fixture on 1 May got

'Crasher' Myhill lives up to his nickname. (Auto-Motor Journal)

Preston's home campaign underway with another victory. The team for the first home fixture was Ham Burrill (capt.), Joe Abbott, Jack Chiswell and George Reynard, with Frank Smith at reserve. The opening league match was followed by three support events. The first was the Preston Handicap, a controversial event which sometimes had as many as six riders in a race. It is interesting to note that the first three places in the final of this event were taken by riders who were only on the fringes of the team, Jack Tye, Eric Airey and 'Crazy' Hutchins. The Stokes Trophy, presented by James. A. Stokes, the new director of speedway at Farringdon Park, was won by Joe Abbott after a terrific tussle with Ham Burrill and the junior race was won by F. Hesmondhalgh.

Frank Charles made a victorious return to Preston for an individual meeting on Saturday 3 May, while the team suffered their first league defeat riding away at Edinburgh on the same day. The Preston team were a different proposition on their home track though, and reversed the result in the return fixture on 8 May. Ham Burrill was the outstanding rider that night, winning the Preston Handicap and the All Stars race too. Eric Airey continued to impress, beating Jack Tye and Harry 'Crash' Fraser in the final of the Golden Armlet.

Tommy Price, Ham Burrill and Frank Varey dominated the individual meetings in May and Preston continued their winning ways beating Barnsley 25-10 on 22 May. All six heats were won by Preston riders and so comfortable was their lead that reserve Claude Rye was given rides in the last two heats. There was a sensational ending to the Golden Sash event that followed the league clash. Chris Tattersall had been leading the race, but crashed on the last bend. Jack Tye quickly shut off his engine to avoid a collision, but still managed to win the race. With Joe Abbott gaining ground very quickly, Tye used his feet to propel his bike across the finishing line for the narrowest of victories. Frank Smith won the Stokes Trophy ahead of B. Halstead and Jimmie Carnie.

In an attempt to provide some variety and attract a bigger crowd, a series of match races between riders representing the cities of Preston, Liverpool and Manchester was held on 24 May. After three exciting races, the Preston pairing of Ham Burrill and Jack Chiswell won the meeting, with Frank Charles and Syd Newiss of Manchester in second place and 'Ginger' Lees and Larry Boulton bringing up the rear for Liverpool.

Saturday 31 May was a busy day for the Preston riders. They pulled off a shock 18-17 victory at the White City track in Manchester during the afternoon. Joe Abbott was the star for Preston, winning all three of his heats in the league encounter and winning the Silver Helmet during the second half. Unfortunately, Ham Burrill was injured at White City and couldn't ride in the individual tournament at Preston in the evening. Joe Abbott continued his winning ways, winning the Golden Sash and beating Cyril 'Squib' Burton in a series of match races.

It was around this time that the Preston management began to run into financial difficulties. In the late 1920s, almost half of the Preston workforce was employed in the textile industry. The effects of the recession following the Wall Street Crash of 1929 began to hit the cotton trade very hard and by mid-1930, the Lancashire cotton mills were beginning to close down at a rapid rate. Many of the Preston fans ended up on the dole and were unable to afford two trips to the speedway every week. To add to their difficulties, the Star riders were demanding high appearance fees and the Preston directors were well known for their generous bonuses!. It cost around £700 to run a speedway meeting at Farringdon Park and eleven meetings were held in May 1930. It didn't take a mathematician to work out that the track was being run at a huge loss. Following the home match on 14 June, Preston Speedway only ran on Thursday evenings.

The following week was a very busy one for the Preston riders. Starting on Monday 16 June, Preston lost 14-22 in a league match at Wombwell. On the following night, Joe Abbott, Ham Burrill, George Reynard and Jack Tye represented Preston in a series of challenge races at Bristol, before moving on to Cardiff on the Wednesday night for a challenge match at the White City Stadium on Sloper Road. Then it was back up to Preston for a challenge match against a Welsh select side on 19 June, which Preston won 48-15, before finishing their hectic schedule with a league victory at Warrington on Friday 20 June.

With meetings being held less frequently, crowd levels showed some improvement and over 14,000 saw Preston beat Warrington on 26 June. The meeting against Glasgow on 3 July was the first to fall victim to the atrocious summer of 1930 and a week later, Preston faced the Hall Green team from Birmingham in a nine-heat challenge match.

The promoters needed crowds of around 14,000 just to break even, so the appearance of the legendary Lloyd 'Sprouts' Elder on 17 July was expected to attract another bumper crowd. In the event, only 8,000 spectators turned up for what proved to be an excellent night's racing. Elder was an easy winner of the Golden Armlet, but the biggest surprise of the night came when the American star was beaten by Claude Rye in the heats of the Flying Twelve.

Claude Rye came to prominence when he beat American Ace 'Sprouts' Elder on 17 July 1930.

The Preston team that beat Liverpool on 24 July 1930. (Left to right): Tommy Price, Jack Chiswell, Joe Abbott, George Reynard, Claude Rye and Ham Burrill (captain).

In a deal that saw Frank Chiswell move to Liverpool, Tommy Price returned to Preston in time to face his former team mates in a £200 'grudge' match on 24 July. The two-legged match was arranged by the Preston manager to avenge their league defeat earlier in the season. In a sensational first heat, Ham Burrill was knocked from his machine and had to withdraw from the meeting. Tommy Price, determined to put one over his old team, rose to the occasion with a splendid three ride maximum, including a vital win in the last heat that gave Preston victory by a single point. The meeting also featured a match between the Preston and Liverpool reserve sides, Jack Tye and Jimmie Carnie proved their potential by winning all of their rides.

Tragedy struck in the closing stages of the meeting though, when Carnie became the third rider to be killed at Farringdon Park in fifteen months.

The fatal accident occurred in the second heat of the Golden Helmet, the final event of the evening. Claude Rye was originally drawn to ride in this heat, but was having problems with his bike. In a gesture of goodwill, the two riders had agreed to swap races. Carnie caught Chris Tattersall's back wheel as he tried to overtake him at the Ribbleton end of the circuit and was flung against the fence. As he fell back on the track, he was struck by George Reynard. Carnie was still alive when the ambulance men carried him from the track, but died within half an hour from a fractured skull. It was revealed later that twenty-three-year-old Carnie was due to retire from speedway later that week. He wanted to concentrate on a new car sales business, the only means of support for his recently widowed mother! Despite the black cloud hanging over the team, Preston went to Liverpool on 30 July for the return leg and won 29-25 in Jimmie's honour.

Joe Abbott in conversation in the Preston pits (Auto-Motor Journal).

On the following evening, Belle Vue visited Preston for one of the most thrilling matches ever seen at Farringdon Park. In heat four, with the scores level, Ham Burrill's chain broke just as the starters flag fell. In another heat, Joe Abbott was forced to retire after clashing with Eric Langton and in the penultimate heat, the steward could not separate Claude Rye and Clem Court and awarded a dead heat for third place. This left Preston needing maximum points from the last heat to secure victory. Tommy Price won the heat in great style, leading from start to finish, but despite a typically battling performance, Jack Tye could only finish third, meaning that Belle Vue won the match by a single point!

With the club falling deeper and deeper into debt and the directors now publicly squabbling with each other, a challenge match featuring the stars of Lancashire and a team of crack Australians was arranged for 14 August. The meeting went to another thrilling last-heat decider, Australia finally winning the match 25-23. Despite the action on the track, crowd levels were still too low to make speedway financially viable. Some of the riders had not been paid and a creditors' meeting was held on the morning of 11 September. The directors of Preston Speedway laid their cards on the table and offered to pay out 5 shillings in the pound or go into liquidation. Very sportingly, the creditors accepted the deal and the club went ahead with a league match against Leicester later that evening.

Not all of the riders were happy, though. Tommy Price and Ian Ritchings moved to Leicester Super and Crazy Hutchins announced that he was going to ride in Copenhagen. Claude and Percy Rye headed back south, 'where the money was better'. Claude signed a contract to ride for Wimbledon, where he blossomed into one of their most outstanding riders of the pre-war era. Jack Chiswell announced his retirement from the sport, but the biggest shock was the retirement of the skipper. Ham Burrill revealed that he had quietly married local girl Gladys Wilkinson on the previous Tuesday and was opening a motorcycle business in Whiston. He told the gathered crowd that he would be leaving Preston on 13 September to combine a honeymoon with some riding at the Hamburg track. It wasn't all down to money for Ham though; recent injuries had affected his form and Jimmie Carnie's death had really upset him.

Following Burrill's departure, Joe Abbott took over as skipper and led the team to victory against Leicester. Ivor Creek, frustrated at the lack of rides at Belle Vue, was signed in a bid to bolster the weakened team. Ivor had ridden at Preston a week earlier and had beaten 'Sprouts' Elder in one of the best races ever seen at Farringdon Park.

Preston's troubles came to a head following the league match against Leicester. The proposed match against Sheffield on 16 September was cancelled, as was the individual meeting planned for 25 September. Once again, Preston failed to complete all of their league fixtures, but, still managed to finish in fourth place. It looked like the end of the line for Preston Speedway, but in an amazing twist of fate, their biggest rivals at Liverpool proved to be their saviours.

During the 1930 season, the Liverpool promoters had tried to introduce on-track betting in a bid to attract bigger crowds. Not only did the ACU refuse this request, but the landlords of Stanley Stadium were so annoyed that they terminated the lease on 10 September and refused to have them back for another season. The entire Liverpool promotion, along with former Preston manager Norman Jackman, relocated to Farringdon Park for the 1931 season, taking over the Preston name and the contracts of some of the current Preston riders as part of the deal. The new faces at Farringdon Park included 'Ginger' Lees, Les 'Smiler' Wooton and Larry Boulton.

With a new board of directors, the 1931 season opened with an individual meeting on 3 April. Sheffield's Dusty Haigh won the race for the Golden Helmet on opening night and Frank Varey won the Golden Sash at the second meeting on 9 April. The

Harold 'Ginger' Lees became a Preston rider when the Liverpool team relocated to Farringdon Park in 1931.

new-look Preston team opened their league campaign with a defeat at Belle Vue on 11 April, but they had their revenge five days later at Farringdon Park. With only six teams contesting the 1931 Northern League, teams would face each other twice at home and twice away in order to make the league more attractive.

Although Preston were a hard team to beat at home, they could never repeat their form on their travels. Of their 8 completed home fixtures, Preston won six, drew one and only lost once, against Belle Vue on 25 June. It was a completely different story away from Farringdon Park, however, where Preston lost all 9 of their matches.

The draw with Leeds on 11 June ended in controversial style when Eric Airey was excluded from the final heat, depriving Preston of the point they needed to secure victory. It was all taken in good spirit, though, and the Leeds team were actually applauded for their spirited performance.

Possibly the most outstanding Preston performance of the season came in the National Trophy, a new competition sponsored by the *Daily Mail* featuring teams from both the Northern and Southern Leagues. The trophy was run using a twenty-one-heat format and favoured teams with greater strength in depth, which is probably why Preston performed so well. In the first round Preston faced against White City (Glasgow) and surprisingly beat the Scottish team 52-43 on their home track on 26 May. In the return leg, Preston totally outclassed the visitors, romping to a 70-26 victory. Following the match, Jack Chiswell made a return to the track and gave a spectacular display of broadsiding, but the demonstration ended suddenly, when Jack's rear wheel collapsed.

In the second round of the National Trophy, Preston were drawn against High Beech from Essex. The home leg on 2 July saw Preston build up a comfortable 34-point lead, which saw them safely through to the semi-finals on aggregate. Preston were the only Northern team to get beyond the second round, but they met their match in the semi-final, losing home and away to the Stamford Bridge side from London.

Programme cover from the National Trophy match against High Beech on 2 July 1931.

1931 Preston team (Left to right): Jack Tye, 'Ginger' Lees, Eric Airey, Joe Abbott, Larry Boulton, Norman Jackman (manager), Les 'Smiler' Wooton and Gustav 'Bill' Kellner.

Preston's run in the Northern Knockout Cup was halted by Belle Vue in another tense tussle. Preston had already disposed of Leicester Super in the first round and gone within a point of beating Belle Vue on their home track in the first leg of the semi-final. In the return leg, though, Belle Vue did the unthinkable and reversed the score exactly, leaving the teams level on aggregate. Both matches were replayed, but there was to be no fairytale ending for Preston, who were beaten home and away by the Manchester team.

With Liverpool and Preston now combined, Belle Vue had taken over the mantle of the team the Preston fans loved to hate! The Preston manager, Norman Jackman, expressed his disappointment that three Belle Vue riders had been chosen to represent England against Australia in July, but there was no place for any of the Preston team. He wrote a letter to the Belle Vue supremo, E.O. Spence, challenging the Belle Vue trio of Eric Langton, Frank Varey and Walter Hull to meet a Preston trio (chosen from Ginger Lees, Joe Abbott, Smiler Wooton and Larry Boulton) in a home and away challenge, just to prove who had the best riders.

As an England selector, Spence could not turn the challenge down and the grudge match was arranged for Belle Vue on 17 June with the return leg at Preston on the following day. The challenge was run under league rules and at the end of the first leg, much to the home crowds' displeasure, Preston led 14-11. In the return leg at Farringdon Park, the home side repeated the feat and beat Belle Vue 14-8. Mr Jackman was justifiably pleased with the result.

Further excitement fuelled the Preston *v.* Belle Vue league match on 25 June, when Jack Tye and Frank Varey came to blows in the pits. Later in the match, Varey was

Ready for the off – heat one of the Preston v. Belle Vue match on 25 June 1931, the only time Preston were beaten at home all season. (Auto-Motor Journal)

excluded for dangerous riding after he had beaten 'Ginger' Lees. Even Lees could not understand that decision. Despite that one minor setback, Belle Vue were the better team on the night and inflicted Preston's only home league defeat of the season.

Joe Abbott's season was cut short when he suffered one of many racing injuries that would interrupt his career. The White City track in Manchester had closed down in July 1930, and most of their riders were transferred to Belle Vue. Two of them, Norrie Isbister and Alfie Williams, were then 'loaned' to Preston to cover for their injured number one rider.

The rising level of unemployment in Preston meant that crowd levels at Farringdon Park were way below the 'break-even' mark. For the third season running, Preston failed to complete their league fixtures and ended their season early with a challenge match against an Australian select on 24 September. They finished fifth out of six teams in the final league table and were in deep financial trouble again. Preston Speedways Ltd was wound up at the end of the 1931 season and all of their contracted riders were put up for sale to pay off their creditors. Tommy Price, Larry Boulton, Joe Abbott and Eric Airey were all transferred to big rivals Belle Vue, 'Ginger' Lees went to Wembley and 'Smiler' Wooton found his way to Birmingham.

Jack Tye's sponsor, William Jones of the New Cock Yard Garage, became the new managing director of Preston Speedway in 1932. The season opened on Good Friday, 25 March with the traditional individual meeting. In the programme notes, William Jones explained that he was sorry to see that a number of star riders had left Preston, but promised the supporters that he would be signing some equally good riders in the near future. It was also suggested that he wanted to enter a Preston team in the new National League. He finished his notes with an appeal for continued support to enable him to bring star riders back to Preston.

The next meeting on Easter Monday 28 March saw the return of former Preston favourites Larry Boulton, Joe Abbott, Eric Airey, Claude Rye and 'Ginger' Lees. The meeting also heralded the return of Ham Burrill, refreshed after a year out of the sport. Ham had missed the thrill of riding and had already been offered trials at West Ham and Crystal Palace, but in the end he decided to return to his former track. A third meeting, planned for 7 April, was rained off and rearranged for the following week, 14 April, when Wal Phillips of Stamford Bridge won the race for the Golden Armlet. By this time, even the local newspapers were beginning to lose interest in Preston Speedway and even though a meeting was advertised for 21 April, the papers do not report any results.

The new Preston team was due to be unveiled in a challenge match against Sheffield on 19 May, but the meeting was cancelled due to the abysmally small crowds. A further meeting was advertised to take place on 2 June, but it is highly unlikely that the match ever took place.

Earlier in the year, the rugby club had been approached by another syndicate, who were interested in introducing greyhound racing to Farringdon Park. As the rugby club only had a couple of years remaining on their lease, they sold up, raising enough money to purchase their own ground at Lea. Farringdon Park was eventually sold and the site of the speedway track now lies beneath Farringdon Crescent, adjacent to Ribbleton Cemetery.

A greyhound track did open on 5 May 1932, but on a new site just off Acregate Lane. The track was very close to Farringdon Park and no doubt contributed to the demise of the speedway. The possibility of speedway racing being introduced to Acregate Lane was mentioned in 1937, but as far as I am aware, nothing ever materialised.

Speedway was rumoured to be returning to Preston again in 1971, when promoter Vic White sought planning permission from the local council, but his application was turned down, and like so many other towns and cities in the north-west, Preston seems destined to be lost to speedway.

Programme cover from the final speedway
meeting at Farringdon Park, 14 April 1932.

4

TOWNELEY SPEEDWAY, BURNLEY

Towneley Speedway had it all: big crowds, a fabulous stadium and three of the top dirt-track riders in the north. But it was not to be. Towneley Speedway opened on 30 March 1929 and closed less than four months later, on 20 July 1929.

Towneley Stadium was on the drive to Towneley Hall, just off Todmorden Road and close to the footpath known as 'Rabbit Walk'. It had originally opened as a greyhound track on 3 September 1927 and offered two covered grandstands on the home straight, three covered shelters on the back straight and electric floodlights.

Early in 1929, the Burnley and District Dirt-Track Racing Association Ltd was formed to promote motorcycle dirt-track racing at the stadium. Amongst the directors of the company was one Arthur Taylor, a well-known steward for the North-Western Centre of the ACU.

On 9 March 1929, it was announced that nearly forty riders, all with a local connection, had been signed up to ride at Towneley. They included Frank Charles (whose uncle lived at nearby Brierfield), Harold 'Ginger' Lees, (the nephew of the Mayor of Burnley), Arthur, Cyril and Fred Wilcock from Nelson, Jack Lund from Hapton and local riders Joe Abbott and Les Martin. These riders would form the nucleus of the Burnley team, which had been entered into the newly formed English Dirt-Track League.

Towneley Speedway opened its doors to the public on the afternoon of 30 March, the first of a two-day extravaganza over the Easter weekend. The first meeting was an open invitation event featuring some of the top northern dirt-track stars. Around 12,000 spectators packed into the stadium to see Councillor H. Lees formally open the track and his wife cut the tapes to start the first race, a Stars Challenge match race between Arthur Franklyn and Arthur Wilcock. The two principal events of the afternoon were the Golden Helmet, won by Arthur Franklyn from the White City track in Manchester and the senior scratch race won by 'Ginger' Lees. Other competitors included Harry Whitfield, Mark Sheldon, Frank Charles, Jack Chiswell, Ham Burrill and 'Crazy' Hutchins. Amazingly, the only casualty of the day was Arthur Wilcock, who injured his hands and face after a spectacular fall on the first bend.

A young bike racer from Galgate, near Lancaster, destined to become one of Britain's greatest speedway stars, made his dirt-track debut in the junior scratch races on that afternoon, too. Riding a stripped down 350cc Sunbeam, William Kitchen finished

*Harold Riley 'Ginger' Lees was the captain of the
Burnley speedway team and the nephew of the
Mayor of Burnley, who formally opened the track.*

second in his heat behind Eric Airey, another young hopeful from the Lancaster area.
The final of the junior event was won by Les Martin, who later found fame in the Isle of
Man TT races.

The Easter Monday attendance of 4,000 was disappointing considering the huge
turnout on the previous day, but the racing was still as thrilling. Frank Charles showed
the crowd exactly why he was so highly rated, and won both the Stars Challenge race
and the senior scratch race, setting a new track record in the process. The junior final
was won by another local rider, E. Francis.

Burnleys first league match was ridden at Lundwood Speedway, Barnsley on 6 April.
It was a victorious debut as they beat the home side by 17-11 in a match raced over four
heats. Frank Charles and Arthur Wilcock scored top with 6 points each, Cyril Wilcock
scored 3 points and Joe Abbot scored 2. The reserves, Eric Airey and Jack Lund, did not
ride. 'Ginger' Lees was away riding in Copenhagen at the time.

The third home meeting was on 13 April, another open individual event, which only
attracted a crowd of around 3,000. Once again Frank Charles was in invincible form to
take the Golden Gauntlet event. Charles was also on course to win the final of the
Golden Helmet, too, but he momentarily lost power on the last lap, allowing Cyril
Wilcock to go around him and register his first trophy win at Towneley. Les Martin took
the honours in the junior scratch race.

By the time Burnley raced their second league fixture, the format of the English Dirt-
Track League had been altered. The original company behind the EDTL had gone into
liquidation and a new company, the Northern Dirt-Track Owners Association, had
taken over the running of the league. From this point on, matches were run over nine
heats with teams made up of six riders and two reserves. Even though the new league
didn't officially start until 20 April, the result of the Burnley *v.* Barnsley match was
allowed to stand.

The first match under the new format was at White City (Manchester), but Burnley were well and truly beaten by the Manchester team 49-13. Scorers were 'Ginger' Lees 4, Joe Abbott 3, Frank Charles 3, Cyril Wilcock 2, Jack Lund 1 and E. Ingham failed to score.

The next home meeting was scheduled for 27 April, but this had to be cancelled due to building work at the stadium. Amongst other improvements, a new car park was being constructed to cope with the amount of spectators turning up for the speedway and greyhound racing.

In a bid to strengthen the league team, Burnley signed Billy Howard in time for their third league fixture at the Stanley Stadium, Liverpool, on 4 May. This time Burnley got it right, beating the home team 35-28. Frank Charles was invincible for the visitors, scoring a 12-point maximum from his three rides (4 points were awarded for a win in the EDTL). He had solid support from his team partner Joe Abbott, who followed him home for second place in all three of their heats, Captain 'Ginger' Lees weighed in with 9 points, whilst Arthur Wilcock, Cyril Wilcock and Billy Howard shared the remaining 8 points between them.

Things were looking good for Burnley and over 10,000 spectators turned up for the first league match at Towneley on 11 May. The team chosen to represent Burnley in their home debut against Salford Albion was, 'Ginger' Lees, Frank Charles, Joe Abbott and Arthur and Cyril Wilcock. Billy Howard beat Jack Lund and E. Ingham in a special three-man challenge race to decide who would be the sixth member of the team. The visitors simply had no answer to the scoring power of Charles, Abbott and Lees and were soundly beaten 41-22.

Following the league match there was a 'best of three' match race series between Frank Charles and 'Ginger' Lees to decide who was the 'Champion of Burnley'. Lees won the first leg and Charles levelled the score in the second leg. In the third and final leg, Lees hit the front from the start but fell on the second bend. Rather than finish the race alone, Charles coasted to a halt and called for a rerun. At the second attempt, Lees

The Burnley English Dirt-Track League team (left to right): Frank Charles (kneeling), Arthur Taylor (manager), Arthur Wilcock, 'Ginger' Lees, Jack Lund, Cyril Wilcock (on bike), (unidentified), Joe Abbott, (unidentified).

made the start again but Charles overtook him on the third lap; Lees then came around the outside to try and regain the lead, but he overcooked it and fell off again. Charles lost his concentration and came to grief himself, allowing Lees to remount and coast across the line for an easy but hollow victory.

Despite the success on the track, things weren't going quite so well behind the scenes. The Burnley promotion had been trying to get local businesses to invest in the speedway and had even asked the local council for support, but just about all of their requests had fallen on deaf ears. Even though they had seen crowds of over 10,000 for two meetings, outside financial investment was needed if they were to avoid bankruptcy. An advertisement in the *Burnley Express and Advertiser* on 18 May announced that there would be no further meetings at the track, 'owing to insufficient support and consequent financial losses. Negotiations are proceeding for the sale of the track and meetings will hopefully recommence on 25 May'.

On the very same night as the announcement was made, the Burnley league team were in action at Hanley in Staffordshire. Once again, Burnley's top-end strength saw them win by an impressive 49-13, moving them into third place in the league table behind Leeds and White City. To rub salt into the wounds, Frank Charles and 'Ginger' Lees took all of the silverware in the support events, too.

The promised sale never materialised and a shareholders meeting was held on 27 May. To puts the minds of the fans at rest, a press release stated that, 'There is no doubt that racing will continue at Towneley and it is practically certain that the track will reopen on 1 June with a league match against Hanley followed by another league match against Liverpool on the evening of 4 June.

It took until 26 June for the sale of the track to be completed and Percy Blatt, managing director of Rochdale speedway, was announced as the new owner. In the meantime, all of Burnley's league encounters had been cancelled and 'Ginger' Lees had been banned from riding by the sports governing body for appearing at the unlicensed Audenshaw track, near Manchester. Joe Abbott and Jack Lund had gone to Preston on loan, but this was only on the condition that they would return to Burnley when it reopened.

The first meeting under the new promotion was held on 29 June, when Burnley faced Leicester in a league fixture. As an added incentive for the fans, admission costs were reduced. Burnley raced into an early lead, but the meeting had to be stopped after just 20 minutes due to excessive dust. The riders were riding almost blind and the crowd couldn't see anything. The country was in the grip of a heatwave at the time, and water rationing was the order of the day. Because of the ban, Burnley corporation had refused Towneley Speedway the use of any water for the track. After heat three of the Leicester match, efforts were made to utilise the stream which passed under the stadium, but the pumping engine would not work. In the circumstances, the meeting was abandoned with Burnley leading 13-8. Frank Charles and Joe Abbott had both won their first heats, Fred Wilcock had scored 2 points and Arthur Wilcock, Jack Lund and E. Ingham had scored 1 point each.

What turned out to be the last speedway meeting in Burnley was held on 6 July 1929. It was scheduled to have been another league encounter against Leeds, but Arthur and

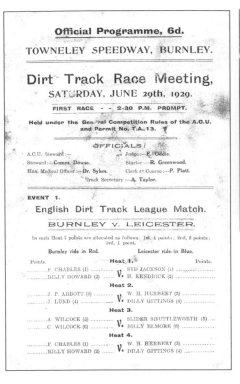

Above: *Joe Abbott was arguably the most successful local rider to emerge from the Burnley track. During his career he rode for Preston, Belle Vue, Harringay and Odsal and also represented his country on numerous occasions. Sadly, Joe was killed in a track crash in 1950, a few days after his Silver Wedding anniversary.*

Left: *Programme cover from the league match against Leicester on 29 June 1929. The match had to be abandoned after the third heat due to the excessive dust.*

Cyril Wilcock and 'Ginger' Lees had been booked to ride in Hamburg on the same weekend. The league match was subsequently cancelled and replaced with an individual programme. The promoters had been advised against running during the Burnley 'holiday weekend', but they chose to ignore the advice and suffered the consequences when a very poor crowd turned out to see the racing.

Matters were made worse when the star attraction, 'Squib' Burton, failed to appear and was replaced by Rochdale's Ron Thompson and only four riders contested the junior scratch races. Frank Charles dominated the whole meeting, beating Joe Abbott and B. Higginbottom in the Flying Nine final, winning all of his heats and setting a new track record. His only defeat came in the final of the Golden Helmet when he suffered an engine failure, allowing Joe Abbott to take the honours.

Percy Blatt suffered a huge financial loss by running this meeting against good advice and it was announced on 20 July that Burnley had formally withdrawn from the English Dirt-Track League and cancelled all of their remaining fixtures. On 24 July Joe Abbott and Jack Lund returned to Preston on loan, and Frank Charles joined them in a similar deal three days later. 'Ginger' Lees remained in Hamburg for the remainder of the season and on their return, the Wilcock brothers found a new home at Salford.

I have heard stories about local riders using the Towneley track for practice sessions long after the speedway had closed, but there is no documentary evidence to support this. Towneley Stadium did continue to host greyhound meetings until the stadium closed down for good in 1933 and was sold. The site of Towneley Speedway is now home to a more sedate sport and lies under part of the municipal golf course.

5

WHALLEY

By the summer of 1929, speedway was booming and tracks were being opened in virtually every major town in the UK, but one of the more unusual and lesser known venues was at Whalley in Lancashire, a picturesque village between Preston and Burnley.

Whalley is probably more famous for the ruins of its ancient Abbey, but back in 1929 it was also home to 'Jazzland', a riverside amusement park run by John William Dean of Clayton-le-Moors. 'Jazzland' was situated at the foot of Whalley Nab, on the banks of the river Calder (the same river that ran past Towneley Stadium in Burnley). A sixpence admission fee would give you unlimited access to swings, see-saws, a helter-skelter and rowing boats on the river. It also boasted its own tea rooms (constructed from two First World War army huts) and was very popular with courting couples and the young motorcyclists from Billington, Great Harwood and Clitheroe. Amongst their number was Cliff Walmsley, who was only sixteen at the time and rode a 250cc Ivy.

Speedway tracks had opened at nearby Burnley and Preston in 1929, so it comes as no surprise to find that these motorcyclists were all speedway fans too. One of the young lads bought a dirt-track Douglas and kept it in a garage at Whalley. His friends all took turns riding in the fields, but they all found it a bit slow, until one of them noticed a small lever and pushed it forward to see what it was for; the bike instantly took off! They had been riding the bike with the ignition retarded. The next step was to find a track to ride it on.

John William Dean came to their rescue and let them use the field next to 'Jazzland', but not content with just riding on the grass, they decided to build their own miniature dirt track. Ted Wild, a gold dealer from Great Harwood, used his truck to ferry cinders and ash from the cotton mills in Great Harwood and the others borrowed a donkey and cart to ferry factory ash from Billington. There was no hardcore base, they simply laid the ashes and cinders directly on top of the grass. The track was almost circular in shape and measured approximately 150 yards to the lap; it was narrow too, only measuring about 10ft at its widest point. Cliff recalled that the track used to cut up really badly when it was wet and the earth would often break through the cinders, but it was nothing that a bit of work with rakes and a roller couldn't sort out. When it was warm and dry, though, the Whalley track turned out to be a super little racing strip.

As the months rolled on, more and more aspiring riders turned up at Whalley, so in an attempt to control numbers, the Whalley Amateur Dirt-Track Club was formed. Ted Wild was elected as president, 'Dizzy' Adams, club secretary and C. Jones as captain. Together they laid out some basic rules.

The club was to be limited to thirty riding members, all of whom had to live within a ten-mile radius of Whalley. Professional riders were forbidden to use the track unless invited by the committee. To finance the upkeep of the track, the committee decided that members would have to pay an annual subscription and also pay 5 shillings to ride on the track, which was a big chunk out of a cotton mill worker's wage. No liability would be accepted for any injuries or damage to machines and as the track was so small only two riders would be permitted to use the track at any one time.

Such was the reputation of the little track, it was featured in the northern edition of *Auto Motor Journal*, where it was revealed that Whalley would be hosting properly organised dirt-track meetings in 1930. The first meeting took place on the afternoon of 30 March 1930, when around 4,000 spectators turned up to watch the first 'Whalley Dirt-Track Festival'. Refreshments were laid on in the 'Jazzland' tea rooms and in the Assembly Rooms on the other side of the river.

The committee had invited members of the Preston team to take part in the festival. 'Ham' Burrill didn't find the tiny track to his liking and crashed in practice. The subsequent injury to his arm was enough to prevent him from riding in the afternoon's main event.

The club members entertained the crowd with some enthusiastic riding, and former Burnley rider Jack Lund was in spectacular form until he fell and took no further part. But it was another former Burnley rider who stole the show. Joe Abbott was greeted by loud applause as he rode out onto the track and he repaid the compliment by showering the crowd with cinders as he swept around the tiny track flat out.

Throughout the summer of 1930, the members of the Whalley Club would take turns to practice their broadsiding skills, some progressing to the novice races at nearby Preston. Amongst them were Cliff, (still riding his stripped-down Ivy), 'Dizzy' Adams, who rode an Excelsior with a 250cc Villiers engine and a lad named Smithson from Burnley. Arthur, Cyril and Fred Wilcock were frequent visitors and sometimes the entire Preston team would turn up on a Sunday morning for a few practice laps. The summer of 1930 was certainly a memorable one for the motorcycle enthusiasts in Whalley.

Joe Abbott was the star attraction at the Whalley Dirt-Track Festival and really made the cinders fly! The report in the Auto Motor Journal *described his broadsiding display as… 'bordering on the miraculous'*

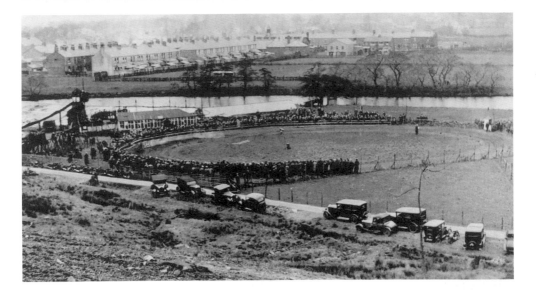

Above: *A large crowd watches the racing at Whalley on 30 March 1930. The helter-skelter, swings and tearooms at 'Jazzland' can clearly be seen on the left of this picture, with the village of Whalley on the other side of the river.* (Mortons Motorcycle Media)

Right: *Take a walk up Whalley Nab today and the shape of the track is still clearly visible in the field beside the river.* (Author's collection)

By the end of the year, however, interest was on the wane. Burnley Speedway had already closed down and Preston was having financial difficulties. The track at Whalley wasn't used much after the summer of 1930 and the site gradually grassed over. The Lancashire cotton industry had been hit hard in the depression and many of the club members found themselves out of work and unable to afford their subs. Some of them found new jobs and moved away, while others simply lost interest. Not Cliff Walmsley, though. Besides being a life long supporter of Belle Vue speedway, he continued to ride in grass tracks, trials and scrambles, becoming a founder member of the Ribble Valley Motor Cycle Club and the Lancashire Grass-Track Riders Club.

Sadly, Cliff died while this book was being prepared, but a few months earlier he had joined me on a walk up Whalley Nab. We stopped and looked down on the field next to the weir. The shape of the tiny track is still clearly visible and for a moment we both imagined the sight of Joe Abbott churning up the cinders on one of the most picturesque tracks in the country.

6

BARROW-IN-FURNESS: IN THE BEGINNING...

Formed in 1901, Barrow AFC played their first three seasons at the Strawberry Ground, followed by a move to Ainslie Street in 1904. Within twelve months though, the club was on the move again, to Little Park, in Roose, but after several seasons playing on the outskirts of town, the club started to look for a more central venue. They set their sights on Holker Street, a ground owned by the Furness Railway Company and the home of Hindpool Athletic.

The Holker Street enclosure was originally a gypsy site, dating back to the nineteenth century. When the gypsies were evicted, they placed a curse on the land, making sure that any new tenants would have a bleak future.

In May 1930, it was announced that dirt-track racing was to be introduced at Holker Street. The Northern Motor Sports Club came to an agreement with the football club to run dirt-track races on Thursday evenings and Saturday afternoons during the summer. The track was specially prepared using ashes laid directly on top of the grass, and a safety fence (of sorts) was made using corrugated steel sheets with sharpened points on top! Harold Jackson, 'Bert' Evans, Stan Ainsworth and the Skirrow brothers held trial sessions during the first week of June and everything was set for Barrow Speedway to open on the evening of Thursday 12 June 1930.

The star of the opening night was Eric Airey from Lancaster, a well-known sand racer who had been booked as a replacement for local rider, Frank Charles, who was on league duty for White City. In the final of the Silver Goblet event, Airey had taken the lead when Harry Skirrow had crashed on the first lap. He pulled away from Harold Jackson and Roger Rogerson and won by over half a lap. Unsurprisingly, Eric established the track record in this race, a time of 95.2 seconds for five laps (one mile) and also set a standing one-lap record of 18.4 seconds.

Airey put on a superb display in his heat of the handicap races, too. Riding off a 16-second handicap, he caught and passed two riders, and finished barely a bike's length behind Harold Jackson on the line. The handicap final produced the closest race of the night. Harold Jackson, 'Bert' Evans and Tommy Simpson were all off scratch and Frank Burgess was given a 4-second handicap. Burgess caught Jackson at the end of the second lap, but Jackson lost concentration and fell. Burgess then set his sights on Evans, passing him on the last lap and crossing the line barely yards in front to win the Soccer Club Trophy. Several riders crashed in the junior race, luckily none were

Above: *Eric Airey from Lancaster was the star of the opening night at Holker Street.*

Right: *Advertisement for the second speedway meeting at Holker Street.*

BARROW SPEEDWAY.
Saturday June 21st, 2-45 p.m.

BATTLE OF GIANTS.
ERIC AIREY, Preston
v.
BROADSIDE DAWSON Copenhagen
Also Special Engagement of the one and only
CRAZY HUTCHINS
who will ride against our best, also
DANK McKEWAN, Preston.

THIS IS THE REAL THING.
YOU WILL BE THRILLED.

seriously hurt. The final, for the Silver Rose Bowl, was won by G. Skirrow ahead of Ernie Whiteside and 'Gilly' Alison. In an interview after the match, Eric Airey remarked that the new Barrow dirt-track was 'much smoother than the Preston track'.

In the weeks following Barrow's first speedway meeting, young lads were seen racing bicycles on an old cinder track on Abbey Road. It was suggested that this would have been a better option than Holker Street, but the NMSC committee were more than happy with the first meeting at the football ground and quickly organised a second meeting on the afternoon of Saturday 21 June.

The meeting was run in the pouring rain, and in a gesture of goodwill, spectators were allowed into the grandstand at no extra charge. Eric Airey managed to shatter his own lap record by over a second and beat Norman 'Broadside' Dawson in a special match race. But the loudest cheer of the night was saved for fifteen-year-old Harry Simpson, a local garage mechanic who upset the form book by beating G. Skirrow, Ernie Whiteside and 'Bert' Evans in the final of the junior race. Skirrow made amends by beating Frank Burgess and Lionel Cordingley in the final of the senior race.

The rain continued to fall throughout the meeting and loosened the soil beneath the cinders. Fresh cinders were laid during the interval, but the conditions became so bad that riders found it difficult to stay on their machines. Both 'Crazy' Hutchins and 'Dank' McKeowan had taken heavy falls during their match race and all four riders came off in the first heat of the handicap race. The ACU steward declared that conditions had become too dangerous and the match was abandoned.

In his meeting report, the steward also drew attention to some flagrant breaches of the rules. Riders were seen to be repeatedly looking backwards during the course of a race, crowding and foul riding and even riding in the wrong direction! Another complaint levelled at the promoters was the class of riders being employed. Riders of a higher standard were needed if they were to be successful.

Nearly fifty tons of black cinders from Vickers Armstrong Ltd were spread on the track prior to the third meeting on Thursday 26 June, which made the track heavy going. The

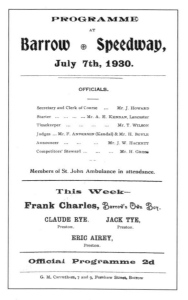

Above: *Programme cover for the 7 July meeting at Holker Street, the first to feature local hero Frank Charles.*

Right: *Frank Charles and Eric Airey prepare for their match race on 17 July 1930.* (Auto-Motor Journal)

programme included a series of match races featuring riders from Preston Speedway. The unfamiliar track conditions led to plenty of crashes. Jack McCauley came off worst of all, spending the night in North Lonsdale Hospital with concussion. Harold Jackson beat Lionel Cordingley and Frank Burgess in the final of the senior race and Roger Rogerson beat Harry Skirrow in the handicap final. The meeting finished with a special challenge race between Bert Evans and Frank Burgess. Evans claimed that he could beat Burgess on a rough track, but the wager backfired when Evans fell off on the second lap.

Over 5,000 Barrow fans turned out to see local hero Frank Charles make his debut at Holker Street on the evening of Monday 7 July. Barrow's favourite son was given a rousing reception when he beat Eric Airey, Claude Rye and Jack Tye in a series of match races. Frankie also smashed Aireys track record, setting up a new five-lap record of 90.2 seconds. The visiting riders easily beat the locals in the heats of the handicap race. The final was a real thriller, ending with Frank Charles and Jack Tye lying on the track after a collision, and Claude Rye cleverly outmanoeuvring Eric Airey to win the coveted Golden Helmet. The junior race for the Silver Rose Bowl was won by G. Skirrow ahead of Foster Williamson, while Harry Skirrow beat Peter Blundell in the race for the Silver Goblet.

Claude Rye and Jack Tye returned to Holker Street on the following Monday (14 July), along with Frank and Jack Chiswell and Jimmie Carnie. Claude Rye clipped one fifth of a second off Frankie's lap record and also beat the Chiswell brothers to retain the Golden Helmet. Local rider Harry Simpson was making rapid progress and won the Silver Rose Bowl. Lionel Cordingley, the grass-track champion from Morecambe, beat Roland Stobbart in the final of the senior race for the Silver Goblet. The most exciting race of the night was a match race between Claude Rye and the spectacular Frank Chiswell. There was never more than a wheel's length between the two Preston riders and they exchanged the lead on nine occasions before Chiswell got the verdict right on the line. Once again the meeting finished with a special challenge race. On this occasion Harold Jackson was the winner, after Harry Skirrow had crashed on the fourth lap.

Another large crowd turned up for the sixth meeting on Monday 21 July, a meeting that was marred by a nasty accident. In the final of the Golden Helmet Handicap race, Claude Rye was leading, with Tony Golding in second place. As Golding came past the grandstand at the start of the last lap, his bike swerved violently and he was thrown across the track. Ham Burrill, a few yards behind, hit Golding's bike and was himself thrown up into the air. The fourth-placed rider, Joe Abbott, could not avoid the carnage and rode over Golding's legs! Miraculously, all three riders survived without serious injury and Claude Rye, who was holding on to a slender lead at the time of the crash, was awarded the race, thus keeping a firm grip on the Golden Helmet.

The heats of the handicap event produced some thrilling races too. Joe Abbott had passed Roger Rogerson in a magnificent last-bend dash and Ham Burrill had produced a similar manoeuvre to pass Harold Jackson. In the senior race, L. Gilbert of Ulverston made a magnificent debut, winning his first race and finishing second to Roland Stobbart in the Silver Goblet final.

Joe Abbott won 2 thrilling match races against Ham Burrill and would surely have beaten Claude Rye's lap record if he hadn't hit a nasty bump in the track. The meeting also featured the debut of former Burnley rider Jack Lund, who was beaten in two

match races by Tony Golding and Claude Rye. For the third time in four weeks, the meeting finished with a special challenge race. This time teenager Harry Simpson threw down the gauntlet to Tommy Newton and beat him in a four-lap match race.

The most exciting racing of the season was witnessed by a record crowd of over 7,000 on Monday 28 July. Two thrilling match races took place between the captains of the two Manchester teams, Frank Charles and Frank Varey, but the deciding leg was abandoned after Varey had injured his foot. Earlier in the evening, Varey had established new one-lap and four-lap track records, only for Charles to break both of them later in the meeting. Claude Rye was unable to defend his Golden Helmet after a nasty looking accident involving Roger Rogerson. Rye was taken to hospital with burns to his hands and face. In the final, Charles raced away from Frank Chiswell to win the Golden Helmet, but Varey had to retire after burning his foot on his exhaust. Roland Stobbart retained the Silver Goblet in the senior race, beating L. Gilbert and Roger Rogerson. Roland also beat Lionel Cordingley in a special challenge race.

After a short run of only seven meetings, the first season of speedway racing in Barrow had come to an end. Not through a lack of support, but because the Barrow AFC football pitch needed returfing in preparation for the new football season.

When speedway returned to Barrow for a second season in 1931, the Northern Motor Sports Club opted to move to a new venue, Little Park, three miles out of the town centre in the village of Roose. This would not be the first time motorcycles had been raced at Little Park, though. Barrow Rugby League Club had moved into Little Park during the First World War and purchased the ground from Lord Cavendish in 1920.

Playing so far out of town had an alarming downturn on the rugby club's finances, so in 1929, they acquired the Jute Works site off Duke Street and began the construction of a new stadium, Craven Park. To offset some of their costs, greyhound racing had been introduced to Little Park in the late 1920s and, on 26 May 1928, the Barrow & District Motor Club had organised a motorcycle grass-track meeting to help fund the ailing rugby club.

Typically for Barrow, it rained! But despite the weather, around 1,500 people turned up to catch a glimpse of the new sport. W.A. Stevens won the two 350cc events, while Frank Charles won all three unlimited events. Frankie and his young partner had also entertained the crowd with some stunt riding during the interval, but heavy rain forced them to cancel their second show, scheduled to take place after the meeting.

The construction of Craven Park took much longer than expected, so the rugby club continued to play at Little Park even though the two grandstands had already been removed to their new ground. With finances stretched to the limit, the rugby club was more than happy to let the Northern Motor Sports Club rent the ground for dirt-track racing in 1931. The promoters laid a new track around the rugby pitch, and in May they applied for admission to the National Speedway Association. Once again, the club acquired around one hundred tons of black cinders from Vickers Armstrong Ltd, and laid them directly on top of the grass.

Five thousand spectators turned up for the opening night on 1 June 1931, a good turn out considering the location, but the promoters had managed to put an attractive programme together. The appearance of local hero Frank Charles (now captain of the Leeds team) would have helped to swell the crowd, too. Frankie had stepped in as a last-minute replacement for the injured James 'Indian' Allen.

Frank Varey officially opened the new track by establishing a lap record of 17.8 seconds and was then set a new four-lap track record of 68.2 seconds in a terrific battle with Frank Charles in the heats of the senior scratch race. Varey went on to win the final ahead of Walter Hull and Eric Airey, but withdrew from the handicap event suffering

Opposite: *Roland Stobbart, winner of the Silver Goblet on 21 July. The young lad holding his trophy is Jack Saul, Roland's mechanic.* (British Photo Press)

Right: *Frank Burgess leads Roland Stobbart at Holker Street Check out the so-called 'safety-fence'!* (British Photo Press)

57

Frank Varey opened the Little Park circuit by establishing a flying lap record of 17.8 seconds.

with a headache. Frank Charles rode brilliantly to win the final, with Walter Hull in second place and Jack Tye third. The junior handicap was won by Bill Kitchen, making his debut at Little Park.

James Howard, clerk of the course, was delighted with the first meeting at Little Park. 'The programme and riding would not have disgraced Belle Vue', he said. 'The track is much faster than Holker Street… as an example of first-class riding under second-class conditions, it was superb!'

During the next week, the top side of the track was relaid with a new turf base. With no time to allow the ground to settle, the track was very bumpy for the meeting on Monday 8 June, and many of the riders complained. Despite the conditions, Jack Tye clipped a full second off Frank Varey's lap record and Eddie Myerscough recorded another fast time to win the Silver Goblet. A blunder by the starting marshal effectively put Jack Tye out of the senior final. Ginger Lees, Gustav Kellner and Eddie Myerscough had all won their heats from rolling starts, but in Jack's heat, the marshal insisted on a standing start. His engine spluttered and by the time it kicked into life, Eric Airey was over half a lap ahead.

To round off a successful evening, Eddie Myerscough produced a splendid manoeuvre to pass Tony Golding and Harry Simpson in the final of the Golden Helmet. Young Simpson had already produced the ride of his life to beat 'Ginger' Lees and Len Myerscough in the heats. Roland Stobbart had a poor meeting, but his seventeen-year-old brother, Maurice, rode magnificently to beat Harry Simpson for the Silver Rose Bowl. Unusually, there were three sets of brothers riding in this meeting: Eddie and Len Myerscough, Roland and Maurice Stobbart, and Tommy and Norman Newton.

A rare engine failure prevented Frank Charles from winning the Golden Helmet on 15 June. The race had to be restarted after Tommy Newton had fallen at the first attempt. In the rerun, Charles had a comfortable lead, but on the last lap, his engine cut out for a brief moment, allowing Len Woods to nip through and win the race right on the line. Harry Simpson finished in third place after another superb performance in the heats.

Earlier in the evening, Charles had beaten Woods in a thrilling match race. The two riders came off the last bend side by side, but Charles got the verdict right on the line. The two riders clashed again in the heats of the race for the Silver Goblet, once again Charles just edged home ahead of the hard riding Australian. The final produced another exciting race. Charles had made up Eric Airey's 1-second advantage by the end of the second lap, but the Leeds captain couldn't find a way past and Airey held on for the narrowest of victories.

Roland and Maurice Stobbart made a complete hash of this meeting and fell off in just about every race they entered, in fact Roland came off twice in his match race with Eric Airey. Roland took no further part in the meeting, blaming engine problems for his poor performance. After the meeting, a reporter asked Frank Charles how he liked the track, he replied 'Champion', spitting out a mouthful of cinders!

The postponement of the meeting on 22 June was a huge disappointment. A spokesman for the promoting club said that the 'regrettable and unavoidable cancellation, pending an ACU inspection of the Little Park track, will have an amicable ending within a few days'.

The end of the month came and went, with no sign of speedway returning to Little Park. Then, on 15 August, an announcement appeared in the *Barrow Guardian*: 'Speedway will recommence at Little Park on 17 Monday of August and weekly meetings will be held for the rest of the season'. The only reason given for the delay was that the club had been waiting for the ACU to give them the necessary permission to resume.

Obviously with racing having been suspended for two months, and very little in the way of an explanation being offered by the promoters, rumours of the track being closed for good were rife. To add fuel to the fire, the rugby club had dug up the pitch and removed 92,000 sods of turf, relaying them at their new ground at Craven Park. Little Park must have resembled a bomb site by this time. But the ACU records have revealed the true reasons behind the stoppage.

ACU regulations at the time declared that a special track licence was only valid for three meetings. NMSC had made a new application to run further meetings, but the new licence never arrived in time and the 22 June meeting had to be cancelled. NMSC did not operate with a 'dirt-track' licence as that would have meant laying a permanent base for their track, so they operated with a 'special' track licence, usually reserved for grass-track events.

The track inspectors at the ACU were confused over what Little Park actually was. If it was a 'grass track', they wanted to know why 'dirt-track' bikes were being ridden there. ACU regulations stipulated that 'grass-track' bikes must be fitted with brakes, and 'dirt-track' bikes should not! Further delays were caused when the entire NMSC committee disappeared off to the Isle of Man TT races for three weeks! In the end, the two parties agreed on a compromise, and the ACU granted permission for Little Park to continue. With the necessary paperwork signed, sealed and delivered, Little Park was due to reopen on Monday 17 August.

The promoters had lined up some of the best riders in the north-west: Reg West, Gustav Kellner, Eric Airey, Jack Tye, the Stobbart brothers and local superstar, Frank Charles. As an added attraction, Gladys Thornhill had been booked to ride in an exhibition race and Reg West was going to give a demonstration in his speedway sidecar outfit. Typically, it rained all weekend and the track became waterlogged. One of the local riders tested the track, but the heavy rain had loosened the soil under the cinders and his bike just skidded all over the place. The ACU steward had no choice but to cancel the meeting.

After a gap of some ten weeks, speedway racing eventually returned to Little Park on Monday 24 August. Despite good weather for a change, a poor crowd turned up to see a series of match races featuring riders from Preston and Belle Vue. Gustav Kellner beat Eric Airey in a hectic four-lap duel, Jack Tye, never afraid to race on a rough track, won a brilliant race with Roland Stobbart and Eric Airey made up for his earlier defeat by beating Reg West in another closely fought encounter. During the interval, seventeen-year-old Gladys Thornhill of Manchester established a ladies' lap record of 23.4 seconds. The ACU had placed a ban on ladies racing competitively in 1930, hence her appearance at Little Park being described as an exhibition! The Barrow promoters didn't want to risk another altercation with the ACU.

The outstanding rider of the evening, though, was Bill Kitchen. Twenty-two-year-old Bill had already gained a reputation as a talented grass-track rider, but his dirt-track experience was fairly limited. That didn't prevent him from beating Eric Airey in the race for the Silver Goblet, and then completing the double by beating Reg West in the Golden Helmet final. A reporter for the northern edition of the *Auto Motor Journal* reported that: 'The clever and cool manner in which he (William Kitchen) scored a popular double gave one the assurance that one day he will become as equally famous on cinders as he is on grass'. Little did he know how famous!

This was the last speedway meeting to ever be held at Little Park; no reason was ever given for the sudden closure, but the timing did coincide with the rugby club moving into their new stadium. Craven Park was officially opened five days later, on Saturday 29 August 1931.

When the speedway club was formed in June 1930, the promoters stated that regular crowd levels of 7,000-8,000 would be needed to fund a league team or sustain star-quality riders. Only once in two years had they reached that figure and crowd levels at Little Park had fallen from 5,000 on the opening night to less than 2,000 for the meeting on 22 August. No doubt, the ten-week delay during the summer had done the club a lot of harm too, or had that gypsy curse followed them from Holker Street?

Greyhound racing continued at Little Park until the ground was sold in 1932. During building work in the early 1970s, remains of the old cinder track were exposed for one last time, before the site was levelled and turned over to housing. The Ship Inn, which was used as changing rooms by the speedway riders and rugby players, still stands, the only reminder of the days when Little Park was a major sporting venue on the Furness peninsula.

7

'OUR FRANKIE'

To coin a modern phrase, Frank Charles was a 'top man'. Not only was he one of the greatest English speedway riders of the pre-war era, he was also a champion glider pilot, a talented accordion player and devoted family man.

Frank was born on 10 March 1907, at 44 South Row, Roose, a small hamlet about three miles west of Barrow-in-Furness. His father, also named Frank, worked in the Barrow shipyards, but to make ends meet, the family also ran a bakery. By the age of fifteen, young Frank was making deliveries on his father's 500cc Dunelt motorcycle and sidecar; so began his fascination with motorcycles.

Tales of Frank's exploits on that old motorcycle outfit are still legend in the shipbuilding town. One of the most popular tales is how he would ride along the parapet of the Jubilee Bridge from Barrow to Walney Island with the sidecar wheel hanging precariously over the edge – all done for a small wager. A similar feat was performed along the wall of his old school. Another story is how he would ride his solo motorcycle down the steps from Michaelson Road Bridge onto The Strand; the wager? A pint, of course!

Far from discouraging Frankie's fascination with motorcycles, his father bought him a brand new 493cc Model 90 Sunbeam for his eighteenth birthday, the top sporting motorcycle of the day. Every weekend Frank would take the bike to Southport, Morecambe, Walney Island or Skinburness and compete in beach races or time trials. He was good, too, picking up numerous trophies and breaking several records along the way. Maurice Stobbart can remember the very first time he encountered Frank Charles. It was back in 1927 and Maurice was accompanying his elder brother Roland to a beach race at Skinburness on the Solway Firth. They were driving down the narrow lane from Silloth when a motorcycle came up behind them and flew past. At the end of the road the motorcyclist didn't stop, he simply carried on at full blat, snaking his way across the sand and coming to a perfect broadsiding halt at the scrutineer's desk. That was Frank Charles and he, too, went home with a bagful of trophies.

Dirt-track racing was the 'big thing' during the summer of 1928 and Frank had his first taste of the new sport at Blackpool's Highfield Road circuit. He dominated the qualifying heats of his first meeting, but in his semi-final, he looked over his shoulder to see where his opponents were… and was promptly disqualified by an overzealous official. Frank had enjoyed the experience, though, and on further visits to Blackpool he won the 500cc final at Highfield Road on three separate occasions and also secured the Golden Armlet at the St Anne's Road circuit. He also became a regular competitor at the Salford and White City tracks in Manchester.

Frank on his Douglas. The picture is from 1930, when Frank was captain of the Manchester White City league team.

At the beginning of the 1929 season, Frank went down to Manchester for trials at the new track in Belle Vue Gardens. Belle Vue were impressed enough to name Frank in their list of riders to enter the new English Dirt-Track League, but Frank had other ideas and started the season riding for Burnley alongside Joe Abbott and 'Ginger' Lees. By July, Burnley had closed down and Frank moved to Preston. His talent really began to shine at the Farringdon Park circuit and he became virtually unbeatable on his home track. At one point in the season, Frank was actually banned from riding because he had entered an individual meeting at Belle Vue, which by this time was operating outside of the Northern Dirt-Track Owners Association. Sense eventually prevailed and his licence was handed back.

This was a period when big prize money was available for the winners of individual competitions, leading to some fierce rivalries on the track. In one such meeting at Belle Vue, Frank was drawn against Frank Varey, the hero of Hyde Road. The race was a real thriller with the two riders knocking each other all over the track. At the end of the race Charles's bike was so badly damaged that there was no way he would be able to take part in the final. Charles threw his machine to the ground and stormed over to Varey. The two riders came to blows, but it was all over in a flash and the squabble ended with the two rivals shaking hands. By way of an apology, Varey offered Charles the use of one of his bikes in the final; Frankie showed his gratitude by winning the race.

For the 1930 season Frank joined White City (Manchester) as the captain of their Northern League team. One of the greatest team battles of that seasons Northern League took place in June, when Frank led White City to a surprise victory at Belle Vue. His prowess on the speedway track did not go unnoticed and although he missed out on the very first Test Match against Australia, he was picked for the remaining four tests and scored a total of 18 points.

White City closed down part-way through the 1930 season, crowds had been falling and there had been discontent amongst the riding staff, too. At one point Frank had expressed a wish to move to the White City track in Glasgow, and transfer fees in excess of £1,000 had been mentioned, but the deal never materialised and Frank finished the season riding for Belle Vue again.

The 1931 season saw Frank riding for Leeds and his unique riding style and superb control made him a local hero at the Fullerton Road track. Frank was one of the first riders to adopt the foot forward technique, but he had a style all of his own. He would take corners standing on the right-hand foot peg and lean right over the handle bars, just as if he was forcibly pushing his bike to the finishing line. 'I just let her buck' is how Frank described it. His stint at Leeds only lasted until July, though, and once again he found himself back at Belle Vue Gardens, riding for the Southern League side, known simply as Manchester. Frank also rode for Belle Vue in their Northern Knockout Cup side, but was forced to sit out the second round when Preston lodged a complaint over his inclusion, claiming that he had already ridden for Leeds in the same competition. Belle Vue had no qualms about reintroducing him for the final, however, where ironically, the losing side was Frank's former team – Leeds!

Frank (far left) with the 1931 Leeds team.

His season ended prematurely, however, when he was injured in a crash at the old Leicester Super track. While he was out of the saddle, Frank took a job as a motor mechanic and earned a few extra pennies playing the accordion in the music halls and cinemas. But Frank was a born racer, and as soon as he felt he was fit enough to ride he was back in training at Belle Vue.

Frank married his childhood sweetheart, Doris Parramore, on 28 March 1932 and they moved into their own house on North Row, Roose. The new speedway season started okay for Frank, and he regained his team place with Belle Vue, but he looked a pale shadow of the rider that had dominated the Northern racing scene in previous years. Sections of the Belle Vue crowd began to heckle Frank and called for him to be replaced. A serious injury to his close friend and riding partner Joe Abbott also affected his confidence, and towards the end of the season he decided that enough was enough and announced his retirement.

Belle Vue found themselves with an injury crisis shortly after the 1933 season had begun, so Belle Vue maestro E.O. Spence turned to Frank for help and persuaded him to ride for the 'Aces' once again. He found it difficult at first, but his confidence gradually returned and during the last few months of the season, he had regained his regular team spot and surprised many of his detractors by winning the Wembley Track Championship, breaking the track record in the process.

Frank came out of retirement in 1933 to began his third spell with the Belle Vue 'Aces'. (C. F. Wallace).

Frank Charles, Furness gliding champion. The sailplane is a two-seater model and the passengers are his wife Doris and his eldest son, also named Frank. (Harry Holme)

Probably inspired by that late season victory, Wembley made an attempt to prise Frank away from Belle Vue at the start of the 1934 season, but Spence was having none of it. Frank was a vital member of the 'invincible' Belle Vue team of the mid-1930s, the team that many consider was the greatest speedway team of all time. The year 1934 was probably his finest season at Belle Vue and his pairing with Joe Abbott became legendary, and not only at domestic level. In the fourth Test against Australia, held at Belle Vue in July, Frank and Joe scored 24 points between them. Tragedy struck at the end of the season, when Frank's father died of peritonitis. Frank senior was instrumental in his son's success, managing all of his affairs and also doing all of all of the tuning and maintenance work on his son's bikes. Young Frank felt that he had no option but to return home and support his family. Once again, he announced his retirement from the speedway scene and this time he opened a grocer's shop!

The grocery trade was a much slower and quieter way to earn a living, so to quench is thirst for speed and excitement Frank took up a new hobby – gliding! He never had any formal training as a glider pilot but took to the air straight away. The story goes that he had read a book on flying and turned up at the Furness Gliding Club with a glider in tow, demanding to be launched. Following a heated debate, Frank finally got his way and was allowed to take off, eventually landing on the beach near Dunnerholme Rock, thankfully in one piece. After only two months he was doing solo flights of over an hour's duration – a feat noted by one of the leading aviation magazines at the time. It wasn't long before Frank had broken all of the Furness Gliding Club's records and eventually became the instructor at their airfield, situated on the moor above Ireleth and Marton.

Above: *The* Daily Sketch *Trophy, won by Frank on Thursday 13 August 1936. Frank won his beat and semi-final before beating Bill Kitchen and Vic Huxley in the final. The trophy is a splendid silver cigar case with a bronze statue of a rider on the lid. (Martin Crooks)*

Left: *Hero of the Wembley fans… Frank on his Victor Martin/JAP, his prize for winning the 1935 Wembley Grand Prix.*

At the start of the 1935 speedway season Frank never gave any thought to returning to the saddle, that is until he was contacted by his old friend Alec Jackson, who was now speedway manager at Wembley. The team had an injury crisis, just like Belle Vue back in 1933. Both Colin Watson and 'Ginger' Lees were unable to ride, so Alec talked Frank into making yet another comeback, but there was one stumbling block. Belle Vue had kept Frank on their retained list and, therefore, Wembley had to pay for his services. An initial £500 was paid as a loan fee, followed by a further £500 to buy him outright. The £1,000 deal was a speedway record that stood until May 1947. Frank described meeting the Wembley director Arthur Elvin as 'more frightening than anything he had ever experienced on the track', but it was another ambition fulfilled. He actually rode his first match as a Wembley Lion suffering from the after-effects of flu, but within a fortnight he was topping the Wembley score chart and leading England to victory against Australia.

It was a magnificent comeback and the 1935 and 1936 seasons were arguably Frank's greatest period in the sport. During his first season at Wembley he was virtually unbeatable and at one point he went thirty-six races without defeat. Throughout the course of the season he won numerous trophies, including the Wembley Gold Cup, the Wembley Grand Prix, which earned him a brand new Victor Martin JAP racing bike and his greatest achievement of all – first place in the Star Championship final, the forerunner of the World Championship. The speedway press quite rightly named Frank as 'The greatest rider of the year'.

His exceptional form continued in 1936. He was made captain of the England side and scored 69 points in 5 international appearances, a record that would not be broken for another three years. This total included a magnificent 18-point maximum at New Cross. He was one of the favourites to become the first World Speedway Champion and bought a new pair of boots especially for the final. He started brilliantly by knocking nearly 1.5 seconds off the Wembley track record in the first heat. He won his second race too, but reared at the start of heat nine and went out of the running. Nevertheless, he still managed to finish in joint fourth place, scoring the same number of points as the American Cordy Milne.

He picked up a further 7 international caps in 1937, one against Australia, five against Overseas and one against the USA, but it has to be said that his form for England was not up to his usual high standards; in fact, *Speedway News* magazine accused Frank of being 'a repeated failure at Test level'. Despite his poor international form, Frank still managed to qualify for his second World Championship final and scored 7 hard-earned points on a very deep track. The Wembley track came in for a lot of criticism after the 1937 final, but Frank was one of the few who didn't make his grievances public. His friend Joe Abbott did though, and he blamed the track for Frank's poor showing: 'Frankie was obviously out to fight, but he got filled up on his first two rides, simply through going out to ride around somebody and give the crowd the thrills they wanted'.

Unlike many of his team mates, Frank did not travel to Australia during the winter months, choosing to spend time with his family. The 1937 closed season was no different and he spent most of his spare time gliding and testing a new prototype for the Yorkshire firm of Slingsbury Sailplanes.

It is interesting to note that when Frank first signed for Wembley, he didn't leave Barrow and preferred to commute by motorcycle. For home meetings that meant leaving home on the morning of a meeting and returning home the next day. That was a journey of over 250 miles each way, and remember, this was in the 1930s, long before the advent of motorways and dual carriageways! Eventually Frank did move south, taking his wife and their two young boys, Frank and Brian, to Dunstable. Not only was he nearer to his home track, but Dunstable was also home to one of the country's top gliding clubs! Gliding was a popular hobby amongst speedway riders and Malcolm Craven, a Wembley novice at the time, became a pupil of Frank's at the Dunstable airfield. Frank's reputation as one of the country's leading glider pilots was beginning to grow and he admitted that, although speedway gave him a good living, his ambition was to set a new world record for long-distance gliding.

He continued to give sterling service for the Wembley 'Lions' throughout the 1938 season and even took his place in the team that faced West Ham on 19 May, despite the fact that he had fourteen teeth removed that morning! Remarkably, he won his first three races before the pain became too much. The return match at West Ham a few days later brought the joker out in Frank. On a rain-sodden track, the match was almost reduced to a farce. Riders were sliding all over the place but none of them complained. Always willing to give a show, Frank made fun of the whole thing and in one heat he gave hand signals as he rode around the bends. As he cruised off the last bend he crouched over his handlebars in true racing fashion and won the heat in a time of 1 minute and 45 seconds; the slowest race ever seen at West Ham!

*The unmistakable style of a champion
– Frank in action for Wembley.*

Frank was a true entertainer and always believed in giving the fans value for money. He would often entertain the Wembley fans by playing his accordion to them during the interval and at supporters' club functions. In fact, the Wembley team were all musically minded and formed their own 'Lions Dance Band', sometimes holding practice sessions on the sacred Wembley turf. 'Ginger' Lees would join Frank on the accordion, accompanied by Eric Gregory on the flute, Cliff Parkinson on the saxophone, George Greenwood on drums, Gordon Byers on the violin and Ted Husband, the Wembley trainer, playing the cymbals. Alec Jackson would take on the role of conductor, of course.

Frank's outstanding form in the league earned him three more England caps, including one as captain in front of his home crowd. Unfortunately, he took a knock on the day before the third Test and returned his one and only international 'duck'. *Speedway News* magazine criticised his inclusion again, saying that he 'should never have been picked in the first place'. A bit of a harsh statement, considering that he had scored 13 points in the previous Test.

Frank had been racing for over a decade by this time, and although he was still a force to be reckoned with at domestic level (186 points from 23 matches) he was starting to struggle on the World Championship scene and failed to qualify for the 1938 World final. At the end of the season it was clear that Frank was considering his future again. He wanted to devote more of his time to his gliding but his demands for the 1939 season seemed unreasonable to the Wembley management and they refused to agree. Neither side would give way, so Wembley went ahead with their team-building plans and brought in Danish rider Morian Hansen as a replacement for Frank.

Frank sold his equipment and returned to Barrow-in-Furness. He bought a house at 26 South Row, Roose, just a few doors away from where he was born, and took up a position as an instructor with the Air Defence Corps. He spent the winter gliding and, come the start of the 1939 speedway season, he went on a camping trip with the air cadets. Then, during May, Frank felt the urge to see a speedway match again. He arrived at the Empire Stadium unannounced and mingled with the crowd. Gradually he made his way down to the pits, where the atmosphere and the instinctive desire to race just got to him again. He found team manager Alec Jackson and announced there and then that he wanted to ride again.

Frank admitted that he just couldn't get the cinders out of his system. Although his work as a gliding instructor was interesting his life had become very slow again and he had missed the excitement of racing motorcycles. Tommy Hall, one of the Wembley mechanics, built him a new frame and prepared an engine. Frank made his third racing comeback on 15 June 1939, in a London cup match against Wimbledon, winning his first three races.

The Wimbledon management protested against the inclusion of Frank in the Wembley team and inferred that either Hansen or Charles should be given to a weaker team. At the same time the New Cross management had also put in an appeal against Frank Charles's inclusion in the Wembley team and requested that either Charles or Hansen should be allotted to them. Hansen allegedly called them both jealous, whilst Jackson said that if New Cross wanted Charles they must pay at least £1,000 for his services, that's assuming Charles would want to go!

Frankie just kept his views to himself and got on with the job he was employed to do – racing speedway bikes. Within a fortnight of making a devastating comeback, he was picked to represent England, reforming that famous partnership with Joe Abbott. Frank repaid the selectors' faith with a 9-point haul, helping England to a narrow 55-53 victory against Australia. He was included in the squad for the third Test at Harringay on 15 July, but Frank turned down this opportunity as it would clash with the National Gliding Championships at Camp Hill, Great Hucklow in Derbyshire.

Frank fixing the wing on to KK1, a prototype sailplane made by Slingsbury Sailplanes of Kirkbymoorside in North Yorkshire. (Harry Holme)

*Frank's final resting place, buried with his
father and nephew in Rampside churchyard,
near Barrow-in-Furness. (Author's collection)*

It was a rainswept afternoon in Derbyshire, when Frank strapped himself into his new sailplane in readiness for a soaring test. His plane was launched into the air by autowinch, which seemed to stop when Frank had reached a height of around 400ft. Charles's plane then levelled out and turned downwind. It flew over the airfield, lost a little height and then dropped straight back to earth, killing Frank instantly.

At the inquest it was revealed that the winch operator thought he'd seen a stray dog standing across the launch wire. To prevent the dog from being cut in half, the operator stopped the winch, believing that Frank had reached a safe height. Earlier in the day, Charles had told his colleagues that he was planning to do a high launch. Frank must have realised that he had insufficient height, levelled out and turned back across the airfield, possibly to land and make a second launch. Then tragedy struck. The launch wire was still attached to the nose of Frank's plane, so when it crossed back over the winch, the wire tightened and brought the plane to an abrupt halt. It then somersaulted and nose dived back down to earth from a height of around 300ft. The verdict was accidental death.

Hundreds of stunned listeners in Barrow heard the accident live on the wireless and the tragic news spread like wildfire. That evening Frank's Wembley team mate and protégé, Tommy Price, was riding at Belle Vue. Geoff Pymar walked into the pits to tell Tommy the tragic news, but Tommy instinctively knew something was wrong; 'Its Frank isnt it? Something has happened to him'.

Frank was buried at Rampside churchyard on 19 July 1939, in the same grave as his much-loved father. The funeral was a who's who of the speedway and gliding world, all of them wishing to pay a final tribute to one of the greatest English speedway riders of all time, amongst them Bill Kitchen, Alec Jackson, Cliff Parkinson, Bob Harrison, Lionel Van Praag and Eric Gregory. In a fitting tribute, Tommy Newton, a novice speedway rider who had benefited from Frank's coaching at Holker Street, paid his own final respects by pushing Frank's bike from his house on South Row to the church gates, leaving it as a guard of honour throughout the service. Frank was due to go gliding with his great friend and rival Frank Varey on the following Sunday. Varey described Frank as 'a top-class rider who could win races on any track', a view echoed by Phil 'Tiger' Hart, who also added that Frank was 'a real gentleman off the track too'. But nowhere was his death mourned more than in his native Barrow, where his memory is still revered today.

8

WHITEHAVEN

Strictly speaking, the track at the Colliery Recreation Ground in Whitehaven was never a traditional speedway or dirt track. It was advertised as a grass track, and was run under the ACU rules as such, but this was a grass-track with a difference. The track was a tri-arch, laid out in front of a covered grandstand, and had a thin layer of sand and cinders on top of the grass to improve traction. So, was this a grass-track or a dirt track? Even the local newspaper described it as 'Whitehavens Speedway... the most exciting event in the area for years'.

The 'Recre' is built on eleven acres of marshland, part of the estate of the Earl of Lonsdale. By 1837, an area known as 'The Playground' had been set aside for sports events, including amateur football, athletics, rugby league, cricket, boxing, whippet racing and even cockfighting! A pavilion, which doubled up as dressing rooms, was built in 1898 and the Whitehaven Colliery Recreation Club built a 750-seat wooden grandstand in 1926.

The very first motorcycle race meeting was held as the grand finale of the Whitehaven Carnival on Saturday 15 July 1930. The event was run by the Whitehaven and District Motor Club, and organised by local road-racing hero Harry Meageen.

Dozens of local motorcyclists joined the cream of Cumberland and Westmorland, all hoping to get their hands on the £5 prize money. A substantial amount of money when you consider that the local miners would struggle to earn that much in a week.

Newspaper advert for the first grass-track meeting at Whitehaven in 1930. (Whitehaven News)

IN CONTINUATION OF HOSPITAL CARNIVAL

THRILLS — EXCITING — SPEEDS

MOTOR CYCLE
GRASS TRACK RACES

Under the Auspices of the Whitehaven and District Motor Club,

IN THE

COLLIERY RECREATION GROUND
WHITEHAVEN

On SATURDAY, JULY 5th, Commencing 6 p.m. Prompt.

£26 FOR THREE COMPETITIVE CLASSES

(RECORD ENTRIES.)

Mr. W. H. T. MEAGEEN (Winner of the Amateur T.T., 1928), will give a 5 LAP EXHIBITION of Fast Riding.

Also MATCH for £5 aside between

Mr. D. C. BENSON, of Whitehaven, and

Mr. G. VIRGOE, Workington. 8 Laps (2 Miles).

ADMISSION TO FIELD, 1/-; GRANDSTAND, 2/- (including Admission). Children, 6d. accompanied by Adults.

Opposite: *The silencer fell from Charlie Barbour's 350cc machine during the 1930 meeting at Whitehaven and one of the track marshals ran onto the track to pick it up, obviously not realising how hot a motorcycle exhaust would be! (Mrs J. Davis)*

Left: *Ben Fidler, of Fidler's Grain Mill on Preston Street, Whitehaven. One of the local competitors in the 1930 meeting. (Andrew Fidler)*

The narrow 430-yard circuit provided plenty of thrills (and spills!) for the 5,000 spectators. The sandy surface cut up badly from the outset and the racing got a bit chaotic at times! Very few riders could get the hang of 'broadsiding' their stripped-down machines and when they did manage to get their machine into a slide, most ended up in an undignified heap on the ground!

Bernard Crabtree of Kendal cannot remember crashing, but had the story related to him by the Chief Marshall, J.T. Kessel. Bernard had not taken a helmet, but Frank Allison insisted that he should wear one and lent him his. Bernard was lying in second place and was chasing William Wilson, the son of the local dentist. On the last bend Wilson went wide and Bernard tried to cut up the inside. Unfortunately, Wilson caught his foot in the straw bales and he was thrown over the handlebars. Bernard could not avoid the falling rider and he rode right over him, crossing the finishing line head first! Frank Allisons helmet was flattened and both riders ended up in the same hospital they were raising funds for. Wilson had serious injuries to his left eye while Crabtree and had the flesh torn from his cheek. He can remember nothing at all about the accident, but carried the scars on his face for many years. Neither of them regained consciousness until the next morning, but when they did wake they had been joined by Frank Allison, the same man who had loaned his helmet to Bernard. Frank had slid into the sand bags and broken his collarbone.

The fourth victim to end up in hospital was actually one of the track officials. When the silencer fell off Charlie Barbour's machine the official ran on to the track to retrieve it, not realising how hot it would be! Another heart-stopping moment came when George Skirrow of Ulverston had to jump clear of his bike when it caught fire during a race. No serious damage was done and George got his bike working again to win the

350cc event final, beating his brother Harry and pre-meeting favourite, Roland Stobbart.

The two-stroke event produced some interesting races, none more so than when young 'Nibs' Boyd, a mechanic from Mark Taylor's garage in Whitehaven, rolled up his shirt sleeves and rode his little 250cc Dunelt to a place in the final. Although his lightweight two-stroke could only muster two and a half brake horse power, he was able to make up a lot of ground against the bigger capacity machines on the bends. In the final he had to settle for second place behind Workington's George Vingoe on a 500cc Scott.

Roland Stobbart brought the crowd to its feet with a spectacular ride in the final of the 'Unlimited' event. He was left at the start as he desperately tried to coax his dirt-track Rudge into life. The St John's Ambulance men rushed to his aid with a push start and suddenly his bike roared into life. Stobbart proceeded to thrill the crowd with a superb exhibition of proper dirt-track broadsiding, showering them with sand, cinders and sods of turf as he picked off his opponents one by one. He crossed the line nearly half a lap ahead of second-placed Harry Skirrow, recording the fastest time of the day in the process. Third place went to J.W. Clague of Workington with Harry Eilbeck of Egremont following them home in fourth place.

The meeting also featured an eight-lap match race between local rivals D'Arcy Benson of Whitehaven and George Vingoe of Workington. Vingoe hit the front first and maintained his lead for five laps before Benson, on a 500cc Douglas, skilfully passed him on the last lap. It looked like he had the race sewn up, but he hit a rut in the track and fell on the last bend, allowing Vingoe to roar past for his second victory of the day and another £5 in his pocket.

WHITEHAVEN & WEST CUMBERLAND HOSPITAL.

Continuation of Carnival.

PROGRAMME
— OF —
Grass Track Motor Cycle Races.
Under the auspices of The Whitehaven and District Motor Club.
Held under the General Competition and Special Track
Rules of the A.C.U. Permit No. R 126.
TO BE HELD IN THE
COLLIERY RECREATION GROUND,
— ON —
SATURDAY, JULY 4th, 1931,
COMMENCING AT 5 p.m.

COMPETITIVE EVENTS:
Event No. 1.—MOTOR CYCLES UNDER 350 C.C.
Event No. 2.—MOTOR CYCLES UNDER 500 C.C.
Event No. 3.—MOTOR CYCLES UNDER 500 C.C.
Novice Class for those who have never won a First Prize on any
Grass, Cinder, or other Track in competition.

EXHIBITIONS:
SENSATIONAL RIDING FEATS by WILF. Mc.CLURE
The Belle Vue Speedway Star, riding through Hoops of Fire
and Sheets of real Glass.

EXCEPTIONAL ATTRACTION.
INTER-COUNTY SPEED MATCH,
CUMBERLAND VERSUS LANCASHIRE.
TEAMS OF SIX RIDERS.

ADMISSION to FIELD, 1/-; Grandstand, 1/- extra.
Unemployed, 6d., on production of The National Health
Insurance Card. Children, 6d.
Parking Ground for Cars, 1/-; Motor Cycles, 6d.

PRICE TWOPENCE.

W. H. MOSS & SONS, LTD., WHITEHAVEN.

Above left: *Harry Eilbeck of Egremont finished fourth in the 1930 Unlimited final.*

Above right: *Programme for the meeting on 4 July 1931. (Author's collection)*

Fuelled by the success of their first meeting, Whitehaven and District Motor Club staged a second stadium grass-track meeting on Saturday 4 July 1931; once again it was the last event in the town's carnival celebrations.

The event attracted more than forty competitors from Cumberland, Westmorland and Lancashire, including Roger Rogerson from Scotforth, Lionel Cordingley from Morecambe, a couple of juniors from Preston Speedway and a young racer from Galgate in Lancashire, called William Kitchen. Les Edmondson, the TT rider and sand-racing expert from Keswick, should also have been riding, but he had taken a nasty tumble in practice and had to withdraw from the meeting on doctor's advice.

The most experienced rider taking part was Frank Burgess, who was riding for the famous Belle Vue speedway team at the time. Burgess was described as being able to 'corner at great speed without ever being thrown'. An added attraction for this event was the appearance of Wilf McClure, a team mate of Frank Burgess at Belle Vue. He wasn't there to ride in the main event, though Wilf provided the pre-match and interval entertainment by riding his bike through sheets of glass and hoops of fire!

With the addition of more experienced riders it was decided to introduce a new 'Novices Handicap' for riders who had never won a first prize on any grass, cinder or other track. The eventual winner was William 'Nibs' Boyd, the local mechanic who had endeared himself to the crowd twelve months earlier. Albert Simister from Ulverston gave him a hard battle in the eight-lap final, but Boyd held the inside line to claim a well-deserved victory. Another local rider, Joe Norman, crossed the line in second place after the over-enthusiastic Simister had fallen on the last bend.

The 350cc event produced a few surprises. Harold Roberts from Cleator Moor, the oldest rider in the field, had entered the event with a twenty-year-old 350cc Douglas. The bike had only cost him 15 shillings, but in his heat he managed to maintain a steady speed throughout the race and surprisingly beat Charlie Barbour and William Sharpe to reach the semi-final. His luck didn't hold out, however, and the vintage machine stubbornly refused to start in his next race. Bill Kitchen, on his brand new 350cc Velocette, showed his class in the final, easily beating Cuthbert Whiteside, Hugh Tatham and Joe Ormrod.

The 500cc event provided the best action of the evening. D'Arcy Benson had been loaned a dirt-track Douglas by the Bristol factory and nearly caused a sensation in his semi-final, holding off the challenge of Frank Burgess for most of the race. Burgess, on a 500cc Scott, had to call on all of his dirt-track experience to overhaul the local rider on the last lap. Maurice Stobbart, Roland's younger brother, made one of his earliest public appearances at this meeting and also played his part in one of the most thrilling races of the evening. In his heat in the 500cc class he was challenging Cuthbert Whiteside for the lead. For six laps he tried to find a way past his opponent and on the final bend he made one last valiant attempt, but lost control and fell in an undignified heap. Luckily, nothing more than his pride was hurt and his newly acquired dirt-track Douglas was undamaged too.

George Brockerton was an Irish road racer from Coleraine who competed in both of the 1931 meetings at the Recreation Ground. He came to Whitehaven to work for Cumberland Motor Services and was given the honour of driving the first bus out of Whitehaven Bus Station;, unfortunately he crashed into the steel barrier, causing extensive damage to the brand-new bus! Brockerton hit the headlines again during the Second World War when he rescued a party of British soldiers trapped in a cellar at Dunkirk. (FoTTofinders)

Les Edmondson of Keswick was a top sand racer in the 1920s and also rode in the TT as a works rider for OK Supreme. He made his grass-track debut at Whitehaven in 1930, but was injured in practice prior to the July 1931 meeting and had to withdraw. He returned for the August meeting and also competed in the 'Cinder Track' meeting at Workington on the same day. He was sadly killed in a road accident near Cockermouth a few years later, testing a new racing Norton for his friend Harry Meageen. (FoTTofinders)

The 500cc final brought together four of the top riders in the north-west. Bill Kitchen and Roland Stobbart were the first to show out of a tight first bend tussle and were fighting for the lead when their machines touched, throwing both riders to the ground. By the time they had remounted, Roger Rogerson and Frank Burgess had roared past and were over half a lap ahead, engaged in another exciting duel. Rogerson held onto the inside line to claim victory over Burgess, while behind them Stobbart set a new lap record of 19 seconds trying to catch them, leaving the much-fancied Kitchen to coast home in fourth place.

Another new event at this meeting was an inter-county Test Match between Cumberland and Lancashire. The match was run over three heats and used the scoring system of 3 points for a win, 2 for second, 1 for third and zero for last place. Not surprisingly, the more experienced Lancashire team took the honours by 10 points to 8. For the home team, Hugh Tatham was the only heat winner scoring 3 points, Vingoe and Benson scored 2 each and Cuthbert Whiteside scored 1 point. For Lancashire, Burgess and Rogerson scored 3 points each, Lionel Cordingley scored 2, Bill Kitchen and G.Dawson scored 1 each and Harold Lawton failed to score.

Five weeks later, on Saturday 15 August 1931, Whitehaven featured in a West Cumberland double-header. During the afternoon, the West Cumberland Motor Club had staged the county's very first 'cinder track' meeting on the old banked cycling track at the Workington Town football ground. Many of the competitors arrived at Whitehaven battered and bruised after the afternoons racing. Frank Burgess was suffering with a bruised foot and swollen ankle, Bill Nichol was still sore following a heavy crash, and George Mortimer had to strip and rebuild his engine before he could race at Whitehaven.

The formula of the meeting had been changed from the July meeting. Two individual classes were being contested, one a handicap event, the other a scratch event. Both classes were for bikes of up to 500cc, but to even things out, the riders of 350cc machines were allowed a 5-second advantage over their bigger rivals. A second Inter County Test Match was also included in the programme. Despite the appearance of a number of experienced dirt-track riders from the Preston and Barrow tracks, the racing didn't quite live up to expectations and certainly didn't provide as many thrills as the previous meetings at the 'Recre'.

The Test Match actually provided some of the evening's best racing. Maurice Stobbart, spectacular as ever, brought down Lancashire's G. Dawson and was excluded for 'ungentlemanly conduct'. At the end of the three races, the scores were level at 9 points each. A run-off was quickly arranged to try and split the rival teams. George Mortimer won the heat for Lancashire, but Roland Stobbart and Bill Nichol combined to keep Bill Kitchen at the back. The heat points were shared again and the match was declared a draw. Roland Stobbart finished as top scorer for the home team with 5 points, Bill Nichol scored 4, Hugh Tatham 2 and Jim Fewster 1. Maurice Stobbart and D'Arcy Benson both failed to score. For Lancashire, George Mortimer scored 5, Bill Kitchen 3, Frank Burgess 2, C. Wearing and G. Dawson scored 1 point each and Harold Lawton failed to score.

An advert for the third and final meeting at Whitehaven in August 1931. (Whitehaven News)

77

Roland Stobbart from Aspatria was one of the most successful competitors to appear at Whitehaven in the 1930s and recorded the fastest ever time at the Recreation Ground.

Inspired by his modest success in previous events, 'Nibs' Boyd had bought a more competitive 350cc Cotton. In the heats of the handicap event he was given a 7-second advantage and managed to beat Maurice Stobbart and in his scratch heat he made the most of a 5-second advantage to beat the injured Frank Burgess. His luck did not hold out in the semi-finals, though, as he was easily beaten by Bill Kitchen in the handicap event and crashed out the in scratch event.

The day belonged to Bill Kitchen, who won both the scratch and handicap finals. His victory in the scratch final was a fortunate one, though. George Mortimer had taken the lead from the start, but his bike broke down less than 20 yards from the finish line allowing Kitchen, Bill Nichol and Rol Stobbart to steal the first three places respectively. In the handicap final, Kitchen made no mistake and finished ahead of Stobbart, George Mortimer and Foster Williamson of Kendal.

There is no doubt that the grass-track races had been very popular with the people of Whitehaven; crowds of 4,000 or more were excellent for such a small town, but no more races were held at the 'Recre' after 1931.

Whitehaven Miners Welfare acquired the Recreation Ground from the Earl of Lonsdale in 1944 and four years later, the new Whitehaven 'Colliers' Rugby League club agreed a thirty-year lease with the landlords for the use of the area in front of the ageing grandstand. A new pitch was laid, destroying all evidence of the dirt-track and only in recent years has the wooden grandstand been strengthened with a steel framework. The pavilion, which was used by the riders as a changing room in 1930 and 1931, was finally demolished in 1986.

Ian Thomas and Jeff Brownhut had the Recreation Ground on their short list of possible venues when they were looking for somewhere to build a new track back in 1969. On arrival at the stadium, they were greeted by a gentleman who obviously had no idea what they were talking about. When Ian and Jeff explained their plans, the gentleman pointed them in the direction of the gravel path that ran around the outside of the stadium! Fortunately for us they had better luck when they came to the next venue on their list – Workington's Derwent Park.

9
WORKINGTON:
THE LONSDALE PARK YEARS

Lonsdale Park was just part of a larger area known as the 'Cloffocks', an open area that has always been used for sport and recreation. There is evidence that there was once a horse-racing course here and Workington Zebras Rugby Club played their home matches here from 1898 to 1909. County and Representative matches were also played on the 'Cloffocks' in the early part of the twentieth century.

Workington 'Reds' AFC adopted Lonsdale Park as their home from 1884 until they folded in 1911 and Workington Athletic played there during 1914-15. Workington AFC reformed in 1921 and returned to Lonsdale Park, which now had a pavilion and a covered stand. In 1923, a new cinder cycling track, banked at one end, was laid around the pitch and when Harry Hurrell bought the stadium from Lord Lonsdale in 1926, he had a new covered grandstand built on the river Derwent side of the ground.

The idea of speedway racing at Lonsdale Park was first mooted by Rol Stobbart at the AGM of the West Cumberland Motor Club on 23 March 1931. The intention was to stage meetings on a weekly or fortnightly basis, depending on the level of support. The first meeting was due to be held in May 1931. But this would not be the first time that motorcycles had raced around Lonsdale Park. On the afternoon of Saturday 28 September 1929, the West Cumberland Motor Club held a Grand Motor Cycle Gymkhana to raise funds for Workington AFC. Numerous motorcycle events were held

George Vingoe's trophy for winning the Lonsdale Park 'One Mile Track Race' in September 1929. (Author's collection)

but it was the 'Track Race' on the 450-yard cinder cycle track that provided the first taster of dirt-track racing. Nine riders entered the time trial, each riding one at a time around four laps of the track from a standing start. The winner was George Vingoe of Workington, who recorded a time of 94.6 seconds on his Scott. In second place, riding a Triumph, was Harold Dunn, also of Workington, who completed four laps in 95.2 seconds and third place went to AJS mounted Roland Stobbart from Aspatria in a time of 97.4 seconds. The remaining six contestants all recorded times in excess of 100 seconds.

Vingoe had no previous experience of track racing and had run the whole race with his Scott in second gear, but his time was well under Alf Edmondson's record, set before the First World War. Meanwhile, the 1921 Triumph, ridden by Dunn, had been used on the roads for the previous eight years!

Following the event, Harry Meageen, the famous motorcycle racer from Whitehaven, could not resist the temptation to have a go. He borrowed Stobbart's machine and completed five laps wearing plus-fours and smoking a pipe, coming home to a rousing reception.

May 1931 came and went without any sign of speedway taking place, but eventually, the very first speedway meeting did take place, on Saturday 15 August 1931. This was followed by a grass-track event at Whitehaven in the evening (covered in detail in the previous chapter). Both meetings featured the same riders, meaning that Workington's first ever speedway meeting actually formed the first half of a West Cumbrian 'double-header'.

A crowd of over 2,000 turned out to witness the birth of speedway in Workington and to see thirty-two competitors from all over the north of England take part in scratch and handicap events. In the semi-final of the scratch event, Maurice Stobbart got into an uncontrollable slide, hit a post and suffered a puncture. His brother Roland reached the final but his engine seized on the second lap, leaving George Mortimer and Bill Nichol to take first and second place respectively. It was a very successful day for Barrow's George Mortimer, who had been riding speedway at Sheffield and Liverpool. He also set the fastest time of the day (89.1 seconds) when he beat Bill Kitchen and George Vingoe in the final of the 500cc handicap race. Maurice and Roland Stobbart did have their revenge though when they both beat Mortimer in an inter-county match race.

The banked, narrow circuit (recorded as being 439 yards to the lap), had provided fast and exciting racing despite its width restricting races to only three riders. Although this inaugural meeting was regarded as a success on the track, it turned out to be a financial disaster for the organisers, and consequently there were no more meetings held at Lonsdale Park in 1931.

In early May 1932, it was announced that the Border Sports Club were going to reintroduce speedway meetings at Lonsdale Park. They declared that, 'with adequate covered accommodation for over 2,000 spectators it was a very suitable venue in which to stage the sport'. However, in order to meet the requirements of the ACU, they would have to make some alterations and improvements to the track, including the erection of crash-proof fencing.

The first meeting under the new promotion took place on Saturday 14 May at 7 p.m. and featured riders competing for the Golden Gauntlet Handicap and the Golden

Helmet scratch trophies. Despite the high rate of unemployment in West Cumberland, over 3,000 paying spectators turned out to see the Mayor of Workington, Councillor F.W. Iredale, officially open the new season.

Not everybody paid to get into Lonsdale Park, though. At least one octogenarian could recall sneaking under the gates to watch the racing for free, even though his mother had strictly forbidden him to go! He used to watch the racing from behind the fence on top of the banked first and second bend. When the riders hit the bend, he had to duck down to avoid the shower of flying cinders that rattled the woodwork. When he got home his mother knew exactly where he had been as his face was black and his hair was full of cinders!

Over the course of the evening a four-lap track record was established at 82.6 seconds by Mortimer and then equalled by Roland Stobbart in the scratch final. Meanwhile, a one-lap track record was set at 19 seconds, by Preston's Jack Tye, who ended the night in the nearby infirmary after crashing and being run over by Mortimer in the scratch races. Tye was found to have sustained a fractured collarbone and superficial head injuries. In the next hospital bed to Tye was Dudley Pryor, the Secretary of Preston Speedway. Pryor was injured when he went to assist a fallen rider and was then run into by another rider following behind. Luckily for Pryor he only suffered bruising.

Jack Tye of Preston set a one-lap track record on 14 May 1932 that was never beaten.

G. Goodall of Preston Speedway won the Golden Gauntlet beating Bill Kitchen and George Mortimer, while the Golden Helmet was won by local star Roland Stobbart ahead of Mortimer. The local press later described the night's proceedings as 'Probably the finest evening's outdoor entertainment that the West Cumberland people have been provided with for many a year'.

Originally, the plan was to hold meetings every fortnight, but the organisers were so pleased with the success of the opening meeting that they hastily made plans for an extra meeting to be held on the following Saturday. Officials went down to the troubled Preston track to sign riders, but in the event, the second meeting did not take place until 28 May when a crowd of 2,000 people turned out in steady drizzle. The star of the show was Stobbart, who won both the Golden Sash and the All-Star Knockout.

Roland's younger brother Maurice was second in the final of the All-Star Knockout but was unfortunate to fall in his heat of the Golden Sash, when Fred Winstanley of Blackpool clipped his back wheel trying to cut in between Maurice and Eric Airey for the lead. In the same race, Airey's and Winstanley's machines broke down on the last lap and both riders pushed their machines to the finish before collapsing with sheer exhaustion. Unfortunately, their efforts were in vain as the slowest heat winner was automatically eliminated from the final!

: PROGRAMME :

AT

Workington Speedway

Lonsdale Park,

Saturday, July 9th, 1932

At 7 p.m.

Held under the General Competition and Special Track Rules of the A.C.U.

OFFICIALS :—

Secretary and Clerk of Course :
Mr. D. Mounsey.

Chief Steward :
Mr. J. M. Renney.

Starter and Timekeeper :
Mr. P. Goman.

Judge :
Mr. J. T. Kessel.

Announcer .
Mr. T. Carruthers.

Competitors' Stewards :
Mr. D. G. Benson.
Mr. I. Conkey.

Medical Attendance by Dr. Clarkson.

Members of St. John's Ambulance in attendance.

THIS WEEK :

H. Robinson. Rochdale.	Norman Griffiths, Liverpool.
E. Brown, Audenshaw.	E. Young, Belle Vue.
Ron Thompson, Rochdale.	G. B. Mortimer, Sheffield.
Peter Waterhouse, Liverpool.	M. Stobart, Preston.

OFFICIAL PROGRAMME   2d.

The Workington Star Ltd., Printers, Workington.

Above left: *Roland Stobbart, the 'King' of Lonsdale Park.*

Above right: *Programme cover from 9 July 1932. (Author's collection)*

In the final of the Golden Sash, a loose rear wheel caused Preston's Billy Yates to crash, allowing Stobbart to ride to an easy victory. Earlier in the evening, Stobbart had established a new four-lap (one mile) record of 1 minute, $19\frac{1}{5}$ seconds, at an average speed of 45mph.

Subsequent weeks saw Roland Stobbart emerge as the man to beat around Lonsdale Park, but a host of other riders became crowd favourites too. Quite a few of them were from the recently closed Preston track, notably Eric Airey, Billy Yates, Ted Shepherdson, Ron Thompson, Peter Waterhouse and a rider who became a real crowd favourite, the 6ft 2in tall, Jack 'Tiger' Woods of Manchester, who wrecked his bike on his debut at Lonsdale Park. Meanwhile George Vingoe, the winner of the track race at the Motor Cycle Gymkhana event back in 1929, became a regular competitor in the junior races.

The meeting on 11 June was the first to feature team racing at Lonsdale Park, a three-team tournament featuring Cumberland, Lancashire and Yorkshire. All three teams were evenly matched and the final score was Cumberland 9, Lancashire 9 and Yorkshire 8. Roland went through the programme unbeaten and on two occasions he even slowed down on the last lap to let his opponent catch up before racing away again to take the chequered flag .

Roland was unbeatable once again in the meeting of 25 June, where it was also announced that he had been signed to ride for West Ham, a move which would restrict his appearances at Lonsdale Park in future weeks. It was a night of bad luck for Jack Woods, though, as his engine failed him on three occasions and he finished the night riding somebody else's bike.

The match race between George Mortimer and Ron Thompson on 9 July was reported as the most exciting race ever seen at Lonsdale Park. The two riders raced side by side for three laps until Thompson hit the fence on the last lap. It transpired that he had been racing with a flat rear tyre! Once again young Maurice Stobbart suffered bad luck, losing his steel shoe in one race and blowing his engine in another. In the final of the Golden Armlet, Ron Thompson shed a chain while leading, the sixth time this had happened to him in two meetings!

The meeting of 30 July was memorable for a spectacular crash involving Ted Shepherdson. In one race, he clipped George Mortimer's back wheel, somersaulted into the air and landed head first on the track. Eventually the doctor reported that he was okay and that his helmet had saved his life. Woods, yet to win a race on his own bike, also crashed out of the Golden Sash event and wrecked his bike yet again. He eventually got Ted Shepherdson's bike fixed up and put in a magnificent display to beat George Mortimer in the final of the Golden Armlet.

Billy Yates, Dick Hayman and George Mortimer were all involved in a three-man pile-up during the meeting on 13 August, Yates ending up in the local infirmary. Crowd favourite Ron Thompson was excluded from the final of the Golden Helmet as the slowest heat winner. This incensed the crowd, who jeered the referee and time-keeper for quite a while, but their jeers turned to cheers when 'Tiger' Woods finally won a race on his own bike beating Australian Vic Ctercteko in the final. During the interval, eight-year-old Tom Meageen, Harry's youngest brother, entertained the crowd by riding his mini-bike on the centre green wearing George Mortimer's helmet.

Above: *The 1932 Workington Speedway Championship Trophy, won by Vic Ctercteko. (Neil Ctercteko)*

Left: *Vic Ctercteko was from Perth, Western Australia and had ridden in the first speedway meeting at the famous Claremont circuit in 1927. (Neil Ctercteko)*

The eighth and final meeting of the 1932 season was the 1932 Workington Speedway Championship held on Saturday 27 August. West Australian rider, Vic Ctercteko (pronounced Ter-chee-ko) took the honours ahead of Peter Waterhouse and Dick Hayman. Meanwhile the evening's support events – the Golden Armlet and the Flying Nine series for the Golden Helmet – were both won by Lonsdale Park regular George Mortimer. He defeated Geoff Walmsley and 'Ham' Burrill in the final of the Golden Armlet, and Vic Ctercteko and Dick Hayman in the final of the Flying Nine.

Despite the success of the 1932 season there was, surprisingly, no place for speedway in Workington during 1933. Instead, a greyhound syndicate stepped in to secure the lease on Lonsdale Park, with the first greyhound meeting taking place in May. The greyhounds only lasted a couple of years though, and by 1935 Workington AFC were the sole tenants at Lonsdale Park.

A Scottish syndicate, headed by J. Fraser Crichton, took over the lease of Lonsdale Park in 1937 and reintroduced greyhound racing. They also appointed Roland Stobbart as speedway manager, and, after a gap of over four years, the dirt-track bikes returned to Lonsdale Park Stadium. Promoted by the Solway and District Motor Club, a total of thirteen meetings were staged during the 1937 season on what was normally a fortnightly basis.

The first of these, the Lonsdale Park Handicap Cup, was held on Saturday 24 April and played out in front of a crowd of over 3,500. Councillor Isaac Armstrong, the Chairman of the Corporation Gas & Electric Committee, performed the official opening ceremony of the speedway.

Oliver Hart won the final of the Lonsdale Park Handicap Cup, from Jack Hargreaves and Stan Hart. Meanwhile local rider Roland Stobbart, who was now riding for Bristol, established a four-lap record of 81.2 seconds with six spokes missing from his rear wheel. However, when Maurice later rode the same machine he was not so fortunate. Maurice covered two laps neck and neck with Hargreaves in the semi-final of the Handicap Cup before his brother's machine wobbled on the straight and shed its driving chain. Then, the rear tyre burst, the rear wheel collapsed altogether, and Maurice was thrown onto the track. Amazingly, he escaped injury and treated the whole incident as a huge joke!

A crowd of over 3,000 turned out for the second meeting, the £100 Championship for the King George VI Coronation Cup, won by the former Preston and Liverpool rider, Tommy Price. Price rode unbeaten throughout and beat Oliver Hart by a single point.

The fourth meeting, held on 10 June, featured the first genuine team match. A north *v.* south affair, which saw the south emerge victorious 32-20. Top scorers for the south were Charlie Spinks, Dan Lee and Wilf Plant, while the bulk of the north's points came from Maurice Stobbart and Alex Ramsay, a local junior from nearby Silloth.

In the opening heat of the scratch event, which followed the team match, Australian Test star Spinks crashed heavily with Leicester's Lal Fulham, ruling both riders ruled out of the remainder of the meeting. The scratch event was won by Maurice Stobbart, who was now starting to carve out quite a reputation for himself. Victory in both the Golden Helmet scratch final and the Derwent handicap event at the next meeting only served to enhance his reputation.

Speedway at Lonsdale Park continued to draw crowds of around 3,000 for each meeting and the promotion were always trying to introduce variety into their fixtures. Meeting number seven was due to feature a Best Pairs Championship, but injuries to some of the listed competitors saw it changed to an individual event which was won by

*Advertisement for the first
meeting of the 1937 season.*

Maurice Stobbart had retired after a poor season at Wembley in 1933, but made a comeback when Workington reopened in 1937 and didn't take long to recapture his old fire. His home-made bike was affectionately known as 'Leaping Lena'.

Bill Desmond, ahead of Maurice Stobbart and Australian Steve Langton. At the end of the meeting, former rider Jack Tye persuaded the promoters to allow him to have 'just one more ride' (Tye's one-lap track record established in 1932 had not yet been beaten). Mounted on Maurice Stobbart's machine he set off on a flying lap only to crash and be thrown some 40ft through the air. After medical attention he was found to have suffered a sprained ankle, but he vowed to return.

On 14 August a team representing Workington made its first appearance on track to take on a team from Lancaster. The home team, (known as the 'Reds', just like the football team) was managed by Roland Stobbart, who was unable to ride after breaking his collarbone a few weeks earlier. Representing Workington were Maurice Stobbart (captain), Sam Marsland, Bill Desmond and Albert 'Aussie' Rosenfeld. The Lancaster team included Norman Hargreaves, Geoff Walmsley, Billy Pilkington and Jim Gordon. Both Walmsley and Pilkington had ridden regularly at Lonsdale Park back in the 1932 season, whilst Hargreaves was having his first competitive rides. Workington proved to be too strong for their opponents, winning by 28-6, with the home riders finishing first in all six heats. Stobbart, Desmond and Marsland were all unbeaten.

The same four riders represented Workington 'Reds' at the next home meeting when stronger opposition in the form of West Ham reserves came to town. (Roland Stobbart had been part of the West Ham squad from 1932 until his transfer to Bristol at the start of the 1937 season). On this occasion the match resulted in a draw, each side scoring 18 points. The local press described the meeting as the grandest evening's

The Workington 'Reds' who beat Lancaster 28–6 on 14 August 1937. Left to right: Bill Desmond, Sam Marsland, Roland Stobbart (manager), Maurice Stobbart, and Albert 'Aussie' Rosenfeld.

entertainment since Mr Roland Stobbart took over the management of the speedway. Floodlighting provided by 100 powerful electric lights, was used for the very first at Lonsdale Park during this meeting and was judged to be an immediate success.

Maurice Stobbart was again the star of the show, racing to six victories in his 7 outings. However, his most notable feat was during the Workington *v.* West Ham match. Maurice's exhaust broke on the opening lap and was dangling on the ground. Officials waved flags to attract his attention and get him to stop, but Stobbart ignored them, raised the pipe off the ground with his right foot and accelerated to take the lead and win the race!

The penultimate meeting of the 1937 season saw Workington 'Reds' take on the Belle Vue 'Merseysiders' in another challenge fixture in front of 2,500 spectators. This time Workington were represented by Maurice Stobbart, Sam Marsland, Norman Hargreaves and Albert Rosenfeld. Despite running out comfortable winners 28-8, the match produced some of the closest racing seen since the season began. All of the riders had been competing at the Moorville track in Carlisle earlier in the day, yet another Cumberland 'double-header'.

Lonsdale Park's final meeting of the 1937 season took place on 25 September, when the Second Workington Speedway Championship was held. Sam Marsland won this from Norman Hargreaves, Denny Pye and Charlie Oates. However, a sporting gesture by Maurice Stobbart ultimately deprived him of a place in the final. Maurice was about to take the lead on the last lap of his semi-final, when he crashed. He remounted and finished in second place, but only because Sam Marsland had broken down and pushed his machine some 300 yards home for third place. Rather than take his place in the final, Stobbart insisted on the toss of a coin to decide whether he or Marsland should progress. Marsland won the toss and even rode Stobbart's machine to victory in the final to bring down the curtain on a successful 1937 season.

Workington AFC moved out of Lonsdale Park in September 1937 and into neighbouring Borough Park, a ground they shared with Workington Town Rugby League Club until 1956. The speedway promoters took the opportunity to undertake several changes to the banked Lonsdale Park circuit with a view to making it wider and safer for the competitors. An application was made for ACU recognition, which necessitated an inspection of the track prior to the 1938 season. The promoters also declared their intention to enter a Workington team in the Northern League. The ACU had always frowned upon the Lonsdale Park track, but on Tuesday 17 May 1938 Mr Ware, the official examiner for the ACU, visited the track and declared it safe and suitable for dirt-track racing.

The first meeting of the 1938 season took place on Saturday 28 May, a three-team challenge match featuring Workington, Nottingham and Sheffield. Watched by a crowd of 3,000, Nottingham won the contest easily, scoring 23 points, with Workington on 17 points and Sheffield on 12. Representing Workington were Maurice Stobbart, Ken Tidbury and Canadian Bruce Venier. George Greenwood was the star of the match, winning all of his 4 outings for Nottingham.

Advert and programme cover for the match against the Belle Vue 'Merseysiders'.

Club Secretary, John Stirling with Bill Desmond (on bike) in the Lonsdale Park pits.

Spencer 'Smoky' Stratton was tragically killed on his way home from Lonsdale Park on 4 June 1938 and is buried in Cockermouth cemetery.

Unlike the previous season, Workington Speedway had planned to hold meetings on a weekly basis for 1938. The second meeting saw a Workington side entertain The Old Canadians. The Canadian visitors won the eight-heat match 13-11, but events that followed the match later that evening made the result of little consequence. On their way home after the meeting, the vehicle carrying the Canadian riders and their team manager, former New Zealand rider Spencer Charles 'Smoky' Stratton, was involved in a collision with another vehicle at Brigham, some seven miles from Lonsdale Park. Thirty-three-year-old Stratton was killed, while riders Ellwood Stillwell, Bruce Venier and Robert Sparks were all injured. Stratton was subsequently buried in nearby Cockermouth cemetery with many speedway personalities, including the legendary speedway pioneer Johnnie Hoskins, present at his funeral.

Workington entertained and defeated a team from Birmingham the following week, with both Maurice and Roland Stobbart starring for the home side, before a second match was arranged against the Canadians. With the riders wearing black armbands as marks of respect for the late Smoky Stratton, the Canadians were defeated 19-29 by Workington in the eight-heat match. All three of the riders who had been involved in the accident took part in the meeting, with their side completed by Norman Newton. Workington had both Roland and Maurice Stobbart in their line-up along with Ken Tidbury and rising star Norman Hargreaves.

Workington's reliance on the Stobbart brothers was emphasised at the next meeting when a team from Belle Vue beat Workington 26-16. The Stobbart brothers were unavailable as they were both on league duty for Newcastle. On this occasion, Workington were represented by two of the Canadian riders, Bruce Venier and Ellwood Stillwell, along with Ken Tidbury and Butch Williams.

Further team matches took place over the next two weeks against combined sides. Firstly Workington defeated a side made up from Middlesbrough and Birmingham, and then a combined side from Newcastle and Middlesbrough. In the latter match, seventeen-year-old Fred 'Kid' Curtis from Newcastle was involved in a spectacular accident. His machine continued to run on for some yards and knocked down two of the official pushers, who somehow escaped unhurt.

The following week, Saturday 23 July, Workington entertained Newcastle in another team match, a meeting that turned out to be the last speedway meeting to ever be held at Lonsdale Park, although nobody in attendance would have realised that this was the case at the time.

Workington won the match 23-21, but the most memorable races of the evening were the clashes between Maurice Stobbart and Newcastle's Canadian star George

Canadian star George Pepper was a friend of Rol and Mo Stobbart and raced in the last ever meeting at Lonsdale Park in 1938. During the Second World War, George was a pilot with the Royal Air Force Volunteer Reserve and was awarded the DFC and Bar, but he was killed in a tragic flying accident in November 1942. He was just about to take off on a test flight when a head-on collision occurred with another fighter coming in to land. (FoTTofiners)

The derelict Lonsdale Park stadium shortly before demolition in 2003. The banking of the 1930s cinder track is clearly defined on the left of the photograph. (Author's collection)

Pepper. They met four times during the evening with honours even at two victories each. In the final event of the night, the Workington Scurry, it was Reg Hay of Newcastle who had the distinction of winning the last ever speedway race at Lonsdale Park.

Ten days after the Newcastle match an article appeared in the local press stating that there were to be no more speedway meetings at Lonsdale Park until further notice. This had come from Mr J. Lees, the manager of the West Cumberland Stadium, Lonsdale Park.

His statement said that:

> dirt-track racing at Lonsdale Park is not paying and that there will be no more meetings until we have had time to think things over and see what can be done. We have been getting the best available riders, and some of the meetings have produced riding as good as may be seen on some of the first-class tracks. But it has made no difference to the attendances, and the surprising thing is that the directors have gone on losing money for so long. Even now they have not given up the ghost, for I have instructions to go carefully into the matter and see what can be done to put speedway racing at Workington on a paying footing. There is, therefore, a possibility that the racing will be revived.

But, racing was not revived and Alex Moffat of the Cumberland Greyhound Company became the sole leasee at Lonsdale Park. Greyhound racing finally ceased in the 1990s and the stadium quickly fell into a state of dereliction. The covered stand on the 'back straight' had long since been demolished but the main grandstand and the banking of the original speedway track were still clearly visible until very recently.

Time has finally run out for Lonsdale Park though. The site has recently been cleared and plans have been put forward to build a brand new 'Super Stadium' on the site for both Workington Rugby League club and Workington AFC. The plans are unlikely to include speedway though, which has found a new home, just across the road at Derwent Park.

10

MIDGETS FROM AMBLESIDE...

Guns are dangerous things: Harry Skirrow used his to steady himself while climbing a gate, the gun went off and Harry lost an arm! So ended the career of one of the region's most promising pre-war motorcycle racers.

Harry Skirrow (his real name was Henry) was one of the prime movers behind the resurgence of the Westmorland Motor Club in 1927 and rode a variety of motorcycles in beach races, reliability trials and grass tracks. He had been runner-up in the 350cc and unlimited finals at Whitehaven in July 1930 and also won the Silver Goblet at Barrow Speedway a few days later. His brother was pretty good too. He had beaten Harry in the 350cc final at Whitehaven and won the Silver Rose Bowl in the very first speedway meeting at Holker Street in June 1930. The Skirrow brothers didn't just ride to make up the numbers, they were amongst the best riders in the north-west.

Following his unfortunate accident Harry opened his own motor business, Skirrow Garages on Lake Road, Ambleside, where one of his colleagues was Walter Mackereth from Kendal. Between them they designed and built a midget speedway car, the 'Skirrow'. The four-wheel drive car was powered by a 996cc vee-twin JAP engine and cost around £185 to buy. It is estimated that Harry built and sold more than fifty Skirrows between 1934 and 1938.

Midget-car racing was born in the United States in the early 1930s, and made its UK debut at Crystal Palace in 1934. Over the next few years its popularity grew, leading to a national speedway car racing league featuring teams from Wembley, Hanley (Stoke), Belle Vue (Manchester), Coventry and Lea Bridge (London). Harry was also a partner in the Stanley Speedway in Liverpool and was behind plans to introduce midget-car racing (or doodle dicing, as it was called) to the Mooreville Speedway track at Carlisle.

As well as designing and manufacturing the cars, Harry was a successful driver too, utilising a hook on the end of his artificial arm to help him compete in trials, hillclimbs and speedway car racing. His colleague Walter Mackereth was even more successful. It is reputed that he won three times as many races than any other midget car driver at the time and won the title of European Champion at a meeting in Rotterdam in 1937. Mackereth also captained the Coventry team, all of whom drove 'Skirrows'.

A number of former speedway riders changed to the four-wheel cars during the 1930s. Frank Chiswell, the former Preston rider, was a team mate of Mackereth at Coventry and Jack 'Tiger' Woods, who had been such a favourite at Workington in 1932,

Former Preston Speedway rider Frank Chiswell in his Skirrow at Coventry in 1937. (Roy Chiswell)

regularly drove at Belle Vue alongside Charlie 'Ginger' Pashley and Syd Plevin. Hugh Tatham, the veteran all-round motorcyclist from Barrow, had a go at midget-car racing in a 'Skirrow', too; at least it made a change from driving his milk float!

Skirrow, Mackereth and Chiswell were all selected to represent England on a tour of Australia over the winter of 1939/40, but the outbreak of war meant that their visit had to be cancelled. Following the war, the 'Skirrows' reappeared at The Hague in Holland in October 1946, and at the Buffalo Stadium in Paris in 1947, but they weren't seen in the UK again until August 1949.

An East Midlands baker, Dave Hughes, was a big fan of midget-car racing and believed he could turn it into a major spectator sport. He bought up as many 'Skirrow' speedway cars as he could find and invested a small personal fortune in a purpose-built speedway car racing stadium at Brafield, in Northamptonshire. Five meetings were held in that first season before Hughes took the 'Skirrows' on tour in 1950. At the tail end of 1951, a Midlands Midget Car League was formed featuring teams from Coventry, Leicester, Birmingham and Cradley Heath, but it only lasted a few weeks before atrocious weather caused the league to be abandoned. Unperturbed, Hughes continued to take his team of 'Skirrows' around the speedway tracks and even took them to Holland and Italy, but by the end of the 1950s, the cars themselves were becoming increasingly unreliable. Without any spare parts as back-up, some of the 'Skirrows' had to be cannibalised to keep the others going. Eventually, Hughes had to admit defeat when he was unable to field enough cars to stage a meeting.

Dave Hughes sold his last remaining 'Skirrow' in 1971. The car had originally belonged to Syd Plevin, who sold it to Frank Chiswell in 1938. Hughes acquired it in 1951 and drove it himself until he called time on his speedway car meetings in the late 1950s.

11

THE GALGATE CONNECTION

To the world of speedway and grass-track racing, the Lancashire village of Galgate really is a 'Cradle of Champions'. It's incredible to believe that so much talent could have come from just one tiny village. Without a doubt, the most famous son of Galgate was Bill Kitchen, probably the UK's first grass-track superstar and one of the greatest speedway riders this country has ever produced, but there is a much bigger story surrounding the speedway dynasty of Galgate.

The villages of Galgate and Ellel were built around three silk spinning mills, all originally powered by water wheels. The earliest of these mills can be traced back to 1790 and was still working in the early 1960s. In 1881, a young man named Richard Burgess left his home in Pudsey, Yorkshire, to take up employment as a card minder in one of the mills. It was at the mill he met Mary Ann West, a young girl who had moved to Galgate from Congleton in Cheshire. Richard and Mary subsequently married and had fifteen children, eight girls and seven boys (Mary actually gave birth to twenty-two children, but only fifteen survived).

When Richard left the mill, he opened his own bicycle workshop, later expanding the business to include motorcycles and, eventually, cars. The garage proved to be a wonderful playground for the children. Two of the boys, Fred and Frank, were fascinated with the motorcycles in their father's garage, so it came as no surprise to find them racing bikes on the beaches and grass tracks when they were old enough. When dirt-track racing became popular in 1928, Frank went along to the White City track in Manchester and later rode for both Liverpool and Warrington in the English Dirt-Track League. In 1930, he signed a contract to ride for Belle Vue. Most of his appearances were for the 'Manchester' team that rode in the Southern League during 1931, but he did make a few appearances for Belle Vue in the Northern Knockout Cup. In one memorable race at Belle Vue Gardens, Frank's bike caught fire just after he crossed the finish line. Luckily both man and machine escaped undamaged. Another brother, George, was one of the first bus drivers in the Lancaster area, and one of the fastest too. On one journey to Cheshire he was caught speeding at an average of 22mph when the legal limit was 12mph! In the mid-1950s, George and his son Charles opened their own motor garage in Galgate. G. Burgess & Son continued to trade until 1985, when George finally retired. Charles's son, also named George, continued the family tradition of motorcycle sport, competing in trials events. A fourth brother, Thomas (but known as Tim) had a cheese stall on Lancaster market, which is still trading today.

Above left: *Frank Burgess at Scale Hall, Lancaster in the early 1930s. His younger brother George is standing to his left and his nephew Jack Kitchen (Bill's brother) to his right. (George Burgess)*

Above right: *Frank Burgess with his dirt-track Scott in the Belle Vue pits, 1931. (C.F. Wallace)*

Richard's and Mary's eldest daughter, Margaret, married the village butcher, William 'Pop' Kitchen. They had two sons, John and William, known to their friends as Jack and Bill. Richard doted on his two grandsons and gave each of them a hand-built bicycle. Bill took his bicycle everywhere, and even rode it around the Blackburn Rovers football pitch whenever his father took him to watch a game – almost a taster of things to come!

Being from such a large family, there was a big age difference between Margaret and her younger brothers. Her own sons were about the same age as her younger brothers Fred and Frank; in fact, Bill was nearly two years older than his Uncle Frank. Naturally, the four boys grew up together and got into trouble together. Fred and Bill built their first motorcycle from bits and pieces they managed to beg, borrow or steal from the garage; unfortunately, the local policeman caught them on the road to Conder Green while they were out on a 'test run'.

At the age of eighteen, Bill was given a brand new 350cc side valve Sunbeam, which ended up wrapped around a telegraph pole on Main Road in Galgate. Using parts from his grandfather's garage, the Sunbeam was resurrected and raced in Lancaster & Morecambe MC events. Bill also used the Sunbeam for his first rides on a speedway track. Bill and his friend Lionel Cordingley rode over to Burnley on the Easter weekend of 1929 for the opening of the Towneley Speedway and talked the promoter into letting them ride in the novice races. Despite finishing second in their respective races, Bill decided that he would wait until he could afford a proper dirt-track bike before he tried again, but Lionel was hooked and signed up as a novice at the Preston track.

Lionel was originally from Haslingden, where his family ran one of the biggest motor dealers in the county. With the business established, Lionel's father retired and moved to Morecambe, where he eventually became Mayor. After leaving Lancaster Grammar School, Lionel took up an apprenticeship at the Ribble Bus Company, where he met Bill Kitchen. Following their first taste of speedway at Burnley, Lionel bought a 500cc Rudge and raced it at Preston, Barrow and Workington. He used the same bike in grass tracks too, winning the coveted Golden Helmet at Scale Hall and was twice crowned Lancashire Grass-Track Champion. Spending so much time with the Kitchen and Burgess brothers, Lionel became part of the 'scene' in Galgate, and married Ethyl Tyson from Salford Road.

Lionel's father had never approved of his son's fascination with the dirt tracks and eventually tempted him away with a brand new factory-prepared Norton road-racing machine. Following successful races at Donington Park and Ireland, Lionel entered the 1933 Senior Manx Grand Prix, but was seriously injured when he crashed at Quarter. Despite setting a course record at Saltburn Speed Trials in 1934, Lionel never really recovered from that crash on the Isle of Man and gave up motorcycle racing soon after.

Lionel Cordingley on his Norton at the 1933 Manx Grand Prix. (Stan Cordingley)

Bill Proctor, Alf Armistead and Frank Burgess outside Richard Burgess's garage in Galgate. The building is now the village Spar shop. (George Burgess)

His marriage to Ethyl didn't survive either and after they split, he moved back to Haslingden to work in the family firm. The Manx Norton is now owned by his only son, Stan, who became a successful trials rider in his own right and still lives at Cockerham, not far from Galgate.

Peter Blundell and Dennis Tong were two more motorcycle enthusiasts from Galgate, who worked at the Ribble Bus Company. Peter won a few grass-track meetings on his Model 90 Sunbeam and also rode in speedway meetings at Barrow and Preston, but it was Dennis who unwittingly gave Bill Kitchen his big break. Bill was always pestering Dennis to let him ride his two-stroke Scott, eventually Dennis relented and allowed Bill to ride the bike in a sand race at Middleton in 1929. Bill duly obliged by winning the Novice event and finishing second to Clarrie Wood in the senior race. This unprecedented success landed him a 'bonus' contract from a leading oil company – an early form of sponsorship. For every first place he secured using their oil, Bill received a bonus of 50 shillings. Bill rattled up 75 first places on Dennis Scott that year and even rode the bike in the Amateur TT, although they forgot to inform the organisers of the change and the records still show the name of the owner, D. Tong, and not the rider, W. Kitchen.

Bill earned enough money in 1929 to buy his own bike, a 350cc Velocette. He rode it in his first grass-track meeting, at Scale Hall near Morecambe, and before long he was he was picking up even more trophies and bonuses. He still wanted to race on the dirt tracks however, so, brimming with confidence, he contacted the Scott factory asking if they would loan him a bike for speedway racing. Whoever opened his letter must have been impressed with Bill's credentials, as he was immediately signed up as a works rider, but on one condition, he was not to ride speedway! As a work's rider, Bill partnered Oliver Langton in the 1930 Scott Trial and was on the leader board at the 1930 Senior TT until he crashed at Bradden Bridge.

By 1931, the effects of the Wall Street Crash had hit Lancashire hard. Bill had to leave the Scott works and return home to help his father and brother in the new family business, W. Kitchen & Sons, an engineering works and motor garage on Main Road in Galgate. Bill supplemented the family income with bonuses from his grass-track and beach-race victories, but everything centred on the Isle of Man TT during the first week of June, where Bill was riding in the Lightweight and Senior TT. Bill finally got to realise his dream of becoming a speedway rider in 1931, too. He started to go along to the practice sessions at Preston Speedway, where his friend Lionel Cordingley was already riding in the handicap events. Speedway came easy to Bill, and in no time at all, he was beating many of the more experienced riders. During August he won a junior event at Belle Vue and was runner-up in the 500cc handicap race at Workington's first 'Cinder Track' meeting. Nine days later he went to the final meeting at Little Park, Barrow and cleaned up, winning the Silver Goblet and the Golden Helmet.

Bill returned to the Isle of Man again in 1932, riding a 350cc Rudge in the senior and lightweight TT, but his greatest success was retaining the Yorkshire Grass-Track Championship at Harrogate, beating Frank Varey and Frank Charles in the final. 'Bronco' Dixon's father watched Bill's masterly performance from the centre green and urged 'Pop' Kitchen to take his son along to Belle Vue speedway for a trial. Bill's speedway activities had been curtailed after Preston and Barrow had both closed down, but when the 1933 Belle Vue training sessions were advertised, Bill booked himself a place and took his Rudge down to Hyde Road. The Belle Vue manager, E.O. Spence, was impressed and offered him a contract there and then.

Bill Kitchen at the 1932 Isle of Man TT. (FoTTofinders)

Bill with his very first speedway machine in 1933. (Mrs M. Proctor)

At first Bill used a two-year-old speedway JAP that his father had bought from Tommy Gamble. His brother Jack and Oliver Hall, an employee at the factory, did their best to make the bike competitive, but Bill's real breakthrough came when they purchased a brand new Victor Martin JAP. Within weeks he was beating many of the established top stars and settled straight into the rigours of league racing. He developed a superb partnership with Max Grosskreutz and, by the end of July, Bill had earned his first England cap. His progress was slightly hindered by a foot injury, but he still finished the season with a League Champions medal, just like his Uncle Frank two years earlier.

The year 1933 signalled Bill's last appearance on the Isle of Man, riding his trusty 350cc Rudge to fourteenth place in the lightweight TT. Speedway and grass-track racing were taking up more and more of Bill's time and he still had commitments to the family business. Eventually, he took over the running of the motor garage and joined his father as a partner in the Liverpool Speedway when it returned to the Stanley Stadium in 1936, but it was on the track itself that he found his real fame and fortune. Bill was virtually unbeatable at Hyde Road and became a master of the art of team riding. He rode with a typically Northern upright style and favoured the inside line, where he could cover his partner and keep the opposition behind him. Towards the end of the decade, he adopted one of the longest helmet peaks imaginable, a trademark that remained until he retired.

In 1935, Bill reached his first Star final at Wembley, then shocked everybody when he announced that he wanted to join the London club. The move never materialised, however, and Bill stayed with Belle Vue right up until the outbreak of the Second World War. He qualified for his first World Speedway Championship final in 1937, and travelled to Australia with the England team during the winter of 1937/38. In 1938, he qualified for his second World final and was appointed captain of the England team. The 1939 season began in fine style too. In 5 Test Match appearances for England he amassed a record 70 points and his league form was outstanding. The Southampton management were so impressed that they tried to tempt Bill away from Belle Vue, but naturally, E.O. Spence blocked the move. The intervention of the Second World War probably

Above: *A scene from the Belle Vue pits. Left to right: Mr Langton, 'Pop' Kitchen, Oliver Langton, Bill Kitchen and Eric Langton.*

Left: *Bill Kitchen, 'international TT and speedway rider – at your service'. A scene from Bill's garage on Main Road, Galgate.*

cost Bill his best chance of becoming World Champion. He was one of the hot favourites to take the World title at Wembley on 7 September, but war was declared on 3 September and the event was cancelled.

During the war years, Bill was lucky to be stationed near to his Lancashire home, which meant that he could still ride at Belle Vue on a regular basis. He won the Northern Championship in 1940, the Belle Vue Grand Prix in 1941 and the British Individual Championship in 1945. When the war ended, ENSA arranged for a NAAFI speedway team to entertain the troops in occupied Germany. Bill was appointed 'Commander' of the combined Army and RAF team and his brother Jack travelled with the team as chief mechanic. In December 1945, Bill won the Hamburg Individual Championship and was crowned the unofficial Champion of Germany at the Hanomag Stadium.

League racing returned to Britain in 1946 and all of the available riders were pooled. Surprisingly, the Belle Vue manager chose Jack Parker as his number one, allowing Alec Jackson to swoop for Bill and appoint him as captain of the Wembley Lions. Bill did everything that was asked of him at Wembley, leading the side to seven league titles in eight years. On the individual front, he finished second to Tommy Price in the 1946 British Riders Championship and lost out to Jack Parker in a run-off for the 1947 title. During the winter of 1946/47, Bill led the England team on a tour of New Zealand, but breaking his arm in April kept him out of the saddle for most of the British season. He spent the summer recuperating on the South Coast, where he spent his time coaching the Plymouth team at Pennycross Stadium.

Bill reached the final of the World Championship again in 1949 and true to form scored 9 points, just as he had done on the previous two occasions. From this point on Bill's scoring power started to decline, but he still loved his racing and was content to ride at reserve for his team until he finally retired at the end of the 1953 season. When Wembley were looking for a new manager in 1970, Bill Kitchen was at the head of their list, but he took a position as the Speedway Control Board's first official track inspector and machine examiner instead. One of his first jobs was to inspect and approve the new track at Derwent Park in Workington, but seeing the track just lying there and doing nothing proved too great a temptation and he couldn't resist a couple of laps, just for old times sake. He continued in this position for many years until the SCB decided that his 'services were no longer required'. It is such a pity that a man with so much experience could be cast aside like that.

Wembley snapped up Bill Kitchen from the 'pool' when league racing recommenced in 1946. Bill led the Lions to seven league titles in eight years.

A teenage Dick Fisher fettles his bike. (David Alderson)

Bill died in May 1994 aged eighty-five. During his twenty-one years as a professional speedway rider he had tasted glory as an individual and as the captain of two legendary teams. His ability to control a race and shepherd his team mate home was one of the reasons why Belle Vue (pre-war) and Wembley (post-war) were so successful. During the 1930s he was probably Lancashire's finest all-round motorcyclist and arguably Britain's first grass-track superstar.

Bill's son Eric didn't quite follow in his father's tyre tracks. He rode as a junior at Belle Vue in the early 1950s, but made his name as a trials rider in the North-Western Centre. Very often he would find himself competing alongside Stan Cordingley and George Burgess, all continuing a long-standing Galgate tradition. Eric was also a renowned motorcycle photographer, having a lot of his work published in the Lancaster-based *Trials and Motocross News*. In later years he founded E.K. Brakes, a successful motor spares business with branches all over the north-west. Eric has since retired, leaving the business in the capable hands of his son Anthony.

When Bill moved south to join Wembley, Jack stayed in Galgate to work at the factory, subsequently taking over the running of the workshop when 'Pop' retired. Jack and his wife Ada had five children. Margaret, Jean, Elaine, Christopher and William. Jean was the first to get involved with the speedway racing world when she married another aspiring young racer from the village named Dick Fisher. Christopher also followed the family tradition and became a speedway rider at the famous Belle Vue track.

Dick was actually born in Cowan Bridge, on 13 January 1933, but moved to Galgate at an early age. Growing up in the village, it was inevitable that Dick would get the bug for racing motorcycles and by the age of sixteen he was competing in grass-track races at Warton. After showing up well in the North Lancashire club meetings, Naaman Baldwin invited Dick to try his luck at speedway. So, in May 1951, Dick signed a contract to ride for the Fleetwood 'Flyers', where Naaman was manager and Jack Kitchen was machine examiner. He started off with some impressive displays in the novice races and on 20 June he beat veteran Charlie Oates to win the scratch race final. Dick made his league debut for Fleetwood against Southampton on 1 August 1951, but failed to score from his two rides.

With doubts surrounding the future of Fleetwood Speedway, Dick moved to Belle Vue at the start of the 1952 season, initially riding in second-half events. Dick got his first team call up in the summer of 1953 and underlined his potential with a magnificent 10-point return in the final match of the season. He finally broke into the team proper in May 1954, but didn't make the progress expected of him. That big score at the tail end of 1953 was starting to look like a fluke until a match-winning performance against Wimbledon at the tail end of 1955. Dick had only scored 1 point from his first 3 outings but he completely upset the form book by winning a last-heat decider.

Following a tour of Eastern Europe over the winter of 1955/56, Dick finally made the breakthrough and started to really rattle up the points. Much of this was down to the advice he was getting from his mentor, Bill Kitchen. The connection with Bill wasn't confined to the speedway track, either. In partnership with Phil Bowker, Dick had bought Bill's garage on Main Road, Galgate and also married his niece, Jean.

Bill's advice really began to pay dividends and Dick qualified for his first World Championship final in 1956, scoring 6 points. But the season ended with the first of a number of injures that would affect his form over the next two seasons. A broken collarbone hampered his scoring for much of the 1957 season, then, just when it looked like his confidence was returning, a broken leg kept him out of the saddle for 9 matches during the middle of the 1958 season. With Dick on the sidelines, another young hopeful from Galgate finally got his chance to ride for Belle Vue.

Far left: *Dick Fisher joined the Belle Vue 'Aces' in 1952 and stayed with them until he retired in 1966. (Wright Wood)*

Left: *Jack Kitchen got his chance to ride for the 'Aces' when his brother-in-law was sidelined in the middle of the 1958. (Wright Wood)*

Jack Kitchen made the breakthrough when he was loaned to Sheffield in 1960. He is pictured warming his bike up in the Sheffield pits.
(Sheffield Telegraph & Star)

Christopher John Kitchen (known to his friends as 'Bud') was born in Galgate on 2 August 1938 and had his first taste of speedway at the Belle Vue training schools in the mid-1950s. If the name doesn't sound familiar, that is because 'Bud' became known as Jack in speedway circles. He always insisted that the reputation of his famous uncle had no bearing on his decision to become a speedway rider. His fascination with the game actually started at Fleetwood, where his father was the machine examiner in the early 1950s. Young 'Bud' loved being amongst the action in the pits and convinced his father to buy him a bike once he was old enough.

Jack rode in 9 League and Trophy matches for Belle Vue during 1958 but apart from a 5-point return against Norwich on 5 September, he failed to make much of an impression and spent the best part of the next season riding in second-half events. Jacks career really began to take off when he joined Sheffield in 1960. He was one of the most outstanding newcomers in the Provincial League that year, scoring 122 points in 16 matches and reaching the final of the Provincial League Riders Championship. During August he scored 10 points in the Northern Riders Championship and beat Trevor Redmond for the Silver Sash match race title too. Belle Vue were impressed with his progress and decided to recall him for the 1961 season.

During the winter, Jack married Eileen Makinson, a girl he'd met in Lancaster while playing darts at her father's pub. Eileen had a Galgate connection too. Her father was born there, and Makinsons Row in the village is named after the family.

Unbeknown to his legions of fans, Dick had been suffering from a long-term illness that had been wearing him down. After a couple of steady seasons as a dependable heat leader, Dick unexpectedly announced his retirement in October 1962, but during the winter he learnt that he had made a complete recovery and rescinded his decision to retire. Jack hadn't been having much luck either. Just when it looked like he was about to make the breakthrough, injuries to his leg and ankle knocked him back again. His confidence only returned when he was given another spell in the Provincial League, this time with Bradford. Pressure from his father to take over the family business led to Jack announcing his retirement at the end of the 1962 season, but Ken Sharples, the Belle Vue manager, eventually persuaded him to change his mind and the two brothers-in-law were back in the Belle Vue fold when the tapes went up on the new season.

Just like the old days, everybody in the village wanted to lend a hand. Oliver Hall was never far away when mechanical help was needed and Jimmy Gowdy and Ken Parker both helped Dick and Jack with the preparation of their bikes. Jimmy was sadly killed in a motorway accident, but Ken eventually opened his own garage in Morecambe.

Back to full fitness, Dick had his best ever season in 1963, topping the 'Aces' averages and playing a major role in bringing the National League title back to Hyde Road. His team-riding with Gordon McGregor was a revelation and on the individual front, he qualified for his second World Championship final. Writing in the *Speedway Graphic*, Frank McLean reckoned that Dick Fisher was 'an outside bet for the World title itself' and that he had blossomed into 'one of the top six riders in the country'. In the event, Dick was outclassed and only scored 5 points.

Jack was still struggling to score points in the higher league, so part-way through the season he reverted to Provincial League Sheffield. Jack was obviously happier in the

1963 was Dick's finest season, topping the Belle Vue averages and qualifying for his second World Championship final. (Wright Wood)

lower league and finished runner-up in the Provincial League Riders Championship. His scintillating form earned him his first England cap too, playing a starring role against Scotland at Middlesborough. In his World Championship qualifying round, Jack scored a magnificent 10 points, but he could easily have won the meeting had he not stalled at the gate in his very first ride of the night.

The disappointment that both riders suffered in the World Championship was nothing compared to the tragedy that occurred on Friday 20 September, though. Peter Craven, the former World Champion and hero of Belle Vue, crashed at Edinburgh and died as a result of his injuries. Dick and Jack were both close friends of Peter Craven and it was feared both would quit the sport again. Thankfully, Dick returned as captain of the Belle Vue team in 1964 and Jack went back to Sheffield, where he started the new season in blistering form. Once again, his season was interrupted when he suffered multiple abrasions in a car crash. He made a comeback before the end of the season, but it took him a while to recapture his form.

Dick continued to be a potent scorer home and away and qualified for his third World final in 1964, at Ullevi in Sweden. Once again he flattered to deceive, finishing third in his opening ride and failing to score in his remaining heats. It was around this time that Dick became involved with Mike Parker's plans to reintroduce speedway to Blackpool. Many felt that Dick would leave Belle Vue and join the new Blackpool team when it opened, but the venture never came to fruition and Dick stayed at Hyde Road for the remainder of his career.

When the tapes went up on the 1965 season the two leagues had combined. Jack was riding better than ever and scoring points at the highest level. He averaged over 9 points per meeting and qualified for the British League Riders Championship. At the end of the season, though, it was announced that he was taking over the running of the family business in Galgate, and would not be riding in 1966. Sheffield struggled without Jack and team manager, Frank Varey, tried every trick in the book to persuade him to ride again. It took him until June to change Jack's mind and when he did come back, it took him no time at all to start knocking up the points again and turn Sheffield's season around.

On 22 September 1966, Belle Vue were the visitors at Sheffield. Dick was drawn against his brother-in-law in his first ride but the race was stopped when Dick fell and injured his shoulder. Dick had received a knock to the shoulder back in 1965 and damaged it again in 1966. After the second injury, Dick took some time off to recuperate, but when he did come back, the shoulder was obviously a burden and Dick struggled to score points. This time he left the track in agony and headed straight for hospital for emergency surgery. Dick's season was over. It came as no surprise when Dick announced that he would not be riding in 1967. Not only was his shoulder permanently dislocated, but he had bought out Phil Bowker's share of the car sales business and was spending more and more time at work.

Jack finally hung up his leathers for good at the end of the 1966 season too, taking over the day-to-day running of the family engineering works with his brother William. Once again, Jack and Dick were working side by side, not on the track this time, but in the engineering works and car salesroom, right next door to each other in Galgate.

Rival captains… Jack Kitchen greets his brother-in-law prior to a Sheffield v. Belle Vue league match. (Wright Wood)

Deep down Jack always wished that he could have carried on racing for a few more years, but even if he hadn't retired, Sheffield would have released him to make way for their new signing, Brian Bett.

Dick sat out the whole of the 1967 season, but he missed the thrill of the racing and declared his intention to ride again in 1968. During pre-season practice sessions at Hyde Road, Dick put in some very fast times, almost equalling the track record in one session. He was named to ride in the opening-night challenge match against Newcastle, but sensationally withdrew from the 'Aces' team less than twenty-four hours before the match. It was later revealed that Dick had not been issued with a racing licence as he didn't have the necessary insurance. Rather than take out the usual cover, Dick had requested additional cover to safeguard his family and business commitments. The request was refused and Dick decided to stay in retirement for good.

Sadly, neither of them lived long enough to enjoy a full and happy retirement. Dick passed away in December 1986 and Jack died from a brain tumour in 1990. None of their children have ventured into the speedway scene, although Jack's daughter, Angela, became something of an international BMX (Bicycle Moto-X) starlet until a neck injury curtailed her racing. Her brother David had no interest in motorcycle racing, but he did work for his father in the engineering works.

Take a trip to Galgate today and you will find plenty to remind you of Galgate's speedway dynasty. The silk mills have long since closed and Richard Burgess's original bicycle and motorcycle garage is now the local Spar shop, but 'Pop' Kitchen's engineering workshop is still there. William Kitchen (Jack's brother) still owns the building, although the business is now in the hands of new owners. Dick Fisher's house in Ellel bears the name 'Ullevi', after the stadium in Sweden where he rode in his last World final and his car sales business is still trading next door to the engineering works. It has changed a lot over the years and the modern, plush showroom bares no resemblance at all to the original garage that was run by Bill Kitchen in the 1930s. Thankfully, the business has remained in the family and R.M. Fisher Ltd is now run by Dick's daughter and her husband.

12

FLEETWOOD –
THE TRACK OF A THOUSAND THRILLS

The story of Fleetwood Speedway begins in April 1948, but the origins of how speedway came to Fleetwood actually began in Wigan twelve months earlier. Wigan 'Warriors' were based at the Poolstock Stadium and entered the Second Division of the National League for the first time in 1947. They gave quite a good account of themselves too, but still finished the season one place clear of the wooden spoon. Wigan were preparing for a second season at the Greyhound Stadium when a dispute erupted between the stadium owners and the speedway promoters. The owners had been running greyhounds at the stadium on a Saturday evening, leaving the speedway free to operate on Fridays, but a change in the law for 1948 opened the door for weekday greyhound meetings and the owners claimed Friday evenings for themselves. Initially, the speedway was all set to run on Tuesdays, but after due consideration, it was decided that running mid-week was going to be too much of a risk. So, with the start of the 1948 season almost upon them, the promoters began the search for a new and more viable venue.

They found the perfect venue in the north-west of the county, Highbury Stadium, the home of Fleetwood Football Club. In early March it was announced that the local council were supporting plans to bring speedway racing to the Lancashire fishing port and a seven-year tenancy was granted to Blackpool-based promoters, James Wolfenden and Joseph Waxman.

It took less than a month to create a new track around the football pitch and by mid-April, the Wigan Warriors were transferred lock, stock and barrel to Fleetwood. The deal included the team manager, Dudley Marchant, and the contracts of all but two of the Wigan riders – the two exceptions being the injured Harry Welch and new signing Don Houghton, who decided to return home to Australia. Meanwhile, the season had begun and 'Wigan' had already completed their first 3 fixtures away at Norwich, Newcastle and Glasgow. On 13 April the team formerly known as Wigan Warriors officially became the Fleetwood 'Flyers' and more than 11,000 people flocked through the gates of Highbury Avenue Sports Ground to see what all the fuss was about. Following the official opening of the track by the Mayor, football stars Stan Mortensen and Stanley Matthews rode a lap of the track to rapturous applause, then it was on with the racing. The Flyers' opponents on that historic night were Edinburgh, another new team to the league. Surprisingly, the visitors won the meeting 49-35, but then, the

Scottish side had been granted an entire afternoon of practice, which in hindsight must have given them an unfair advantage over the 'home' side.

For the next few weeks, Fleetwood relied heavily on Norman Hargreaves and Dick Geary, their only two recognised heat leaders. Cyril Cooper and captain Jack Gordon added some weight to the middle order, but the rest of the team was woefully weak, especially away from home. Possibly the lowest point of the season came at Middlesborough, where the Flyers were mauled 65-19 by the Tigers. Fleetwood came very close to scoring their first home win on 11 May, but sheer bad luck in the last two

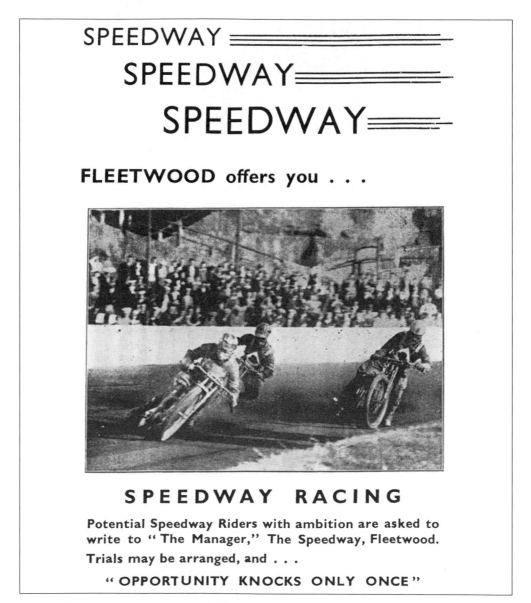

A *1948 advertisement inviting interested riders to come to Fleetwood for trials.*

Percy Brine, a former movie stunt rider and a member of the 1948 Flyers team. (Voyle-Lipson)

heats robbed them of the necessary points. The final heat was marred by a nasty accident involving Bristol's Mike Beddoe, who had grabbed the vital third place right on the line. He crossed the line at such speed that he clattered into the fence with dire consequences. His single point had given Bristol a narrow 42-41 victory, but he left the stadium in an ambulance and had part of his foot amputated on the next day.

An extra fixture was slipped into the fixture list on Whit Monday, 17 May, with Middlesborough beating the Flyers again. The visitor's top scorer, Wilf Plant, became the subject of one of the quickest transfer deals the sport has ever known. On the very next night, Wilf lined up for Fleetwood and led them to a 44-39 victory against Newcastle – their first ever win at Highbury Avenue. From this point onwards, Fleetwood seemed to step up a gear, knocking up some impressive scores at home, but they still struggled on their travels.

The second new signing was Ernie Appleby, who joined Fleetwood from Birmingham at the beginning of July. Ernie took longer than expected to settle down, but began to rattle up some excellent scores towards the end of the season. July also saw the departure of team manager Dudley Marchant and there was a shock transfer request from Dick Geary, who wanted to move nearer to his London base. Luckily, Geary remained faithful to Fleetwood for the remainder of the season, taking over the captaincy from Jack Gordon in September and finishing the season as the club's leading points scorer. Unfortunately, Dick had a painful end to an otherwise successful season, falling and breaking his arm in the last meeting of the season.

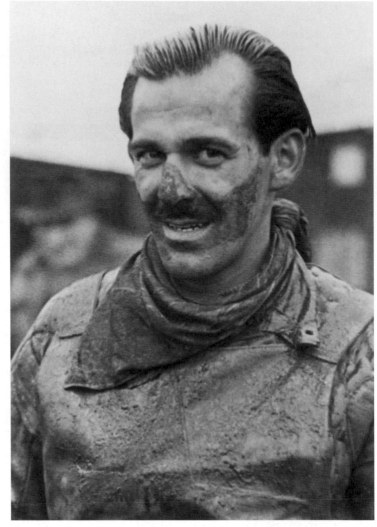

Right: *Dashing Dick Geary rode for the Flyers in 1948, returning for a second term in 1950.* (Wright Wood)

Opposite: *A highly collectible programme from Fleetwood's first season.*

Fleetwood finished their first season in the same position as Wigan had the year before – one place off the bottom. A disappointing result considering many of their defeats had been close-run affairs. A little more luck and Fleetwood could definitely have finished mid-table.

During the closed season, Dick Geary was granted his transfer and joined Walthamstow in a £1,000 deal. Jack Gordon and Jack Winstanley departed too, both of them joining Coventry. In their place came the spectacular leg-trailing George Newton, (making a racing comeback after ten years out of the sport with tuberculosis) and a promising young novice from Blackpool named Don Potter. There were some substantial alterations to the track too. Banking was introduced to the third and fourth bends, extending the circuit to 425 yards.

Fleetwood got their second season underway on 1 April at Bristol, where they went down 22-62. Their next fixture saw them lose again at Newcastle, but at least there were

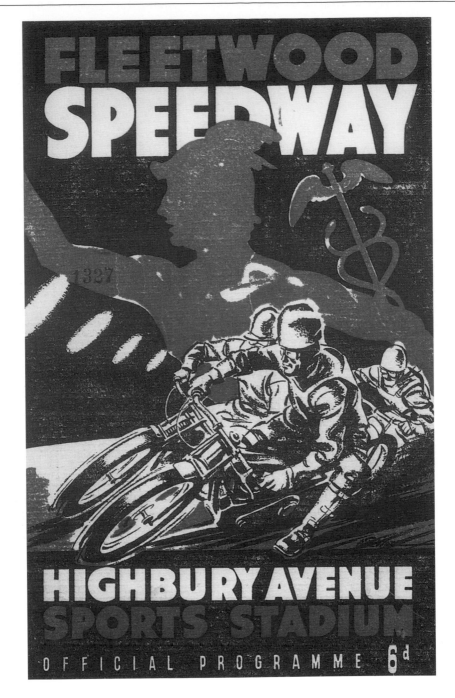

some excellent individual performances from 'Wee Georgie' Newton (12-point maximum) and Wilf Plant (11). The first home match of the season on 13 April saw the Flyers beat Newcastle 47-37 with George Newton in invincible form again. This signalled the beginning of a ten-match unbeaten run at home, but they had to contend with complaints from visiting teams about the state of their track. Bristol were most

More was expected of Reg Lambourne, who lost his place shortly after the start of the 1949 season.

unhappy after their defeat at the Highbury Bowl on 5 May and lodged a letter of protest with the Speedway Control Board.

Australian Frank Malouf was the first new recruit to the team, replacing Reg Lambourne early in the season. Larry Young and Percy Day were also given a chance to shine following Ron Hart's injury in May. Percy certainly repaid the faith that had been shown by scoring a magnificent 14 points against Cradley Heath on 15 June. The 64-18 score line certainly gave a shock to ex-Fleetwood manager Dudley Marchant, who was in charge of the Black Country team. The Flyers were looking a much better side than they had done at any time in the previous season and by the end of June they were actually in third place in the Second Division table.

If June was a month to remember, then July was definitely a month to forget! Defeats at Sheffield and Ashfield were followed by a shock 46-60 defeat at home to Bristol, the same team who had complained so bitterly about the Fleetwood track earlier in the season. To make matters worse, Wilf Plant broke his collarbone whilst riding at Newcastle on 18 July and Ernie Appleby broke his thigh in one of the worst racing accidents ever seen at the Highbury Bowl. Wilf Plant did return to the saddle in late August and kept up his excellent form, but then he rocked the club with a transfer request.

During this difficult time, Fleetwood were still attracting huge crowds making the promoters very happy (and very wealthy!). They could count on some big names amongst the supporters too; world-famous entertainer George Formby, football legend Stanley Mortensen and TT star Bill Doran were all regulars at Highbury Avenue. The promoters had approached the local council with a proposal to extend their current lease, but were turned down. On the back of this disappointment, Waxman and Wolfenden turned their attention to Blackpool. After all, if they could attract crowds in excess of 8,000 at Fleetwood, just think what they could achieve in the heart of the famous seaside resort. These ambitious plans seemed to have an unsettling effect on the riders and the Flyers season went into a sharp decline. In a complete reversal of the first half of the season, the Flyers could only manage six victories from their remaining 21 league fixtures. Fleetwood dropped down the table and finished ninth out of twelve in the Second Division, but at least they finished the season on a high. In the final match of the season they beat Ashfield 52-30 and George Newton recorded his seventh full maximum.

Right: *The all-action style of George Newton. (C.Massey)*

Below left: *Australian Frank Malouf, a great favourite with the fans.*

Below right: *As well as riding for Fleetwood, Australian leg-trailer Percy Day also tuned the engines for Jeff Crawford, Harold Bottoms and Wally Leighs.*

Fleetwood had problems getting a team together for the 1950 season. George Newton suffered a relapse in his health and requested a move nearer his home in the south, Cyril Cooper had joined Coventry and Wilf Plant insisted that he wanted to remain on the transfer list. The only new faces were Bill Reynolds and Graham Williams, both from Australia, and Alf Parker, signed from Sheffield.

The month of April saw Fleetwood succumb to four heavy defeats away from home and their first home meeting of the season was cancelled, leaving them rooted at the bottom of the table from the outset. May wasn't much better either – the team could only muster 6 points from 11 matches, promising reserve Ron Hart moved to Coventry on a free transfer and George Newton made his transfer request official. A rider exchange deal was struck with Walthamstow which saw 'Wee Georgie' move south and an unhappy Dick Geary return to his former club.

The club's fortunes started to improve in June. Two home victories against Newcastle and Yarmouth and a magnificent 46-38 win away at Hanley actually lifted them to sixth place in the Second Division table. Dick Geary's confidence was beginning to return and it really looked like the tide was turning, but five successive defeats in July saw the Flyers start to slide back down the table again and August saw Fleetwood suffer their heaviest defeat ever, going down 15-69 at Norwich.

A succession of novices were tried in the team during 1950, including a young Polish rider named Max Rech, who later had some success at St Austell, but only locally based Geoff Culshaw made any real impression. Norman Hargreaves continued to lead the

Graham Williams returned to Australia after one season with the Flyers, but returned to the UK to ride for St Austell in 1953.

*Geoff Culshaw, the best of the
1950 novices* (Sport & General).

team by example, scoring consistently wherever he went, but the highlight of the season had to be the phenomenal rise of Don Potter. In less than two years, Don had progressed from a raw novice to the club's top scorer. Wilf Plant had obviously been unhappy all year and this was reflected in his form, dropping to reserve for part of the season. Wilf had been in constant dispute with the promoters and he appealed to the Speedway Control Board over the exorbitant fee that Fleetwood were asking for his transfer. Unfortunately, the SCB turned down Wilf's appeal and he was forced to see out the season at Fleetwood. If they hadn't suffered enough misfortune, Dick Geary broke his arm again towards the end of the season, and, as a last resort to plug a broken team, Angus McGuire was brought in on loan from Liverpool. It was all too late, though, and Fleetwood finished the season in the same position they had started – rock bottom. Things could only get better!

During the closed season, Wilf Plant reaffirmed his intention to leave, publicly stating that he would rather retire than have to ride for Fleetwood again. He made a second appeal to the SCB, who this time looked on Wilf's case favourably. In no time at all, Wilf was allowed to leave and Fleetwood's loss became Coventry's gain. Joining him on the exodus from Fleetwood were Graham Williams and Bill Reynolds, who both decided to return to Australia, and Dick Geary, who unsurprisingly decided to call it a day. This left Norman Hargreaves and Don Potter as the only recognised heat leaders, with only Alf Parker capable of giving them any consistent support. The remaining places were filled by novices from the second-half events and Angus McGuire's move was made permanent. But a team comprising five reserves was never going to pull up any trees. It seemed to many that the current management were happy to let riders go but were reluctant to spend any of the transfer money on bringing new riders in; even the speedway press were referring to Fleetwood as 'unambitious'.

Once again, the season got off to a bad start – four consecutive defeats away from home before a narrow but thrilling victory against Ashfield in the Northern Shield got their home programme underway. Victory over Newcastle in the second home fixture suggested that the team may not be as weak as many had feared, but they were soon brought down to earth when they crashed 29-55 to Edinburgh on 25 April.

The arrival of veteran Wilf Jay added some much needed strength to the top end, taking some of the pressure from Hargreaves and Potter. Some of the reserves were beginning to improve too, especially Ray Harker, a farmer from Appleby-in-Westmorland, and Jeff Crawford, but their lack of experience on other tracks led to some crushing defeats away from home.

Once again, the Highbury Avenue track came in for some heavy criticism from visiting teams and the SCB were receiving letters of protest on a regular basis. Ian Hoskins had to more or less blackmail his riders to race there and many of them refused to ride in the second half. Things must have been bad for riders to effectively turn down money in the early 1950s.

The Fleetwood team manager, Naaman Baldwin, a former novice rider himself, was a firm believer in nurturing young talent and, in conjunction with Don Potter, organised regular training sessions on the Highbury Avenue track. One rider to benefit in this way was teenager Dick Fisher, from the village of Galgate near Lancaster. Dick came on leaps and bounds during his first season, making his first team debut against Ashfield on 1 August, but with uncertainty surrounding the future of Fleetwood Speedway, he decided to move to Belle Vue at the end of the season. Trials were also given to another raw novice from Liverpool named Peter Craven. Although he had bags of enthusiasm, Craven spent more time sitting on the track than riding round it, so Baldwin decided

Opposite: *Wilf Plant with the Fleetwood 'management'.*

Right: *Don Potter, raw novice to number one in less than two years.*

not to persevere with him and let him move on again. As we all know, Peter Craven went on to become one of the greatest riders this country has ever produced. Nicknamed the 'Wizard of Balance', Craven was twice crowned World Champion before he was tragically killed in a racing accident at Edinburgh in 1963.

Ernie Appleby made a brave comeback with Fleetwood in mid-season, but unsurprisingly, he lacked confidence and took a few matches to settle down again. Ernie's return to the track was all too brief. Another racing accident left him with a broken ankle and Ernie decided to quit racing for good.

Despite some good performances at home, Fleetwood were always going to struggle on their travels and were often criticised for being 'unattractive opposition'. This was probably justified as they often struggled to score more than 20 points away from home. Their only notable performance away from the Highbury Bowl was a truly remarkable 42-42 draw at Newcastle in September. Even more remarkable was the fact that Don Potter had failed to arrive, leaving the team one man short. As everyone had come to expect, Fleetwood ended their season in fourteenth place, two places clear of the wooden spoon.

By this time, Waxman and Wolfenden had been searching for a new venue in Blackpool for a couple of years. Therefore, when it was announced that they had been given outline planning permission to build a new track and stadium at Marton, it really looked like the end of the road for speedway in Fleetwood. Worse was to come. Following an SCB investigation into the running of Fleetwood Speedway, and then taking into account the amount of protests regarding the state of the track, the Flyers were expelled from the league during the closed season. There has been much speculation as to why Waxman's and Wolfenden's licence was taken away, but finances

Norman Hargreaves was the only rider to turn out for Fleetwood during each of their league seasons (1948-51) and also in 1952.

must have been at the heart of it. Naaman Baldwin had been persuaded to invest in the promotion twelve months previously, and lost the lot when Waxman's and Wolfenden's company eventually folded.

When the attempt to take speedway to Blackpool failed, Naaman Baldwin and Don Potter were amongst the first to apply for a new licence to keep speedway at Highbury Avenue. The SCB rejected Don Potter's application for a league licence, but a probationary 'open' licence was eventually granted to Blackpool businessman Mr W. Roberts. Naaman Baldwin was retained as the general manager of Fleetwood Speedway Ltd and plans were made for a new beginning.

Ironically, Wigan had also reapplied for a league licence in 1952, this time at the Greyhound Stadium on Woodhouse Lane. They too had their application refused, but a probationary open licence was granted to one Peggy Waxman (does the name sound familiar?), only to have it suspended again in August. Halifax, Newcastle and Walthamstow had all failed to reopen for the new season, the latter claiming that Second Division racing was just not financially viable. Despite the fact that speedway was heading towards a national decline, Fleetwood still managed to buck the trend and draw large crowds to the Highbury Bowl.

The nucleus of the new non-league Fleetwood Knights was Wilf Jay, Norman Hargreaves, Don Potter, Jeff Crawford and Ray Harker, supplemented by numerous novices, guest riders and ex-Flyers. Besides fulfilling their obligations to turn up to ride at Fleetwood every Wednesday, Wilf Jay and Norman Hargreaves were loaned out to Glasgow Ashfield, and Don Potter joined Liverpool in a similar deal.

The new season began on 30 April with a challenge match against Liverpool. It was a very wet night, but the track stood up well and the two teams put up a great night's entertainment, the Knights winning 43-40. The home side's top four of Hargreaves, Potter, Jay and Harker all scored well, but ex-Flyer George Newton, riding as a guest, was a pale shadow of his former self and picked up a solitary point.

In fact, 1952 actually turned out to be Fleetwood's most successful season on the track. The Knights were destined never to lose on the Highbury Bowl and home riders took top honours in most of the individual events too. A new track surface was laid prior to the second visit of Liverpool. Don Potter found himself riding for the opposition on this occasion, whilst Derek Close stood in as a guest for the Knights. Close had shown his liking for the Highbury Bowl the week before, equalling the track record set up by Les Hewitt in August 1950, but on this occasion he was magnificent, 17 points from six rides, dropping his only point to partner Wilf Jay.

Don Potter was the winner of the first qualifying round of the Highbury Individual Championship on 9 July, but Wilf Jay could count himself unlucky, losing 3 points when he fell ahead of Potter in heat nine. A week later, the Knights continued their winning ways beating Cardiff in another thrilling challenge match. Don Potter was immaculate, scoring a 12-point maximum, but it was the scorer of another maximum that made the headlines. Young Jeff Crawford was improving at a rapid rate and this performance proved just how much he had progressed.

The second qualifying round of the Highbury Championship, scheduled for 23 July, had to be cancelled when Fleetwood had their licence suspended for a week. The SCB wanted to clear up some financial irregularities left over from the previous promotion,

Jeff Crawford made a real breakthrough in 1952, scoring his first full maximum and winning the Best Pairs competition in September, the last meeting ever held at Highbury Avenue.

1952 Fleetwood 'Knights'. Left to right, back row: Don Potter, (unidentified), Norman Hargreaves, Jeff Crawford, Naaman Baldwin (manager). Front row: Ray Harker, (unidentified), Wilf Jay (on bike) and Harold Bottoms.

but this minor hitch was soon cleared up and racing resumed on 30 July with the rearranged individual trophy meeting. Evergreen Norman Hargreaves secured first place, but only after a run-off with the young pretender, Jeff Crawford.

The meeting of 6 August was a Best Pairs competition and, once again, Derek Close showed his liking for the track, partnering Stan Bradbury to first place. A week later, the final of the Highbury Individual Championship took place. The meeting was supposed to be contested by the top eight finishers from each of the two qualifying rounds, but Harry Welch, Gil Blake, Peter Robinson and Willie Wilson all dropped out and Ray Harker was unable to ride due to an injury. Despite fears of the meeting turning into an anti-climax, the 7,000 spectators were treated to some of the most thrilling racing ever seen on the Highbury Bowl. Heat fourteen was an absolute cracker. There was never more than a yard between Norman Hargreaves and Jeff Crawford as they tried in vain to catch Bruce Semmens. At the end of a breathtaking race, the two Knights crossed the line side by side and the referee had no option but to award a dead heat, costing Crawford a place on the rostrum by half a point! Wilf Jay emerged as the deserved winner, dropping his only point to Alf Parker in the opening heat.

As the season drew to a close, Fleetwood began to run out of 'friendly opposition'. The Knights beat a team of 'All-Stars' on 20 August and Liverpool returned for a third time on 27 August. Jeff Crawford capped his most successful season to date by partnering Harold Bottoms to victory in a Best Pairs competition on 2 September, beating former Flyer Cyril Cooper in a run-off after the two pairings had tied on 20 points apiece.

SOUTH WALES TROPHY

Fleetwood

v

Cardiff

Wednesday
July 16th. 1952
at 7-45 p.m.

OFFICIAL PROGRAMME
6ᴰ

Nº 1935

Programme cover from the match against Cardiff on 16 July 1952.

The 1952 Fleetwood season ended just as it had started – in the rain! Unfortunately, on this occasion, the track was unrideable and what should have been the final meeting was washed out.

Sadly, this wasn't just the end of the season, it was the end of speedway in Fleetwood. Running speedway on an open licence was not a viable proposition and Naaman Baldwin's dream of taking Fleetwood back into the league never materialised. Naaman continued to race on the Lancashire grass tracks and helped with the organisation of North Lancashire Motor Club events. When the speedway closed down, Naaman arranged for the staring gate to be removed from Highbury Avenue and relocated at NLMC's grass-track site at Warton near Carnforth.

Wilf Jay, winner of the 1952 Highbury Indiviual Championship.

By 1954, rebuilding work at the stadium had virtually obliterated any remains of the speedway track and, although Highbury Avenue sports ground still exists, it bears little resemblance to the famous Highbury Bowl of the 1950s. That seems to be the end of the line as far as speedway in Fleetwood is concerned. Don Potter continued to have close links with speedway in Lancashire, reopening the old Wigan circuit at Poolstock in 1960, but just eight meetings were held before Potter closed it down again. Ernie Appleby reappeared at Wigan too, holding training schools at Wigan's Woodhouse Lane track in 1953. Ian Hoskins was reported to be looking for a new base in the north-west during the early 1970s and Fleetwood was definitely being considered in 1971. Apart from a long-track meeting on the sands at Pilling in 1972, Fleetwood Speedway only remains as a memory for those who were fortunate enough to experience the 'Track of a Thousand Thrills'.

13

NELSON

During the mid-1960s, Mike Parker wanted to introduce speedway and stock car racing to Lancashire. Initially he had looked at Blackpool, but when his plans were thwarted he turned his attention to Nelson in the east of the county.

Parker could see that speedway needed a lower division and Nelson was going to be the first toe in the water. If he could make a good impression with a season of open meetings and challenge matches, he hoped that others would follow and there would be enough new teams to form a Second Division for the first time in over ten years.

His chosen venue was Seedhill Stadium on Carr Road, the home of Nelson Football Club. In their heyday, the 'Blues' attracted crowds of around 15,000, but by the late 1960s they were lucky to see 100 supporters dotted around the stadium. The directors of the football club welcomed Parker and his brand of entertainment and they could see that a successful speedway team might just help the football club to get back on its feet. The partisan supporters weren't so sure though. There may not have been many of them, but they made sure that their objections were heard. Even the directors at Belle Vue objected to Parker's plan to run on Saturdays. Belle Vue had always been a Saturday track and was less than thirty miles away.

By the end of June 1967, over 400 tons of shale had been laid and the track was complete. A new safety fence was constructed and extra lighting was installed to supplement the football club's floodlights. Parker invited a group of riders from the Belle Vue Training School for a full-scale practice at Nelson on 15 July and it was from these that he planned to form the nucleus of the Nelson team.

On 29 July 1967, Seedhill finally opened its doors to motor sport with a 'Cavalcade of Speed' and the first speedway meeting, the 'Olympiad Trophy', was held a week later on 5 August. Heavy rain on the Friday night had made the track very heavy, and very few riders escaped without falling at least once. None of them suffered any serious injuries though, and the racing improved as the meeting progressed. Australian Alan Paynter adapted to the tricky circuit very quickly and scored 9 points. Not surprising really, as Alan had spent the previous two months helping to lay the track. Dave Parry was programmed to ride in the meeting, but he broke down on his way to the stadium. His replacement, Goog Allan, was the only rider to find a good racing line from the outset and won the meeting with an immaculate maximum.

The next three meetings saw Nelson successfully beat teams from Wolverhampton, Sheffield and Glasgow. The fifth and final speedway meeting of 1967 was the 'Seedhill

Left: *A very collectable programme from the second ever speedway meeting at Seedhill Stadium on 12 August 1967 and the first match to feature a Nelson team. Nelson beat Wolverhampton 51–45.*

Opposite: *The Nelson team that lost 27–50 at Crayford on 12 June 1968. Left to right: Gary Peterson, Paul Sharples, Murray Burt, Laszlo Muncacsi, Alan Paynter (on bike), Dave Schofield and Jack Winstanley. (Wright Wood)*

Trophy' on Saturday 23 September, won by New Zealander Bruce Cribb. The second half of the meeting featured sidecar speedway for the first time at Seedhill, a team match between Nelson and 'The Midlands'. Seeing the sidecars battling around the narrow track in the 'wrong direction' must have been a frightening experience!

The track at Nelson came in for heavy criticism right from the outset. Built around the football pitch, the 360-yard track was very narrow and the corners were almost square. The corners had to be re-laid every Saturday after the football match and the stock cars cut the track up so much that it was never in top condition for the speedway bikes. Journalist Peter Oakes witnessed the 58-37 victory over Sheffield on 26 August and was not impressed at all. In his report he says that heat thirteen was 'the only heat that I would call anything like speedway' and that the match in general was 'hardly speedway as we know it'. To add further fuel to his criticism, the starting gate had failed and every race was started on the green light. His opinion of the Nelson track deteriorated even further when local novice Dave Beacon was rushed off to hospital with a suspected broken leg after he had clattered into the safety fence during the 'Reserves Scurry'.

By the time that the 1968 season opened, Parker's plans for a new Second Division had come to fruition. Eight other teams joined Nelson in the new British League Second Division. The riders selected to represent Nelson in the 1968 Second Division campaign included some familiar faces from the previous year: Fred Powell, Alan Paynter, Murray Burt, Hungarian Lazlo Muncacsi and veteran Jack Winstanley. They were joined by Dave Schofield from Rochdale, Gary Peterson and Terry Shearer from New Zealand and Belle Vue youngster Paul Sharples.

Nelson Speedway reopened on Monday 3 June 1968 with a league match against the previously unbeaten Belle Vue Colts. The 'Admirals' went into that first match minus Paynter and Burt, but pulled off a shock victory beating the Colts 46-32. The Belle Vue fans were astonished and their riders condemned the track as a 'death trap'. As always, it was the same for both teams, especially when you consider that none of the Nelson team had ridden any practice laps and Dave Schofield was riding the track for the very first time.

Three days later Nelson won away at Middlesbrough, followed by another home victory against Crayford on the Saturday. The late opening to their season meant that Nelson raced 8 league matches in four weeks, resulting in four defeats and four victories.

Muncacsi found points hard to come by and was dropped after 4 matches. His replacement, Gerry Birtwell, fared even worse, scoring only 1 point in his 5 outings. Quite a few riders were promoted from the second-half races, including Dave Beacon, Jack Lee and Sid Sheldrick. The most successful was Alan Knapkin, a motorcycle dealer from Eccles. Bespectacled Knapkin was originally a scrambles rider, but had to quit when he was hit by a flying stone and nearly lost the sight in one eye. After a couple of years out of the saddle, he took up speedway. He rode his first match at Berwick in 1968 and then joined Nelson, where he became an instant hit with the fans and his trademark golden leathers earned him the nickname 'the Golden Wonder'.

Nelson's second away match at Reading on 17 June was a real thriller, but it all ended in a farce. In a last-heat decider, Gary Peterson and Terry Shearer had stormed their way to a 5-1 victory to earn a 39-39 draw. The travelling Nelson fans then gasped in disbelief as the referee disallowed the result and ordered a rerun. His reason was that Nelson should not have used Gary Peterson as a reserve substitute in the final heat. The heat was rerun with Gerry Birtwell replacing Peterson, but both Nelson riders fell and another rerun was called for. Shearer was excluded as the primary cause of the stoppage and Birtwell could not take his place as he was injured. Gary Peterson was brought back into the race as a 'legal' substitute, but with only one rider Nelson could only manage a 3-3 at best, turning a hard-earned draw into a controversial defeat. They very nearly pulled off a shock victory at Belle Vue in August too, but Gary Peterson's worst performance in a Nelson bib cost them this match and effectively handed the title to the Colts; sweet revenge for that infamous reversal at Nelson earlier in the season.

An injury to captain Alan Paynter in July cost Nelson dearly. He had averaged over 9 points per meeting in his 7 appearances and was the joint track record holder. The hard riding Australian was difficult to replace and Nelson's early exit from the Knockout Cup at Middlesbrough in August can also be put down to Paynter's absence.

Nelson completed their first season with a clean sheet at home and two away victories. They finished the league campaign in second place, only 6 points behind the Belle Vue Colts.

Dave Schofield and Murray Burt were the Nelson representatives in the Second Division Riders Championship. Schofield had a disastrous meeting, but Burt could have won if he hadn't have fallen off in heat six. Burt also missed out on the Nelson Trophy on 3 August, losing a run-off to John Poyser of Reading. Gary Peterson was undoubtedly the find of the season. He began the term as a relatively unknown reserve, but finished the season as Nelson's third-heat leader. His fence-scraping antics made him a real crowd favourite and he was quite popular with the girls, too. Amazingly, Fred Powell only got to wear the Admiral's bib on four occasions, twice finishing as Nelson's top scorer!

The 1968 season that had promised so much led to a 1969 season to forget. On paper, Nelson had a team strong enough to challenge for league honours. Even though Alan Paynter had decided to stay in Australia and Terry Shearer had moved to Doncaster, Burt, Knapkin, Schofield and Peterson were a powerful top four. Expectations were justifiably high.

The season opened on 19 April with a league match against Rayleigh. Peterson was in blistering form and scorched to a faultless maximum. He equalled the track record during the match, and then set a new record of 62.8 seconds in the second half. Schofield and Burt gave him solid support, but Lee, Sharples and Beacon could only muster 4 points between them and Rayleigh held the home team to a 39-39 draw, the first time Nelson had failed to win a home match since they opened. On the following Saturday, Murray Burt found himself leading a lone battle as Nelson were well and truly beaten 55-22 at Berwick (Peterson and Schofield were both riding for their parent track Newcastle in the First Division). The next home meeting was against Long Eaton on 3 May. Once again Peterson had been recalled by Newcastle and the visitors took full advantage, holding the Admirals to another 39-39 draw. Interestingly, the first heat of this match was won in 85.8 seconds, the slowest time ever recorded at Carr Road, yet in the second half, Dave Schofield set a new track record of 62.4 seconds! The one good point to come out of this disappointing result was the battling 12-point score from Alan Knapkin, riding at number one for the first time.

The next four weeks saw Nelson sink to six successive away defeats and the home match against bottom-of-the-table Kings Lynn was rained off. The biggest disaster happened at Wolverhampton, though, where Gary Peterson's season ended in a

Dave Schofield had suffered serious head injuries while riding for Belle Vue in 1966. After struggling for much of the 1967 season, he was a revelation at Nelson, topping the averages in 1968 and captaining the side in 1969 and 1970. Schofield joined Workington in 1971, but was bundled into the fence by Jack Millen in his very first match and the resulting injuries ended his career. (R. Spencer Oliver)

horrific crash during a World Championship qualifying round. The young Kiwi suffered severe head and facial injuries and was forced to miss the rest of the season. Demoralised by this devastating news, Nelson were dumped out of the cup at Middlesbrough on 12 June, Burt and Knapkin scoring all but 6 of the Nelson total.

The Nelson fans had to wait until Saturday 14 June before the Admirals scored their first home victory, a 45-33 win against Eastbourne. Even though parent club Newcastle had recalled Schofield and Burt, the Admirals were in a determined mood and were helped by a 12-point maximum from guest rider Tom Leadbitter, standing in for the injured Peterson. The next four weeks saw Nelson back on a losing streak. They suffered defeats at home to Belle Vue and Berwick, and lost twice away at Reading and Plymouth. To try and stem the tide, manager Derek Tattersall brought in Stuart Riley and Dai Evans from Crayford, another track in the Mike Parker stable. Both had been injured earlier in the season and were left without a team place when they recovered.

The home win against second-placed Reading on 12 July was the start of the club's best run of the season, seven wins in nine meetings, including a 41-37 win at fellow strugglers Kings Lynn. The Reading match also saw Alan Knapkin score his first full maximum and the fans witnessed a sensational debut by Chris Baybutt, a teenage grass-track racer from Wrightington, near Wigan. Baybutt only scored 6 points, but he did it on his 350cc JAP grass-track machine, complete with rear suspension! Former Belle Vue 'Colt' Peter Thompson also made his Nelson debut that night, scoring a respectable 5 points. But it wasn't all good news. Murray Burt crashed in heat seven of the home match against Romford and was taken to hospital with a broken thigh. Nelson went on to win the match 44-34, but Burt never raced for Nelson again. He returned to New Zealand and eventually made a name for himself racing midget speedway cars.

Peter Thompson was signed from Belle Vue in July 1969 and proved to be a reliable and steady scorer for the Admirals throughout 1969 and 1970. (R. Spencer Oliver)

Stuart Riley once worked with Coventry duo Ron Mountford and Rick France in a Midlands petrol station. He joined Crayford in 1968 but lost his place through injury and moved to Nelson in June 1969. Stuart became a firm favourite with the Nelson fans (especially the girls!) making 22 appearances for the Admirals in his first season and averaging nearly 6 points per meeting. (R. Spencer Oliver)

From then on Nelson became even more of a makeshift team. They had two heat leaders out for the season and parent club Newcastle were adding to their difficulties by constantly recalling riders to cover their own injury problems. Even so, they managed to beat Ipswich, Kings Lynn, Doncaster and Crewe during August, and only lost by 4 points at Crayford, where Stuart Riley scored an impressive 11 points against his old team mates. The enforced absence of the heat leaders meant that youngsters like John Lynch, Norman Truman and Dave Beacon were called up for first team duty. Jack Lee had his moments, but the most exciting prospects were Baybutt and Sid Sheldrick from Sheffield. Sheldrick had ridden for Nelson once before in 1968 and had a few matches for the Admirals earlier in the 1969 season, but after Murray Burt's injury he moved up a gear. The 8 points against Doncaster, 9 against Plymouth and 13 against Crayford, proved his immense potential. Nelson had unearthed another rising star. Baybutt made a total of 4 appearances for the Admirals, his best return being 9 points against Kings Lynn. For the match against Doncaster, his last ride for Nelson, he actually fitted a 500cc ESO speedway engine into his grass-track frame, but only scored 4 points!

Nelson used guest riders on no less than fifteen occasions during the 1969 season and the top seven riders in the end of season averages never rode together! But they did manage to put out a full team of their own contracted riders on 6 September and convincingly beat Middlesbrough 52-25, with Knapkin, Schofield and Riley all scoring double figures.

A rare picture of Belle Vue's Taffy Owen riding as a guest for the Admirals during the injury hit 1969 season. (R. Spencer Oliver)

Over 4,000 spectators crammed into the Carr Road venue on Tuesday 9 September to see Young Britain take on Young Australasia in the second Test of a five-match series. The only riders to really master the awkward Nelson track were Geoff Ambrose, who scored 17 points for Young Britain, Paul O'Neal, the top scorer for the opposition, and home favourite Alan Knapkin, who scored a superb 15 points from his six rides. It wasn't such a good afternoon for Dave Schofield, though. The Nelson and Young Britain captain could not reproduce his domestic form and only scored 5 points. In fact, he pulled out of his last ride and sent out reserve rider Ian Turner in his place. Burnley-based Eric Broadbelt also had a good meeting for the British team, scoring 12 points from six rides. Young England won the match 66-42 and went on to win the series 4-1.

A minor success came Nelson's way on 12 September, when youngster Dai Evans won the British Junior Championships at Wolverhampton, but September also brought another big headache for the Nelson management. They were running out of dates to finish their home meetings! After the Young Britain International, there was only one more Saturday available to run speedway at Seedhill and Nelson had 3 home matches outstanding. A loss-making double-header was run on Saturday 20 September where the Admirals went down 36-42 to Crayford in the first match, but beat Plymouth 45-33 in the second. It was a miracle that the match was run at all, but Tattersall and his team worked all afternoon to dry out a soaking wet track. Sid Sheldrick was the first to master the muddy conditions, slithering to his first ever paid maximum in the match

Sid Sheldrick was another 'discovery' at Nelson, making his debut for the Admirals in August 1968. He started the 1969 season riding at reserve, but his form improved as the season progressed and he scored his first maximum in September. (R. Spencer Oliver)

against Crayford. Captain Schofield finally found his way through the mud in the second fixture and scored another 12-point maximum. The conditions didn't seem to bother former scrambles man Knapkin, though; he revelled in the conditions and scored double figures in both matches!

Following another heavy defeat at Crewe, where they were forced to ride without Knapkin, Schofield or Sheldrick, Nelson were left with 1 match outstanding. Even though the final league match of the 1969 season against Canterbury was officially a home fixture, it was actually raced in Kent! None of the team really had their heart in the match and Nelson slipped to yet another heavy defeat, losing 24-54.

The run of form during July and August had saved Nelson from finishing bottom of the league. Then, Mike Parker successfully appealed against Berwick's illegal use of Peter Kelly in July. Kelly's points were scrubbed from the records and the result was amended to 39.5-37.5 in the Admirals' favour. This unexpected bonus lifted Nelson to thirteenth position in the final league table for the 1969 season – an appropriate position for the unluckiest team of the year.

The rumour that Nelson would not be running in 1970 was already doing the rounds before the dust had even settled on the 1969 season. Bill Bridgett had joined Mike Parker as co-promoter for the new season and both were quick to assure everybody that Nelson would indeed be running in 1970. They did admit that they were having problems arranging all of the speedway fixtures around the demands of the stock cars and the football club, though. Further concern was raised in January 1970 when the directors of Bradford Northern Rugby League Club announced that they were ready to welcome speedway back to the Odsal Stadium.

Nelson were also having problems getting a team together for the 1970 season. Murray Burt was definitely not coming back and nobody knew whether Peterson would be fit to ride again. The original 1970 fixture list had Nelson opening their season with an away match at Doncaster, but there was a last-minute hitch. Nelson still didn't have a team! The Doncaster management were co-operative in this instance and the fixture was cancelled.

One by one, the Nelson team started to fall into place. Alan Knapkin, Dave Schofield, Peter Thompson and Sid Sheldrick all returned and Alan Bridgett, nephew of co-promoter Bill, was signed from Doncaster. Another new signing was Alf Wells from Glasgow. Reserves, Stuart Riley and John Lynch, stuck around knowing that their chance would come. Lynch was so keen to break into the Nelson team that he had moved to Burnley from his home in Plymouth. Another youngster, Mick Barry, travelled all the way from Hull just to have rides in the second half. The best news was that Gary Peterson and Alan Paynter had both been declared fit and were definitely returning to Britain for the 1970 season. With such a strong team, Tattersall was confident that Nelson could win the league. The stadium had been given a makeover too, with new floodlights, better catering facilities, a complete reworking of the infamous Nelson track and even a brand new 'powder room' for the ladies! It really looked like 1970 was going to be Nelson's year.

But things never went according to plan at Nelson. The first big disappointment came when Berwick announced that Alan Paynter had signed for them. Parker hit back claiming that Paynter was still contracted to ride for Nelson. The BSPA intervened and the matter was put in the hands of the Speedway Control Board, which meant Paynter had to miss the start of the season while he waited for the verdict.

Then, Nelson's opening match against Doncaster on 18 April was rained off. Nelson hadn't even started their season and they were already faced with a congested fixture list. Nelson were forced to start their season with 2 away fixtures. Still rusty, they were dumped out of the Knockout Cup at Crewe on 20 April and then went down to a narrow 38-40 defeat at Rayleigh on 25 April. The first home match took place on the following Saturday, an easy 49-29 victory over Reading. Gary Peterson proved that he had completely recovered from the previous year's injuries with a splendid 12-point maximum. This was even more impressive when you consider that he fell off while leading heat four, remounted, and passed his opponents again to win the heat – magnificent stuff! New signing Alan Bridgett scorched to a 12-point maximum, too. The two home riders tossed up to decide who would challenge Reading's Mike Vernam for the Silver Helmet. Bridgett won the toss, and promptly won the helmet too.

The match against Doncaster on 18 April should have been the first home meeting of the 1970 season, but heavy rain meant that the meeting was cancelled and never restaged.

The victory over Reading was quickly followed by an impressive 47-30 victory at Doncaster on the next day. This time it was former Glasgow rider Alf Wells who kept a clean sheet and Bridgett continued his fine start to the season by dropping only 1 point. Crayford became Nelson's next victims when they were soundly beaten 55-23 at Carr Road on Saturday 9 May, with Gary Peterson breezing through his second successive home maximum and Alan Bridgett successfully defending his Silver Helmet against Archie Wilkinson.

Then came the heartbreaking news that everyone had been dreading. Parker wanted to pull Nelson out of the league. The idea was to transfer Nelson's Second Division licence to the new track at Bradford and Nelson would take over Bradford's open licence. If everything went to plan, Bradford would stage their first match on 20 May. The transfer had really come about because of the fixture congestion at Seedhill Stadium. The number of teams had grown for the 1970 league, which meant that Nelson were already stretched to the limit before the season had started. Following the postponement of their very first meeting, the situation had become impossible. Thus, the deal with Les Whalley at Odsal was born. Nelson would provide the licence and a ready-made team and Odsal would provide the track. No money changed hands, it was a straightforward swap. Parker was at pains to add that this was not the end for Nelson. Open meetings would continue to be held at Seedhill throughout 1970 and, subject to sorting out more available dates, league racing would definitely return in 1971. As always, the proposed switch hit a snag. The Speedway Control Board did not approve the switch to Bradford at first and the two promoters lodged an appeal. At least this decision gave the Nelson fans a stay of execution. The SCB did resolve one matter, however. They upheld Liz Taylor's claim that Alan Paynter was not a Nelson asset and agreed that he could resume his career riding for Berwick.

Meanwhile, away from the boardroom, Nelson suffered a narrow defeat at Long Eaton, due to costly falls and engine failures for Peterson, Knapkin and Sheldrick. Alan Bridgett also fell in his defence of the Silver Helmet and lost it to Malcolm Shakespeare. Then came more bad news. Alan Knapkin was involved in an accident at his bike shop after an explosion there, and had suffered serious burns to his hands and face. It was expected that he would be out of action for several weeks, but they are a tough breed

New Zealander Gary Peterson was arguably the first great discovery of the old Second Division and many believe that he had the ability to become a World-class rider, but he was tragically killed riding for Wolverhampton in the 1975 Midland Cup Final.

in the north-west. Knapkin turned up to ride against Rochdale on the Saturday and scored an impressive 11 points as Nelson cruised to an easy 46-31 victory. Gary Peterson continued his impressive form with his third successive home maximum.

On the Monday following the victory over Rochdale, the Speedway Control Board upheld the appeal from Mike Parker and Les Whalley and gave the go-ahead for the switch of Nelson's Second Division Licence to Bradford. The Nelson fans were in uproar. Their team was being taken away from them and moved across the Pennines to the 'old enemy' in Yorkshire, of all places. Work had already begun on relaying the track at Odsal, the fence was already in place and the team had adopted the name Bradford Northern. Parker had already had new bibs made: red, yellow and black on a white background, a homage to the famous Rugby League club that played at the same venue. With everything now going to plan, Bradford set their opening date for 24 June 1970.

Racing continued at Nelson for the next few weeks, but not without more controversy. The league match against Teesside on 30 May had to be abandoned when the visiting riders walked out after four heats. Roger Mills and Dave Durham had both fallen at the first bend and captain Tom Leadbitter claimed that the track was unrideable. The referee, Mike Whittaker, disagreed, and so did Nelson captain Schofield. Even the Teeside manager Henry Atkinson tried to persuade his team to continue, but his riders were equally adamant that they were packing up and going home. So, with Nelson leading 18 points to 6, the referee had no other choice but to call the meeting off. The Nelson management were furious. Tattersall said that he would claim the points and Parker added that he would be looking for some recompense from the Teesside club and wanted disciplinary action taken against their riders.

After all the shenanigans of the previous month, June turned out to be quite productive for the Admirals. The meeting of 6 June was reserved for stock cars, but the speedway returned on 13 June. Gary Peterson and Alan Knapkin were both unbeaten as the home team cruised to a massive 55-22 victory against Long Eaton team. The visitors had turned up with only six riders so Robin Adlington was drafted in to make up the numbers. Although he was described in the Nelson programmes as an Australian, Adlington was actually from New Zealand, the last of a line of young Kiwis to be introduced to the UK scene at Nelson. Adlington scored a single point for Long Eaton on his public debut, but he was handed a reserve spot for Nelson in their final meeting at Carr Road on 20 June 1970. It must have been quite an emotional meeting for everyone associated with Nelson speedway and the Admirals went out on a high. Peterborough 'Panthers' had absolutely no answer to the all-round strength of the Nelson team and were soundly beaten 56-22. Peterson had been recalled by Newcastle and missed the last ever meeting at Seedhill, but Knapkin bagged a another 12-point maximum and Adlington made an impressive debut for his home team, scoring 5 points from three rides. Then it was all over. The Nelson Admirals moved out of Seedhill and out of Lancashire.

On Wednesday 24 June, Odsal Stadium reopened its doors to speedway after a ten-year absence. A crowd of over 10,000 watched the former Nelson Admirals riding as Bradford Northern beat Eastbourne 44-34. Gary Peterson, the darling of Carr Road, quickly made himself at home, chalking up yet another maximum and setting the track

Even though Seedhill Stadium was demolished in 1980 to make way for the M65, only a fraction of the site was ever built on. The pits wall is still standing and even the riders numbers and the words 'NELSON' and 'VISITORS' have survived, all that remains of a once proud circuit. (Author's collection)

record of 71.2 seconds. The Nelson fans began to come to terms with the move to Bradford and regular coach trips to the Yorkshire city were arranged for every 'home' meeting.

In the programme notes for the last meeting at Carr Road, manager Derek Tattersall said that the Admirals would be back again in 1971. Parker added that this was not going to be the last meeting at Carr Road in 1970. The annual rent had already been paid, so it made sense to utilise the available dates. Six open meetings had been planned. The first of these was due to be the star-studded 'Nelson Trophy' meeting on 4 July, but none of the open meetings were ever run. The whole fiasco stemmed from the fact that Bradford had turned down the offer of an open licence, insisting that they would only run on a full-league licence. So there never was an open licence to transfer to Nelson in the first place! The Nelson application was referred to the Second Division management committee but, by the end of the 1970 season, Parker had still not received the necessary licence and speedway never returned to Carr Road.

Seedhill Stadium continued to host stock cars and football until 1978 and was finally demolished in 1980 to make way for the Blackburn to Colne section of the M65 Motorway. A visit to the site today makes you wonder why the stadium was demolished at all. Only a fraction of the site was ever built on and even the riders' numbers can still be seen painted on the old pits wall – an eerie reminder of the days when Nelson had a speedway team to be proud of.

14

BARROW-IN-FURNESS: THE POST-WAR YEARS

Despite a healthy motorcycle scene on the Furness peninsula, it's something of a surprise to learn that there hadn't been any speedway activity in the area since the track at Little Park had closed down in 1931. Local motorcycle enthusiast, Cliff Hindle, had built his own track in the early 1950s and several other riders joined him for practice sessions. They also attended training sessions at Sheffield and Coppul, near Wigan, but Cliff's track never really got going and none of the riders appear to have made any further progress with their speedway racing aspirations.

Speedway did eventually return to Barrow in 1972, surprisingly at the same venue that had first staged speedway back in 1930, Holker Street Stadium, the home of struggling Football League side, Barrow AFC. Whether it's down to that old gypsy curse or not, Barrow AFC have never had the best of fortunes. They had won promotion to the old Third Division in 1967, but they struggled and were soon relegated back to the Fourth Division. The 1970/71 season saw Barrow sink even further. They played 17 games before a victory and not surprisingly finished bottom of the league again.

During October 1971, rumours began to circulate of a new speedway venue in the north. Sure enough, on 18 December 1971, Fleet Street journalist, Peter Oakes, confirmed that he and multi-World Speedway Champion, Ivan Mauger, were joining forces to promote speedway at Holker Street.

On the first day of the 1972 promoters' conference, the application for a league licence at Barrow was refused and Oakes and Mauger were barred from becoming promoters by the British Speedway Promoters Association. On the second day, Wally Mawdsley made an alternative application to run speedway at Barrow on an open licence. This application was approved, with Oakes and Mauger being allowed to have an active role at the track.

Oakes was a busy journalist, Mauger was at the pinnacle of his career and Mawdsley was tied up with his other tracks in the south, therefore the trio needed someone to live in Barrow and run the speedway for them. That man was Australian Peter White, who gave up his job with the Commonwealth Public Service in Sydney to take up the position. His journey would make a story in its own right. A three-hour delay following an engine failure over Singapore was followed by another engine catching fire when it was struck by lightning over Bangkok, and, finally, he had to suffer a twenty-four-hour delay in Bombay. To make matters worse, he arrived at Heathrow with food poisoning – a legacy of that long day in Bombay!

White was met at Heathrow by Mick Page, a young rider from Sydney hoping to break into the Barrow team. They shared a car to Barrow and couldn't believe what they found. The weather was the bleakest either of them had ever experienced. Eight consecutive days of rain and it was freezing, but there was work to be done. Aided by local newsagent Ken Norman, they walked the streets of Barrow poster pasting and knocking on doors. With only one newspaper and no local radio or television stations, the opportunities for publicity were limited, so it was word of mouth nearly all the way.

The track itself was built by New Zealander Colin Tucker, with help from Alan Wilkinson, the locally based Belle Vue rider. The football pitch had to be altered to accommodate the track, but despite the disruption, the football club seemed to be happy with their new tenants and were no doubt looking forward to the extra income. All of the excavation and heavy construction work was carried out by Cliff Hindle, the local enthusiast who had tried to introduce speedway back in the 1950s. Cliff had also built a practice track on land behind his Plant Hire business at Marton, where his young son Ian learnt to ride speedway.

Barrow AFC lost their final match of the season on Monday 24 April, needing re-election for the eleventh time in their history. Following the match, the floodlights were left on and the final few yards of the track were completed in time for opening night on Thursday 27 April.

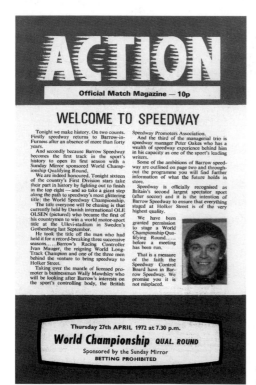

Programme from the opening meeting at Holker Street, 27 April 1972.

Ulverston-based Alan Wilkinson rode for the famous Belle Vue 'Aces' in Manchester and finished runner-up in the World Championship qualifier at Holker Street. Alan was always a popular visitor to Barrow Speedway and helped with the construction of the track.

Barrow became the first track of this sport to open its first season with a World Championship qualifying round. Mauger had pulled off a scoop too. He had invited one of his neighbours to officially open the track, none other than football legend George Best. Official figures tell us that 4,096 spectators turned up for the opening meeting, which is more than George Best did! The Manchester United star had given Mauger the slip at a barber's shop in Manchester and disappeared. Coventry's John Harrhy won the meeting with a faultless 15-point maximum, but the loudest cheers were saved for local hero Alan Wilkinson, who responded with some spectacular riding to take second place. Meanwhile, Coronation Street's Bet Lynch (Julie Goodyear) had agreed to take Best's place, and arrived just in time to present the trophies. It's fair to say that the majority of the crowd on that first night had come to see George Best and many people in Barrow never forgave the speedway for letting them down.

On 4 May 1972 the first appearance of a Barrow Speedway team in a challenge match against Ellesmere Port took place. Lining up for the Barrow 'Happy Faces' on that historic night were Mike Watkin from Gilsland, Ian Hindle from Barrow, Scottish prospects Allan Mackie and John Wilson, Tom Owen from Ormskirk, Geoff Lyon from St Helens and Aussie Bob Campbell. The match ended as a 39-39 draw.

Sponsorship was becoming a very important facet of speedway at the time and Barrow were one of the very first speedway teams in the UK to benefit from such a deal. Duckham's Oils not only supplied financial and material aid to all of the contracted riders, their famous 'Q' logo was also the inspiration behind the unusual 'Happy Face' motif on the team's body colours.

The early weeks were dogged by teething problems. Persistent rain disrupted the fixture list, the public address system kept breaking down and a match at Motherwell had to be cancelled when it was discovered that the Scottish track didn't have a licence! Subsequent attempts to restage the match weren't successful either. The rescheduled fixture on 29 May was abandoned just before the first heat because of pouring rain, and a third attempt to stage the match on 5 June was also rained off. Barrow did mange to complete their home fixture against Motherwell on 25 May – their first ever victory.

Then came two announcements that had huge repercussions on the future of Barrow Speedway. Firstly, Second Division side West Ham closed down when their stadium was sold for redevelopment. Almost immediately, the Barrow management applied to take over the West Ham licence and signed two of their riders, Bob Coles and Mike Sampson. The second major announcement came a day later, when Barrow AFC were thrown out of the Football League. Many of the football supporters believed that it was the introduction of the speedway and the subsequent alterations to the pitch that lost Barrow support at the Football League AGM. The football club obviously needed the revenue from the rent, but this signalled the beginning of an uneasy relationship between the two parties.

On Friday 9 June, Barrow rode their first match as a fully-fledged Second Division side at Peterborough, losing 26-52 in a cup match. Four days later, Barrow lost the second leg at Holker Street, too. This was followed by a victory at Scunthorpe on 19 June (their first official league fixture), but they came crashing down to earth the very next night when local rivals Workington came to Holker Street and won. Like all local derbies, controversy was never far away, but on this occasion it was dissent within their own ranks that had the Barrow faithful up in arms. In a bid to pull back Workington's lead, Peter White dropped Bobby Campbell from his third ride and replaced him with a tactical substitute. Campbell was furious and stormed off to the dressing rooms, refusing to take any further part in the meeting. This left Barrow with only one rider in the final heat and cost them the chance of forcing a draw. Campbell never rode for Barrow again.

At the end of June, Peter White accepted a teaching position near London and was replaced by Maurice Morley. There were more problems on the team front, too; Geoff Lyon had been seriously injured and Mackie and Wilson had both asked to be released, but in the circumstances, their requests were refused. The team had a couple of weeks to regroup at the beginning of July with the only action at Holker Street being the

Mike Watkin from Gilsland was the captain of the 1972 'Happy Faces'. (R. Spencer Oliver)

Eddie Crooks Trophy, an individual meeting sponsored by the former Manx Grand Prix star and won by Sunderland's Jack Millen. When the time came to present the trophies, Eddie emerged from the pits on a Suzuki with his wife Pauline riding pillion. After the presentation, Mrs Crooks turned down Millen's offer of a pillion ride on the back of his Jawa, and took the New Zealander on a victory lap on the back of the Suzuki instead.

Bob Coles and Mike Sampson both lived in the south-west and made the long journey more bearable by travelling to home meetings together. By mid-July they were joined by a third West Country recruit, Chris Roynon. Other new faces included Keith Evans, Harry McLean and another former West Ham rider, Stan Stevens.

Bob Coles and Mike Watkin leading Russ Dent at Sunderland. (R. Spencer Oliver)

At last, Barrow began to make an impression on the league; they won all of their remaining home fixtures, and picked up two more wins and a draw on their travels. There could have been more, but the league match at Boston on 30 July was rained off with the 'Happy Faces' leading 34-20. The Barrow management appealed for the result to stand, but the match was declared void and rearranged for later in the season. The restaging proved to be just as controversial. The Boston management claimed that Ian Hindle was using an illegal nitro-methane additive in his fuel, Mike Watkin failed to arrive and the track doctor ruled that his replacement, Clive Buckler, was unfit to continue after falling in his first ride. To cap it all, the referee refused to let Barrow use a reserve in Buckler's place in heat twelve, a decision that cost Barrow the match! Once again the Barrow management lodged an appeal, this time it was upheld and the SCB ordered another rerun of the match at a later date.

In a moment of pure unselfishness, Stan Stevens asked to be released in mid-August because he thought that he was keeping one of the youngsters out of the team. August also brought another change when Ken Norman became the third team manager of the season. Tom Owen's sixteen-year-old brother Joey made his debut in the junior races during September. His first four public laps impressed the Barrow management so much that a contract was signed before the meeting was over. As a result, Alan Mackie was finally released and returned to his former track at Glasgow.

As the season drew to an end, a two-leg challenge match against Workington was arranged. The Barrow fans enjoyed a 42-36 victory at Holker Street in the first leg, but the evening leg at Derwent Park was a disaster. Barrow crashed to a humiliating 25-53 defeat and were forced to ride without top scorer Bob Coles, who had been injured in a car accident the previous day. The 1972 home season ended on 17 October with victory over new league champions Crewe in a challenge match, and the league match at Boston was finally completed on 22 October with Boston taking both league points.

Despite early teething troubles, the George Best fiasco, an uneasy working relationship with their landlords and an industrial dispute in the town's shipyards, support for the speedway had remained steady. The team could hold their heads up high, too, finishing a respectable ninth out of seventeen in the Second Division, but the highlight of the season had to be the progress of youngsters like Tom Owen, Keith Evans and Ian Hindle. Mike Sampson had come on leaps and bounds too, winning the Duckham's Rosebowl Trophy on 10 October with a perfect 15-point maximum.

Barrow went into the 1973 season with a new promoter, yet another new team manager and a new name. Mawdsley and Oakes had found the travelling too much and Mauger couldn't find the time to fit Barrow into his busy schedule. The new promoter at Holker Street was George Graham, a businessman from Workington and formerly Clerk of the Course at Workington Speedway. The new team manager was Alan Middleton, who actually had his feet in both camps, being the new Clerk of the Course at Workington too. The team were now known as the 'Bombers', paying homage to the old Romford/West Ham Bombers who they had replaced in 1972. On the team front, Bob Coles had been recalled by First Division Exeter and Mike Watkin had retired. New signings included Chris Bailey, wild riding Belle Vue novice Terry Kelly and former Nelson and Bradford rider Sid Sheldrick.

The season opened with a league victory over Ellesmere Port on 20 March but the challenge match against Crewe on 27 March looked like it would have to be cancelled when all electrical power was lost in the stadium. The fault was eventually found and the match got underway, but the new promoter wasn't there to see his side beat the reigning champions. He had suffered severe burns in an accident at work during the week and the injuries were serious enough to keep him away from Holker Street for a number of weeks. April saw Barrow win two more challenge matches, and score league victories over Chesterton and Eastbourne, but the month ended with a narrow 37-41 defeat at Berwick. Poor Sid Sheldrick had arrived at the track with a damaged bike after it had fallen off the back of his car on the motorway! He arrived late and hastily rebuilt his bike, but it only lasted one lap before the engine packed up! Keith Evans put in a magnificent performance to score 10 points from the reserve berth, including a second place in heat eleven with a burst rear tyre, but luck just wasn't on the Bombers' side that night.

George Graham returned to the fold for the match against Peterborough on 1 May, and witnessed one of the closest and most exciting matches ever seen at Holker Street. The lead changed five times, but by heat nine Peterborough were 9 points ahead. The Bombers refused to be beaten however, and clinched the match 4-2 in the very last heat. The final score – Barrow 39, Peterborough 38; you can't get much closer than that!

Ian Hindle was unhappy about being left out of the Barrow side and moved to Scunthorpe in May 1973, where he rapidly rose to heat leader status. (R. Spencer Oliver)

The Bombers continued their winning ways and by mid-May they were sitting on top of the Second Division table, but things were about to take a turn for the worse. Chris Roynon had hit a lean spell and everyone expected Ian Hindle to be recalled to the team in his place, but Hindle was unhappy about being left on the sidelines in the first place and didn't turn up for his second-half rides on 8 May. A couple of weeks later he signed for Scunthorpe and rapidly rose to heat leader status. George Graham criticised the teenager's attitude, pointing out that if Ian had turned up for his second-half rides, he would definitely have been in the side to face Sunderland on 15 May, but Cliff Hindle saw things differently. His son had made steady progress during the 1972 season, but his form had dipped towards the end of the season. Barrow didn't offer him a new contract for the 1973 season, even though they had used him in their first three meetings. His form began to improve in the second-half scratch races, but still no contract was offered. The final straw came when some of the Barrow fans started to heckle the teenager. He decided to switch to Scunthorpe and Barrow lost their only true local rider.

Typically, as soon as Hindle had gone, the injuries started to mount up. Chris Bailey aggravated a neck injury when he took a knock in the match against Teesside on 22 May, Terry Kelly injured his back when his bike reared and landed on top of him and, to cap it all, Tom Owen broke his jaw in a grass-track accident. Joey Owen, Craig Pendlebury and Don Howison were all promoted from the novice races to try and plug the gaps, but Pendlebury ended up on the sidelines himself with a fractured collarbone.

The second half of May brought defeats at Sunderland and Crewe, followed by two defeats in one day against Workington in the Cumbria Trophy on 28 May. Workington's top scorer, Lou Sansom, even had the cheek to return to Holker Street on the very next day and take top honours in the Charlie Williams Gold Cup. Workington paid another visit on 19 June and inflicted Barrow's first home league defeat of the season. If losing to their deadliest rivals three times in two weeks wasn't bad enough, the visit of Boston on 26 June turned into a nightmare. Barrow only managed two heat winners all night and were heavily beaten 27-49. After this debacle, things could only get better.

Shell-shocked and depleted, the Bombers travelled up to Derwent Park for a league match on 29 June and very nearly pulled off the shock result of the season. With two heats to go, Barrow were leading by 6 points and Workington were praying for a miracle – they nearly got one, too. The Comets closed the gap with a 5-1 in the penultimate heat, but Mike Sampson held on to second place in the final heat to grab a sensational draw. Hero of the night was Joey Owen, who scored a magnificent 11 points from the reserve berth. As ever, tempers became frayed on both sides, protests were lodged and fuel samples were taken – you can't beat a local derby to get the blood boiling!

With Terry Kelly fit again, and Tom Owen riding with his jaw wired up and seventeen stitches in his wounds, it was time to get their league campaign back on track again, but the Bombers struggled on their travels. The nearest they came to winning away from home were draws at Workington and Hull and a controversial 38-39 defeat at Canterbury. At home they were a different proposition, though. A crushing 60-18 victory over Scunthorpe on 17 July showed just how formidable they could be. Terry Kelly, Tom Owen, Chris Roynon and Joe Owen were all unbeaten by an opponent and the only heat winner for the opposition was ex-Bomber, Ian Hindle. The depleted visitors even drafted in his father, Cliff, to make up the numbers when they arrived a rider short!

*Tom Owen, Barrow's all-time top points scorer, rode for part of the 1973 season with his jaw wired up and seventeen stitches in his wounds.
(R. Spencer Oliver)*

It was announced in August that Chris Bailey had quit the sport on medical advice, but he wasn't the only one with problems. Keith Evans was missing from the side that faced West Germany on 14 August, allegedly suffering with tonsillitis. It transpires that Keith had actually lost his confidence and was considering quitting the sport for good. George Graham tried to convince him otherwise and allowed him time off to sort himself out. After a few weeks, Evans decided to have another go and Graham booked him in for some second-half rides on 28 August. Evans wasn't happy about being left out of the team and confronted Graham in front of the crowd. He became abusive and demanded a transfer. Graham later explained that even though Evans had bags of talent, he wasn't prepared to put him straight back into the team after missing three meetings. In any case, it would have meant dropping either Chris Roynon or Craig Pendlebury, and that would not have been fair. Evans never did regain his place in the team and Graham refused to let him sign for another track.

The season ended on 30 October with the Hughie Green Knockout Trophy, and it was the turn of the youngsters to steal the limelight, with Chris Roynon beating Joe Owen and Sid Sheldrick in the final.

For a team that started the season as genuine title challengers, it must have been disappointing to finish halfway down the table again, but that can be attributed to the awful run of injuries in mid-season. On the bright side, though, Barrow had unearthed some exciting young talent again and the prospects for 1974 looked good – that's if they still had a track to call home!

Relationships between the football and speedway clubs had taken another turn for the worse. Following complaints from visiting sides and referees alike, Barrow AFC had been forced to postpone 4 of their home fixtures due to the poor state of the pitch. The problem was the four temporary corners of the pitch, which were merely boards with turf on top! Following an inspection by the secretary of the Northern Premier League, Barrow were ordered to play their home fixture against Northwich at the Cheshire club's ground and were told to get the pitch in order or be kicked out of the league. To accommodate the alterations, the speedway club had to modify the shape of the track. Then, it was announced that the speedway had offered to buy Holker Street. This move was crushed by football club director Bill McCullough, who hit back by telling the speedway to get out! The argument was taken all the way to the High Court, where the judges ruled in favour of the speedway, ensuring the future of speedway at Holker Street for at least another twelve months.

The closed season brought team-building problems for George Graham too. Mike Sampson had opted for a move to Eastbourne and Craig Pendlebury had been recalled by Sheffield. Keith Evans was pencilled into the line-up for the opening fixtures, but he didn't ride and it was announced that he had joined Scunthorpe, ironically replacing Ian Hindle, who had moved into the First Division with Belle Vue. At one point, it looked like Terry Kelly might have been on his way too, but Belle Vue agreed to let him stay at Barrow on loan.

To strengthen his side, George Graham tried to sign Dave Baugh from Bradford, but after agreeing terms, the rider decided to stay in Rhodesia. When the season did

The difficult Holker Street track didn't always suit Terry Kelly's exciting style of riding. (R. Spencer Oliver)

eventually get underway on 2 April the only new faces in the side were Mick Sheldrick (Sid's younger brother) and former Nelson junior, Graham Tattersall.

The first four weeks of the new season were a complete disaster: dumped out of the cup by Stoke and only 1 point from 6 league matches, the track was coming in for a lot of criticism as well. Working around the commitments of the football club meant that there was never enough time to prepare the track properly and the corners were cutting up badly. Conditions got so bad that Terry Kelly walked out after two rides in the match against Bradford on 30 April, signalling the start of an unsettled season for the popular Mancunian.

Graham must have wondered what he had done wrong to justify everything that was going against him. The only highlight during the first month of the season was a highly entertaining 54-54 draw between England and Czechoslovakia on 16 April, the first of 3 international matches to be held at Holker Street during the season.

It was obvious that Barrow were missing the firepower of Mike Sampson. An unsuccessful attempt was made to sign Andy Meldrum, but salvation came in the shape of New Zealander Paul O'Neal, tempted out of retirement by a desperate George Graham. O'Neal made his debut against Stoke on 7 May and scored a perfect 12-point maximum as the Bombers tasted victory for the first time in the new season. Six days later, O'Neal scored another maximum, helping Barrow to victory at Scunthorpe. Barrow won again the next day, beating Canterbury 40-38 at Holker Street. O'Neal only scored 2 points on this occasion, however. Impatience at the gate brought him three tape-breaking exclusions and a back injury! The Bombers were feeling confident and, even without O'Neal in the side, they won their next 2 league matches at home, beat Sunderland away and annexed the Formula Furness Trophy after another exciting bank-holiday duel with the Comets of Workington.

149

O'Neal returned to the side on 8 June, inspiring his team to another away win at Weymouth, but the victory came at a price, with both Joe Owen and Sid Sheldrick picking up injuries and having to watch their team lose at Boston on the next day. O'Neal's return was short-lived, though. His flew back to New Zealand when his mother was taken seriously ill and never returned.

By this time, however, the team had found their feet and Sid Sheldrick was having possibly the best spell of his career. The two reserves struggled at times, but even they were capable of picking up points when they were most needed. The progress of the young Bombers did not go unnoticed, and no less than three of the Barrow side were on parade when England beat Poland at Holker Street on 16 July. Tom Owen scored an impressive 12 points and Sid Sheldrick and Joe Owen weighed in with 7 points apiece.

Sid Sheldrick leads into the first bend during the four team tournament between Barrow, Belle Vue, Sheffield and Hull on 30 June 1974. The photograph was taken by Roy Dixon a former member of the Formula Furness MCC and mechanic for Barrow-based road-racer, Les Trotter.

More action from the 30 June 4TT as Chris Pusey leads Chris Roynon into the first bend. Compare this picture with the one of Frank Burgess leading Roland Stobbart in the chapter on speedway in Barrow in the pre-war years. (Roy Dixon)

The Bombers had actually been sitting on the top of the division at the end of June, but just as in the previous season, this signalled the start of a run of bad luck. Tom Owen was injured while riding for England at Derwent Park, and novice, Charles McCormack was drafted in to replace him. Terry Kelly was still unsettled and didn't turn up for the match against Eastbourne on 23 July, ultimately costing Barrow the match. Going into the last heat Barrow were actually leading, but they simply ran out of riders and could only track Chris Roynon in the vital last heat. Eastbourne won the heat 5-1 and stole the match 39-38. To add to their woes, Sid Sheldrick was seriously injured in the match against Weymouth on 6 August and a week later, they dropped another point at home in the local derby against Workington – dropping points against their deadly rivals was always hard to stomach. The lowest point of the season came on 12 August with a near whitewash at Crewe. Barrow failed to win a single heat and lost by a massive 17 points to 61!

With Sheldrick and O'Neal out for the rest of the season, George Graham agreed terms with Newport to take Roger Austin on loan and made another attempt to sign Dave Baugh. The proposed deal with Austin ran into problems, however. Bradford had already been using him on loan and insisted on one month's notice. When the Yorkshire side did eventually sanction the move, Austin couldn't be found to be informed. In the end, it was too late in the season and Austin never did get to ride for Barrow. George Graham finally got his new heat leader, though, and Dave Baugh made his debut for Barrow in the August bank holiday challenge against Coatbridge.

England made their third appearance at Holker Street on 10 September, narrowly losing to Australasia 53-55 in the first Test. Barrow were well represented again, with Tom and Joe Owen scoring 11 and 8 points respectively. Chris Roynon was named as reserve too, but did not get a ride. The 1974 home season finished on 24 September with victory over Workington in a revenge challenge match.

Once again, Barrow finished in mid-table, cursing that dreadful start to the season, another string of injuries and an appalling run of bad luck for their lowly position. More bad news followed the season's end. A protest about the make-up of the Barrow team had been lodged by Scunthorpe, following their defeat at Holker Street on 11 September. The protest was upheld and Barrow had a further 2 points deducted. The record books still show that Barrow beat Scunthorpe 45-33, but Scunthorpe got the 2 league points – make sense of that if you can!

Storm clouds were gathering behind the scenes and relationships between the football and speedway clubs had turned particularly sour. The track was far from perfect and needed a significant amount of work and investment to bring it up to scratch. George Graham was willing to spend up to £4,000 of his own money on moving the safety fence and relaying the track. This would have given the football club enough room to retain a permanent pitch (albeit at the bare minimum dimensions) and the speedway track would be slightly longer with improved bends. All George Graham wanted in return was a new five-year lease at reasonable terms. Instead, the football club offered a three-year lease increasing from £130 per week for the 1975 season to £170 per week for the next year and £200 per week for the year after! Despite Graham's pleas, the directors of the football club basically told him to take it or leave it!

The two parties remained at loggerheads throughout the winter, but hopeful of a resolution, Graham went ahead with his team-building plans and agreed terms with Chris Roynon, Dave Baugh and the Owen brothers. Roynon was so happy at Barrow that he moved there permanently, finding work and joining in with the local scrambles (motocross) scene. The Bombers had all the makings of a formidable looking side, but talks between the football and speedway clubs broke down right on the eve of the new season and it was announced on 8 March 1975 that Mildenhall would be taking over Barrow's Second Division licence and fixtures.

Despondent and frustrated, George Graham moved out of Barrow and took over the promoting rights at Workington, taking Terry Kelly and Graham Tattersall with him. But he fought valiantly to save speedway in Barrow and in April he revealed that he had agreed terms to stage six open meetings at Holker Street, and was confident that more could be arranged later in the season. The supporters' club even had new badges made, but the 1975 season never happened and Holker Street was restored to its pre-speedway condition.

Barrow had built up a hardcore of supporters, who didn't want to see Barrow Speedway just fade away. Ken Norman kept Barrow in the news by supplying regular articles for the speedway and local press. Norman Millard, from Urswick, went one step further and put forward a planning application to build a new track in the town, possibly on Ironworks Road, but it was our old friend Cliff Hindle who finally got the wheels rolling again. He secured the lease on a six-acre site just off Park Road, and built

Chris Roynon has a long history with Barrow Speedway. Originally from Bristol, Chris joined the 'Happy Faces' in 1972 and relocated to Barrow permanently in 1974. He rode for the Furness Flyers in 1977 and 1978 and was behind the relaunch of the Barrow Blackhawks in 1984 and 1985. (Wright Wood)

his own 300-yard track and a humble stadium. Planning permission was granted following noise tests in July 1976 and Cliff had intended to be open the following Easter, but as with all attempts to run speedway in Barrow, nothing was ever straightforward. Negotiations with the council became very protracted and the weather always seemed to be against him.

A competition in the local newspapers to find a name for the new speedway team resulted in the 'Furness Flyers', with a race-jacket design based on Concorde! The Flyers first took to the track in the first leg of the National League Four-Team Competition at Coatbridge on 12 June, but they were completely outclassed. It was the same story in the next two legs at Newcastle and Edinburgh and the home leg was never staged as the track was not completed in time.

Park Road eventually opened its doors to the public on 16 August 1977 with a challenge match against Glasgow. Lining up for the Flyers were former Barrow stars Bob Coles and Tom Owen, Cliff's son Ian, Ross Townson, Les Race and Andy Reid. Completing the line-up was sixteen year-old Mark Dickinson from Askam. Mark had been the Barrow mascot back in 1973 and learnt to ride a speedway bike on Cliff's practice track at Marton; in fact, Mark had been working for Cliff since he left school. Although he was officially a Workington asset, George Graham allowed Barrow to use Mark to give him some real racing experience.

Opposite: *Programme cover for the first meeting at Park Road, 16 August 1977.*

Right: *Former 'Happy Face', Bob Coles made half a dozen guest appearances for the Flyers in 1977. (R. Spencer Oliver)*

A week later, Cliff resurrected the prestigious Eddie Crooks trophy, won by Tom Owen with a 15-point maximum. The biggest surprise of the evening was the return of Chris Roynon, who scored 2 points from 4 reserve outings. Roynon had retired part-way through the 1976 season, but the return of speedway to his adopted home town proved to be too hard a temptation to resist.

The old enemy from Workington made their first visit to the new track on 30 August, led by former Barrow boss George Graham and with Ian Hindle in the line-up. Barrow called up Tom Owen and Bob Coles again, drafted in another locally based rider, Nig Close from Sedbergh, and Mark Dickinson continued to impress with 7 points from the reserve berth. The result was a satisfying one, too; the Flyers beat the Comets 45-32 and Ian Hindle didn't score a single point! The meeting was marred by a nasty accident involving Grahame Dawson, who was rushed to North Lonsdale Hospital with serious injuries that would ultimately end his career.

During September, the Flyers were beaten by Newcastle, but then reeled off victories against Stoke, Ellesmere Port and Teesside. The season was originally due to end on 27 September, but the BSPA approved two further meetings in October. Unfortunately for the fans, the local publican who had been running the beer tent at Park Road pulled out because he reckoned it 'wasn't worth the hassle'.

The Flyers made one more appearance on 4 October, beating Scunthorpe 46-31, and the season ended on 11 October with the 'Mr Junior of the North' competition. Mark Dickinson underlined his potential with a faultless 15-point maximum and looked a class apart from the rest of the field.

Despite some poor crowds, Cliff pressed ahead with his plans for a second season. An application to join the National League was approved, but plans to improve the stadium facilities were less fruitful. Thwaites Brewery had agreed to fund a new club house, and Cliff was prepared to build a covered grandstand, but the planning application had still not been passed when the new season opened in March 1978. On a more positive note, improvements to the pits were completed, despite the best attempts of the Barrow rain to disrupt the work!

Cliff ran into trouble trying to raise a team too. Of the dozen or so riders that had worn the Flyers' race-jacket in 1977, only Geoff Pusey, Andy Reid and Les Race chose to return to Park Road. To complete the side, Andy Heyes and Dave Butt were signed on loan from Belle Vue, New Zealand trialist John Snowdon was thrown in at the deep end for the opening fixtures and another Cliff Hindle protégé, Mark 'Kid' Courtney, was promoted from the junior races. Cliff really wanted Mark Dickinson back at Park Road, but despite a closed-season row with the Workington management over his contractual future, Mark stayed with the Derwent Park outfit.

The new campaign began with a 28-44 defeat at Workington in the first leg of the Formula Furness Trophy. The match was ridden in atrocious conditions and was abandoned after a pile up in heat thirteen. No Cumbrian derby would be complete without an element of controversy and this challenge match was no exception. Cliff Hindle obviously thought that Workington's Dave Baugh was to blame for the last heat pile up, and the two nearly came to blows on the track. The Flyers fared even worse in the return at Park Road on 27 March, losing 26-49 in their first home match of the season.

Andy Reid was the only rider to come out of the opening challenge matches with any credit and it was obvious that Cliff needed to strengthen his side. Chris Roynon returned after the two defeats against Workington, but further heavy defeats at Weymouth and Edinburgh necessitated more changes. Charlie Monk joined the Flyers in time for their first home league match on 4 April, but even his 8-point contribution could not prevent Barrow from losing to Mildenhall by a whopping 28 points! The next rider to be given a chance was Malcolm Bedkobber, who joined the Flyers on loan from Exeter. He scored 7 points on his debut against Glasgow on 18 April, helping Barrow to their first victory of the season. Bedkobber looked like he would become a useful reserve, but the young Australian broke his ankle at Teesside on 4 May and was ruled out for the rest of the season. In a further bid to strengthen the side, Chris Robins and Des Wilson were both signed from Workington during May, but neither lived up to expectations. Wilson only managed 3 points in 5 matches and Robins never recovered from a disastrous debut at Park Road, when he completely wrecked his bike.

It seems as though Barrow always saved their best performances for their visits to Derwent Park, and 1978 was no different. Despite the fact that the Flyers had only won 1 of their previous 18 matches, they took the Comets to a last-heat decider and were

Big things were expected of Chris Robins when he joined the Flyers in May, but he wrecked his bike on his first appearance at Park Road and never really got to grips with the tight circuit.

unlucky to lose 38-40. This fighting performance must have given the struggling side some confidence, because four days later they held Eastbourne to a 39-39 draw. Then, on 13 June, they had the great satisfaction of beating Workington 41-37 in front of their home crowd, with Geoff Pusey becoming the first 'Furness Flyer' to score a full maximum.

Chris Bevan had joined Barrow on loan from Sheffield in mid-June and made his league debut against Rye House on 4 July. At first he looked like another failure, but he scored 9 points in the win against Crayford on 13 July and never looked back. Tony Boyle agreed to join Barrow in August and would probably have slotted straight in at number one, but he was injured a few days before he was due to make his debut and never got the chance to ride for Barrow. With Boyle unavailable, Chris Bevan was promoted to the team proper for the match against Scunthorpe on 8 August and another trialist, Ken Murray, brought some unexpected strength to the tail end.

Bevan and Murray certainly made a difference and despite the home fixture against Newcastle being rained off, August became quite a productive month for the Flyers. They beat Scunthorpe, Boston and Berwick at Park Road (the latter a record 52-25 scoreline) and scraped another draw against Milton Keynes, but they did slip to another hefty 44-point defeat at Ellesmere Port. The start of September brought another home victory, this time against Weymouth, but the final league match at Park Road saw the home side lose 24-54 to a rampant Newcastle side led by former Barrow 'Bomber' Tom Owen.

The season ended with 3 challenge matches. The first, on 19 September, was against First Division Sheffield. The Flyers put up a great fight and were unlucky to lose 38-39.

Geoff Pusey, an inspirational captain and the first Flyer to score a full maximum.

Disaster struck in the second half, though, when Chris Bevan crashed and broke three ribs. A week later Barrow beat Ellesmere Port and the Park Road season ended on 3 October with another win against Teesside.

At the end of a traumatic season, it was no surprise to find Barrow sitting at the foot of the table. They had lost all 19 away matches and only won 8 and drawn 2 at home. The Flyers had used eighteen different riders during the league campaign. Most were ineffective and only lasted for a short time. Roynon and Pusey were the only two riders to appear in every league match and Charlie Monk never missed a match after he joined the club in April. Reid and Courtney missed 2 matches apiece and improved steadily as the season wore on, and everybody wished that Chris Bevan had been at Park Road from the outset. Bedkobber and Murray were the only other riders to show any promise, but neither had the opportunity of an extended run in the team. Considering the team struggled all season and the stadium could only boast very basic facilities, it wasn't surprising to learn that crowd levels rarely reached four figures. The track had been running at a loss for two years, so Cliff Hindle cut his losses and announced that there would be no place for speedway in Barrow in 1979.

Somewhat surprisingly, speedway did return to Park Road in 1981, when the homeless Berwick team were waiting on planning permission for their new circuit. Between 18 April and 13 June, Berwick used the Park Road circuit for 5 league matches and one Knockout Cup match – and as any speedway fan in Barrow had come to expect – 2 other fixtures were rained off!

Two years later, speedway bikes were heard racing around the Park Road track once again. Chris Roynon had been taking gyrocopter lessons and flew over the derelict stadium. It saddened him to see the stadium just rotting away, so he decided to buy it from Cliff Hindle and run speedway himself. Chris enlisted the help of Robin Martakies and John Earnshaw and set about restoring the Park Road Stadium. The terracing was rebuilt, the car park cleared of rubbish and the whole stadium was rewired and replumbed. To comply with new safety regulations, the floodlights had to be taken down and resited, a new safety fence was built and the track was reshaped and relayed. Throughout 1983 and into 1984, Chris ran monthly stock car meetings and organised speedway training sessions. Only two riders turned up for the first session in 1983, but Roynon persevered and local enthusiasm began to grow.

The first official meeting under the new regime took place on Tuesday 17 July 1984, a challenge match between the Barrow 'Blackhawks' and Stoke. Most of the Blackhawks were 'borrowed' from other teams and included a number of former Barrow riders such as Craig Pendlebury, Geoff Pusey and Tom Owen. Also joining the squad were John Walmsley, Sean Courtney (another Cliff Hindle protégé) and veteran Eric Broadbelt. The biggest surprise was the return of Mark Dickinson, who hadn't ridden since his fallout with the Workington management in 1981. Mark still had the short stroke Weslake engine that his father and Frank Whiteway had built for him in the late 1970s, so they decided to build up a bike and give it a go. After some impressive second-half performances, Mark was back in the Barrow team on 21 August.

Mark Dickinson of Dalton-in-Furness made an unexpected comeback for the Barrow Blackhawks in 1984. Mark hadn't ridden since his fallout with the Workington management in 1981. (Tony Jackson)

Seven 'open' meetings were staged at Park Road during 1984, including four home victories for the Blackhawks against teams from Stoke, Hackney, Scunthorpe and Edinburgh. They also rode in 1 away fixture at Edinburgh on 27 July, losing 34-44.

On 26 August, the Barrow 'Braves' took to the track for the first time, in a challenge match against the Halifax junior side. Junior racing was a new venture for Barrow Speedway and allowed Chris Roynon to give trials to a number of youngsters who might not otherwise have experienced team racing. The match ended in a 38-38 draw. John Walmsley was in a class of his own, notching up three easy wins after falling in his first ride. Mark Dickinson suffered with mechanical problems all night, eventually blowing his engine up altogether in the second half. Lee Edwards, the grandson of former Belle Vue legend Ken Sharples, made an impressive debut too, scoring 6 points in the match and reaching the 'Rider of the Night' final. Debuts were also given to Mike Irving of Carlisle, Paul Bickley of Egremont, Scott Cook (the son of Edinburgh promoter Tom Cook) and Adrian Brayshaw. Chris Roynon's biggest disappointment was the poor crowd though – it seems that the people of Barrow just didn't share Roynon's enthusiasm for junior racing.

The Cumbrian Open Championship, held on 4 September, confirmed Eric Broadbelt's return to form when he beat Paul Thorp and Steve Lawson in a run off for first place. A proposed match against an ex-Workington team on 11 September was never run, but permission was granted for one extra match to end the season. This was due to be a challenge match against the Belle Vue 'Aces', a match guaranteed to bring in the crowds, but the British Speedway Promoters Association put a block on the fixture stating that First Division sides were not allowed to race at venues operating on an open licence. So, instead of an attractive fixture against the most famous team in the history of the sport, the match on 25 September became a challenge between Eric Broadbelt's Blackhawks and John Walmsley's 'Lions'. The two teams were made up of some of the regular Blackhawks mixed with some of the more promising junior riders. The top riders were all given either 20-yard or 10-yard handicaps to give the youngsters a fighting chance of scoring some points. The system certainly worked for the Blackhawks' reserve pairing of Mike Irving and Daltons David Price, who both recorded victories over more experienced opposition.

Despite some good racing and the emergence of some promising new riders, Roynon's first season in charge of Barrow Speedway was something of a disappointment. The crowds just didn't come to Park Road in big enough numbers to make it financially viable and the income from the short 1984 season did nothing to recoup any of the money that had been spent on renovating the stadium. Nevertheless, he pressed ahead with plans to enter a team into the 1985 National League, believing that the higher standard of league racing would produce more exciting matches and, in turn, lead to bigger crowds.

Chris Roynon's problems began before the season had even started. His biggest headache was raising a competitive team. Joe Owen, Tom Owen, Kevin Price, Louis Carr and Geoff Pusey were just some of the riders that were rumoured to be coming to Barrow, but all of them chose to ride elsewhere. Mark Dickinson opted against a full-time return to the saddle and Appleby-based Alan Emerson also turned down an offer

Burnley-based Eric Broadbelt made a brave comeback at Barrow in 1984 after being seriously injured riding for Edinburgh in 1982. Eric proved his fitness by winning the Cumbrian Open Championship on 4 September.

to make a racing comeback with the Blackhawks. By March 1985, Chris Roynon had still not been able to assemble a team that met the League's minimum points limit. Eric Broadbelt and Gary O'Hare were the only two riders to return from the previous season and they were joined by Paul Price, Kevin Armitage, Wayne Jackson and old favourites Bobby Coles and Terry Kelly. Hardly a title challenging side, but Barrow were given special dispensation to begin the season on the understanding that the team would be brought up to strength by the end of April.

The first 2 home matches were rained off and 3 league matches at Middlesborough, Edinburgh and Eastbourne ended in heavy defeats. Jackson and Coles were hopelessly out of touch and were shown the door after the first 2 matches. John Walmsley returned for a second spell at Park Road and was joined by Bernie Collier, on loan from Belle Vue. Despite the changes, the Blackhawks went down to another hefty defeat at Exeter in the first round of the Knockout Cup. Things weren't looking good!

The Park Road season finally got underway on 23 April, with the second leg of the Knockout Cup match against Exeter, but even this turned into a nightmare! The match got off to the worst possible start when the first heat had to be rerun three times and Eric Broadbelt was excluded. The worst was yet to come. The lighting generator had been stolen during the previous week, so the promotion had rigged up a system utilising a tractor to power the lights. When the time came to turn the floodlights on, Roynon went over to the tractor and began to rev the engine. The harder he revved the engine, the brighter the lights shone, then there was a loud 'crack' and the lights went out! The match had to be abandoned after heat seven, with the Blackhawks trailing by 6 points.

Incredibly, the next meeting, a league match against Mildenhall, was also rained off, meaning that only seven heats of speedway had been ridden at Park Road in the whole of the month of April. Terry Kelly was the next rider to leave Barrow and his place was taken by guest rider Dave Trownson for the bank holiday challenge match against Berwick on 6 May. The Blackhawks actually won the match 39-36, but this was the last time that the Blackhawks would take to the track as members of the National League. A mid-week tour of the south-east, taking in league matches at Arena Essex, Hackney, Canterbury and Mildenhall was postponed while the league reassessed Barrow's league status. On 16 May, the committee delivered its bombshell decision. Barrow were expelled from the league for fielding an under-strength side. It was hardly a surprise; the 85 Blackhawks were possibly the weakest team to ever have been seen in National League speedway.

It seemed as though everybody was prepared to write-off Barrow Speedway. The speedway press came out with ludicrous statements like, 'Barrow have withdrawn from speedway', and 'unlikely to stage any more matches', but things couldn't have been further from the truth. Roynon was enthusiastic about junior racing, so he and Robin Martaikes came up with the idea of 'Intermediate Racing', challenge matches against junior sides from other tracks.

Kevin Armitage and Gary O'Hare stayed at Park Road to ride at the lower level and Steve Newsham, David Price and former Barrow mascot Lee Gedling were all promoted from the junior races. Eric Broadbelt was loaned out to Glasgow for the remainder of

First-bend action from the Barrow v. Berwick match, 6 May 1985. Left to right: Eric Broadbelt, Rob Grant, Bernie Collier, Bruce Cribb. (Phillip Haynes)

the season, but still played an active role at Park Road coaching the younger riders. The only new faces in the team were Gary Clegg and Kym Mauger, the son of multi-World Champion and former Barrow race controller, Ivan Mauger.

The first 'Intermediate Challenge' match was held on 27 May, when the Blackhawks beat a side from Wimbledon 47-30. A proposed match on 11 June against a Scottish Select side became the fourth match to be rained off, but the Blackhawks returned to action on 11 June with another 47-30 victory against a side from Stoke. Gary O'Hare scored his first ever five-ride maximum in this match, but at the lower end of the team, young David Price fell off in each one of his three rides. The month ended with a narrow 38-37 victory away at Ellesmere Port, with Gary O'Hare reverting to his parent club and riding against the Blackhawks.

Ellesmere Port were due to appear at Park Road in a return match on 2 July, but the Cheshire side pulled out and the fixture was replaced with a Four Team Tournament featuring junior teams from Edinburgh, Halifax and Sheffield. The match was a real cracker, with Halifax emerging as the winners by a single point in a last-heat decider. Barrow travelled to Edinburgh on the very next day, giving debuts to Paul Cooper, Tony Rizzo and Jamie Young, but they lost 29-47.

Eric Broadbelt was recalled to the team when Workington came to Park Road on 16 July. Workington had reopened in April, and, like Barrow, were only operating at junior level. The Barrow top five all performed well and Darren Boocock, riding as a guest at reserve, weighed in with a handy 4 points. John Walmsley was the next familiar face to return to the side when the Blackhawks travelled up to Derwent Park on 28 July. But, once again, the rain came down and the match had to be abandoned after heat six with Barrow trailing 15-18.

The Coventry junior team came to Park Road on 30 July and everybody was expecting it to be another close match. Coventry had only lost 4 out of their previous 19 matches and were sitting on top of the British junior league, but the Blackhawks took control from the outset and the final score of 62 –15 is the biggest ever win by a Barrow Speedway team. Kym Mauger, John Walmsley and Kevin Armitage were all unbeaten by an opponent and Eric Broadbelt only missed out on a maximum when he was excluded from his last heat for breaking the tapes. The highlight of the meeting, though, was a splendid six-ride paid maximum from new reserve Jim Graham, standing in for the injured Gary Clegg, (he had broken his arm riding at Coventry a few days earlier). But victory came at a cost: Lee Gedling and Steve Newsham were both injured when they piled into the fallen Mike Bacon, Gedling aggravated a leg injury and Newsham damaged his collarbone.

Barrow's awful run of bad luck with the weather continued throughout August when two attempts to stage challenge matches against Birmingham were both washed out. Seven matches were rained off in one season, which must be a record even for Barrow Speedway! The rain had dried up by 20 August, when Ellesmere Port were the visitors at Park Road. Barrow continued their winning ways with a convincing 43-35 victory over the Cheshire side. Eric Broadbelt had a magnificent match, scoring 14 points from five rides, but John Walmsley didn't have such a good meeting and unexpectedly announced that he would not be available for the rest of the season.

Opposite: *Rob Grant of Berwick leads the Barrow pairing of Kevin Armitage and Gary O'Hare. O'Hare joined Ellesmere Port later in the season, but returned to Park Road to win the Cumbrian Open Championship on 24 September. (Phillip Haynes)*

Right: *Locally based John Walmsley had been recommended to Barrow in 1984 and improved with every match. He stayed with the Blackhawks in 1985, but retired at the end of August*

Kym Mauger was really beginning to blossom at Barrow, but a prior commitment meant that he had to miss the rearranged match at Workington on 8 September. With Walmsley missing too, it was a weakened Barrow side that went down 28-50, but on the brighter side, Steve Newsham made a successful comeback from his collarbone injury.

As the season drew to a close, the number of available riders was dwindling. Kevin Armitage was the next rider to join the injury list, and 'Rider Replacement' was utilised in the match against Workington on 10 September. Gary Clegg returned to the side and scored 3 vital points as the Blackhawks fought every inch of the way for a narrow 41-37 victory. But the biggest disappointment was the size of the crowd. Once upon a time, local derbies would have guaranteed a bumper crowd, but on this occasion less than 1,000 turned up and the financial loss on the night was astronomical.

The final match of the season was the Cumbrian Open Championship on 24 September. The meeting was run on a handicap basis, with riders starting from scratch, 10, 20 or 30 yards depending on their finishing positions in their previous heats. The handicap system certainly made the meeting more interesting, with former Blackhawk Gary O'Hare emerging as the winner.

The 1985 season had been a financial disaster. Not many promoters would have persevered, but Chris Roynon had real commitment. Some of the more dedicated fans had been asking for the season to be extended into October, but Barrow Speedway couldn't survive on local support alone. At the end of the day, Chris had no choice but to cut his losses and pull the plug on speedway at Park Road.

The only motorsport to be seen at Park Road in 1986 was the monthly stock car meetings and by 1987, Chris Roynon had replaced the speedway track with a greyhound track. Park Road Stadium was demolished in 1994 and a candle factory now occupies the site. Before building work began though, a couple of local motorcycle enthusiasts made use of the derelict track for their own benefit. Martin Crooks took his motocross bike up there for a few practice laps, accompanied by a teenager who wanted to be a speedway rider. Grant MacDonald had been a mascot in the last days of Barrow Speedway and had learnt to ride his own bike on the beach. Throughout the 1990s, Grant rode for numerous teams, including Linlithgow, Cradley Heath, Stoke, Peterborough, Workington, Newcastle and Glasgow, but he has never really fulfilled his early potential.

Chris Roynon still lives in Barrow and maintains his enthusiasm for speedway racing, but his attention is now focussed on nurturing his son. Adam Roynon is considered to be one of Britain's brightest prospects and has already represented Great Britain at 'Under-16' level.

It seems highly unlikely that speedway will ever return to the Furness peninsular. Since 1930 there have been six attempts to establish speedway racing at four different venues. All of them have failed and none of the promoters have lasted past their second season. The history of Barrow Speedway is littered with controversy and bad luck, and then there's the rain! I doubt whether any other track in the history of the sport has had so many meetings washed out as Barrow!

15

WORKINGTON: THE MODERN ERA

It was in October 1969 that news first broke of the planned reintroduction of speedway to Workington at a new venue, Derwent Park, home of Workington Town Rugby League Club. Behind this venture were two Yorkshire-based businessmen, Ian Thomas and Jeff Brownhut.

Derwent Park Stadium is built on reclaimed land, which had once been a tidal estuary known as 'The Saltings'. It's hard to imagine now, but at the start of the twentieth century, fishing boats were moored just about where the grandstand is today and mine workings ran out under the estuary too. Once part of the Lowther estate, it eventually became a council owned landfill site. There is over 3m of ash and rubble underneath the stadium, which has taken many years to settle. Once the landfill was completed, the council granted the newly formed Workington Town Rugby League Club a 199-year lease on the site at a peppercorn rent. The new ground opened in 1947 and by 1954, a 100m terraced stand was completed on what is now the back straight. Construction of the main seated grandstand commenced in 1956.

The winter months of 1969/70 saw the removal of some of the terracing and a slight realignment of the rugby pitch to accommodate a speedway track, which used over 3,500 tons of slag from the nearby steelworks as a base. Meanwhile, Thomas and Brownhut were applying for membership to the Second Division of the British League and trying to assemble a team. Early practice sessions took place at the Belle Vue track in Manchester and amongst the hopefuls were Trials ace Peter Gaunt and grass-track prospects, Maurice Wilson, Tony Sharpe and Alan Bradley. Two of the first definite signings were twenty-one-year-old Mancunian Ian Armstrong and veteran wild man Vic Lonsdale.

The new promotion then suffered a setback when their application to join the Second Division was rejected (along with that of Peterborough), on the grounds that the league already had sufficient teams. Peterborough, promoted by Allied Presentations, purchased Plymouth's licence and so bought their way into the Second Division. Meanwhile, it appeared that Workington would have to run a season of open meetings, which could threaten the viability of the whole venture. So Thomas paid £10 and appealed to the Speedway Control Board. Within three weeks he had won his appeal and had his £10 appeal fee returned, so getting into the league for free!

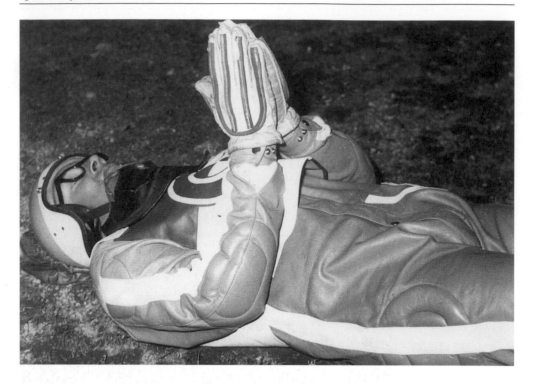

There then followed two weeks of frantic activity at Derwent Park. The track was inspected on behalf of the SCB by the newly appointed 'Track Inspector', former World finalist Bill Kitchen, who couldn't resist the temptation to ride a few laps too! Reg Wilson and Dave Kumeta were signed on loan from Sheffield, Australians Chris Blythe and Lou Sansom were brought over to England, and the promising Ian Armstrong fell and broke his collarbone when demonstrating for the cameras of the local Border Television. The team was to be called 'The Comets'. Having originally chosen the name 'The Cumbrians', Thomas changed his mind and had to think of a new name beginning with 'C' because the body colours, complete with a 'C' motif, were already made.

The gates were opened to an eager Workington public on Friday 3 April 1970, when Berwick Bandits were the visitors in a Border Trophy match. A crowd of over 6,000 turned up, of whom 4,000 paid to get in and 2,000 didn't! One side of the stadium had no perimeter fence, but that was not considered to be a problem as the river ran alongside the stadium. However, there was a large water pipe that crossed the river nearby and hundreds used that to gain access. The following week Thomas greased the pipe and watched as all the would-be gatecrashers fell into the river!

The circuit, which measured 398 yards, proved bumpy and unpredictable on opening night and, in a meeting littered with falls, Berwick ran out 39-37 winners. Top scorer for Workington being Liverpool-born naturalised Australian Malcolm Mackay with 14 points, backed up by fellow Aussie Lou Sansom, and Comets' captain, Vic Lonsdale, with 6 points apiece. Berwick's Andy Meldrum became the first track-record holder with a time of 83.0 seconds. However, despite the home defeat, the Workington public loved the spectacle and support bordered on the fanatical virtually overnight.

Opposite: *Veteran wild man Vic Lonsdale was one of the first riders to sign for Workington in 1970. (Wright Wood)*

Right: *Programme cover from the first meeting at Derwent Park, 3 April 1970.*

It had originally been intended to hold monthly stock car meetings at Derwent Park as well as speedway, but there were considerable problems with the track during the first year and the cars never arrived. Subsidence in the disused mine workings, which pass under the stadium, meant that the track never settled properly and the dates originally set aside for stock cars were filled with even more speedway meetings.

Following a string of early home defeats with a hastily assembled team, the Comets gradually strengthened their squad – firstly with the addition of Australian first-season sensation Bob Valentine, on loan from Sheffield, and then with the experienced Geoff Penniket from Romford. The Comets then ran up an impressive list of home victories and were attractive visitors on their travels; however, they did suffer a blow when Lou Sansom broke his jaw and was out for six weeks. Vic Lonsdale retired due to a loss of form but, late in the season, Taffy Owen was signed on a full transfer from Rochdale.

By the end of the season Workington had a very useful looking side and, considering their late entry into the league, finished a very creditable eleventh out of seventeen. There were impressive returns from Valentine (who was surely the find of the season, attaining a 9.37-second debut average), Mackay, Wilson and Sansom, who all looked destined to improve further in 1971.

Workington finished the season with the second highest crowd in the Second Division (behind Bradford), with an average of 3,850 per meeting, and fully justified Thomas' and Brownhut's brave gamble in bringing the sport to Workington.

The dawning of the 1971 season brought enforced team changes from which the Comets were never to recover. Their 1970 sensation, Bob Valentine, was recalled by parent track Sheffield, Yorkshire-based Reg Wilson wanted to cut back on his travelling and so joined Ian Thomas's new track at Hull, and promising reserve Ian Armstrong retired. The only new signing was Sheffield loan Bernie Hornby.

The progress made by Mackay and Sansom was offset by a succession of injuries to Taffy Owen, a broken shoulder for Geoff Penniket (which was to ultimately end his career) and a broken arm for Bernie Hornby. Once the season was underway, another Adelaide-based Australian, nineteen-year-old Kym Amundson, flew over to join the Comets and veteran Ken Vale was signed as the injury list grew. Mid-season saw the first locally born Comet take to the track. Despite only having sight in one eye, former starting marshal Steve Watson made his debut for his home-town team at the age of thirty-one, and went on to be an ever present for the next three and a half seasons.

The Comets went on to finish a disappointing fifteenth out of seventeen, with five home defeats and a solitary away victory at Sunderland. However, in the Knockout Cup they did provide the shock of the tournament by disposing of league champions elect, the Eastbourne Eagles, in the quarter final, before going out to eventual winners Ipswich in the semi-final.

After a season of consolidation in 1971 a substantial improvement was expected the following year. Gone from 1971 were Bernie Hornby, who had still not fully recovered from his broken arm, Chris Blythe, who joined league newcomers Ellesmere Port, and Ken Vale, who had retired. However, Ian Thomas had adequate replacements lined up for all three. Former Nelson captain, Dave Schofield, was signed from Bradford, a youngster by the name of Lindsay Davies was brought over from Australia, and a local scrambles star, Mitch Graham, was knocking on the door for a team place.

Any optimism was to last precisely eight and a half races, as Dave Schofield was unceremoniously bundled into the fourth turn fence by the late Jack Millen. The outcome was a shattered right ankle, which ended Schofield's career. The Workington faithful were none too happy either. Millen had to be escorted from the stadium by the police after angry fans stuffed chip wrappers under his car and set fire to them!

Meanwhile, Lindsay Davies was a major disappointment and moved on to Boston where he fared no better and returned to Australia. However, Taffy Owen enjoyed a great run of early-season form until a spectacular spill during the Northern Counties Championship at Workington saw him go head first over the safety fence and onto the first-bend terracing. This gave Mitch Graham his chance in the side and he was nothing short of a revelation, scoring solidly both home and away and ending the season with a 6.5-point average.

Opposite left: Taffy Owen joined Workington from Rochdale when Vic Lonsdale retired. Taffy was also a cricket fanatic and had a television installed in his car so that he didn't miss any of the Test matches while he was travelling to meetings.

Opposite right: Bob Valentine was sensational during his one and only season with the 'Comets'.

Right: Former scrambles rider, Mitch Graham, was also in charge of track maintenance at Derwent Park, so it was no wonder it didn't take him long to find the quickest way around the track. (Wright Wood)

June saw fellow Cumbrians, the Barrow Bombers, enter the Second Division when they took over West Ham's remaining fixtures. For the first time the Comets were able to enjoy genuine derby matches, which were never dull and did much to increase interest locally. Towards the end of the season Dave Kumeta retired, giving a chance to another local junior, Darrell Stobbart, son of the pre-war Workington rider Maurice Stobbart, who was still actively involved with the sport as the machine examiner at Derwent Park!

By the end of the season Owen, Sansom, Amundson and Watson had all improved their averages as the Comets finished in seventh position in the league, their highest so far.

All was now set for a 1973 season, when the Comets were expected to mount their first serious assault for Second Division honours. They tracked a septet with only one change from the previous season – Bernie Hornby, who returned to replace Dave Kumeta, while Darrell Stobbart was waiting for an extended run in the side. On the eve of the season, team plans were thrown into disarray when both Taffy Owen and Lou Sansom could not agree personal terms with Ian Thomas. Both riders subsequently missed the opening-night challenge match victory over Bradford, although their differences were soon resolved and they took their place in the Comets line-up.

After 7 matches and seven victories, including away wins at Ellesmere Port and Rayleigh, the Comets entertained Boston (who were also unbeaten in their 7 league matches), at Derwent Park in a thrilling encounter. The Comets, using guest Phil Herne in place of Mitch Graham who was on World Championship duty at Coatbridge, went 8 points down after seven heats. However, they rallied to level the scores at 36 all before Sansom and Mackay raced to a match winning 5-1 in the final heat, putting the Comets top of the league and unbeaten in 8 matches.

However, the Comets had flattered to deceive, and from then on things started to slip. They lost their first league match on 31 May at Long Eaton and then won only 3 more away matches all season, although for the first time in their short history they were unbeaten around Derwent Park. On their travels the Comets were restricted by weak reserves, with both Hornby and Stobbart only averaging 3.5 points per match. Despite this, the Comets finished second in the league, albeit 14 points behind Boston.

Individually, the Comets had the star of the league in Lou Sansom, who finished half a point clear at the top of the averages with a 10.51 figure. Although, disappointingly, he lost out to Arthur Price and Bobby McNeil in a three-man run-off for the Second Division Riders Championship on a rain-soaked Wimbledon track. During the season Sansom scored an incredible 20 full and 2 paid maximums from 42 league and cup matches, held the Silver Helmet on several occasions, and was a prolific scorer and captain for Australasia in their Second Division Test series victory over England.

The year 1973 also saw Workington make their first Knockout Cup final appearance where they met Boston. In the first leg they suffered their heaviest away defeat of the season (19-58), making the second leg a formality. A spirited home performance saw a 47-31 victory, but Comets had to settle for second best once again as their best ever season ended without a trophy. Meanwhile, Sansom increased his average (by 2 points), as had Mackay and Graham; in fact, Graham looked on the verge of great things, but the Comet's weakness in the reserve positions cost them dearly.

Australian Lou Sansom – one of the greatest riders to have worn the Comets' race-jacket. (R. Spencer Oliver)

The arrival of the 1974 season was tinged with disappointment for the Derwent Park fans. Firstly, Lou Sansom had decided to remain in Australia, claiming that he could not make British racing pay. Then, a further blow was dealt when fellow Adelaide-based Australian Kym Amundson also chose to stay Down Under.

Ian Thomas brought the vastly experienced Alan Cowland to Workington from his other track Hull, who had replaced Coatbridge in the First Division. This promotion of Hull naturally caused some resentment amongst Comets' fans, as many felt that after their exploits the previous year the Comets deserved a chance in the First Division. The only other addition to the Comets squad was a sixteen-year-old local schoolboy, Stephen Lawson.

The new-look Sansom-less Comets did well, being unbeaten at home for the second successive season. And, despite dropping to fourth in the league table, they actually scored 3 more league points (from two extra matches), than the previous year when they had been runners up. In the Knockout Cup they went out to losing finalists Eastbourne, having already disposed of Crewe and Berwick before meeting the Eagles. Local rider Mitch Graham did indeed blossom into a star performer with a 10-point average, although he disappointingly crashed out of the Second Division Riders Championship in his second ride, when he had been tipped as a potential winner. New signing Alan Cowland soon settled in, doing the job of a fourth heat leader, although he could never have been expected to replace the scoring power of the absent Lou Sansom. Meanwhile, Mal Mackay remained a tower of strength for the side, but a late season broken leg – while riding as a guest for Barrow at Holker Street – saw his season end prematurely.

Mal Mackay prepares to dive under Russ Dent of Sunderland. (R. Spencer Oliver)

The dawn of the 1975 season saw big changes at Derwent Park as Ian Thomas sold the club to Workington Town Rugby League Club director and local businessman, George Graham. Previously Graham had been the promoter at Barrow, which had now closed following a dispute with their football club landlords. Meanwhile, Ian Thomas was behind the reopening of Newcastle, in addition to operating his First Division side, Hull Vikings.

As well as behind-the-scenes changes, there was plenty of team-building activity too. Mitch Graham and Alan Cowland both joined Ian Thomas at First Division Hull, while Bernie Hornby joined Berwick and promising reserve Darrell Stobbart retired. However, Graham had managed to persuade the prodigal son Lou Sansom to return, along with his buddy Kym Amundson. He brought Terry Kelly with him from Barrow in addition to inheriting Owen, Watson, Lawson and a fit again Malcolm Mackay.

A large opening-night crowd witnessed Sansom falling on the first turn of his comeback ride followed by three straight wins. While a more mature Kym Amundson looked twice the rider he was in 1973 and Mackay appeared as good as ever, it was not to last. The second home meeting saw Mackay crash into the fence in his final ride while chasing a maximum with the match already won. The result, another broken leg for Mackay; eight to ten weeks out of action was the initial diagnosis, in actual fact Mackay had ridden his last ever league race for the Comets.

Graham moved swiftly, signing Robbie Gardner from First Division Hull to cover for Mackay's absence. Then, Taffy Owen broke a thumb and long-serving local rider Steve Watson retired after a lean spell, having set a Second Division appearance record of 123 consecutive league matches for the same club. That, in turn, gave a welcome

Former Workington starting marshal, Steve Watson, made his debut for the 'Comets' in 1971 and went on to be an ever present for the next 122 consecutive league matches. Steve retired shortly after the start of the 1975 season.

opportunity to impressive second-halfer Mick Newton, who had ridden for Stoke the previous season. Newton was a revelation, finishing the season with a 6.5-point average. Meanwhile, with regular double-figure returns, Kym Amundson was scoring like a heat leader. But, in mid-season, he too was lured away to First Division Hull. That was the final body blow that upset the balance of the team. Consequently, Workington suffered their only home defeat of the season (to Scunthorpe), in the very next match. Once again Graham moved quickly, bringing in the experienced Roger Wright from Teesside to replace Amundson.

By mid-season the first signs of financial trouble surfaced at Derwent Park when promoter George Graham launched a weekly fighting fund draw. He reported that on current crowd levels of 1,200 per meeting the club was losing £100 each week and that crowds of 1,700 were needed to break even. This draw was seen as a means of safeguarding the long-term future of the Comets.

The Comets finished the season in sixth position out of twenty in the retitled New National League, despite a best ever six away victories and a highest ever 48 league points; an indication of how competitive the league had become. An unlucky 38-39 home defeat by Swindon in the inaugural Inter-League Cup was offset by another Second Division Knockout Cup final appearance. On their way to the final they had a titanic semi-final battle with Newcastle that went to a replay, in which the Comets subsequently won both legs and so met Eastbourne in the final. But, yet again, the Comets finished as losing finalists following a disappointing, and at times controversial, 52-25 defeat in the second leg at Arlington.

Sansom regained the Derwent Park track record with a time of 71.6 seconds and once again topped the Comets averages, although he couldn't have been expected to reach the levels of 1973 after a year away. However, the early season loss of Mackay and mid-season transfer of Amundson probably did most to restrict the Comets quest for honours.

Following a reasonably successful season despite substantial rebuilding, it was hoped that 1976 would see a settled side challenging for honours once more. However, the hoped-for return of Kym Amundson did not materialise as he remained in Australia. Robbie Gardner reverted to his former base at Ellesmere Port, primarily to cut down on his travelling, and, most disappointingly of all, Halifax-loan and crowd favourite, Mick Newton, returned to his 1974 base, Stoke.

Once more promoter George Graham had entered the transfer market, signing Colin Goad from Ellesmere Port and bringing in youngster Chris Bevan on loan from Sheffield. In addition, Malcolm Mackay was returning from injury having missed virtually all of the 1975 campaign.

After two early season challenge matches, Mackay found that his leg was not up to the rigours of racing and was out once more. In actual fact Mackay, who'd top scored for the Comets at their opening meeting back in 1970, would never ride again. That was the start of a catalogue of injuries, which made their ensuing achievements that season all the more remarkable. Of their first 12 official fixtures only a home defeat by eventual runaway league champions Newcastle spoiled a 100 per cent record. This included four home and four away successes in the league, home and away cup victories over

Steve Lawson from Maryport had joined the Comets squad as a sixteen-year-old in 1974, but really came into his own during the 1976 season, raising his average by over 5 points per match.

Brian Havelock joined the 'Comets' in 1976 as a replacement for the injured Mal Mackay. (Wright Wood)

Coatbridge, and a famous 40-38 Inter-League Cup victory over First Division Ipswich Witches, (who went on to collect the First Division league and cup double), on a never-to-be-forgotten night at Derwent Park. It was a last-heat victory from the back by Sansom, over world number three John Louis, that won the tie for the Comets on probably the greatest night ever seen at the stadium. However, during that spell Owen missed 4 matches with concussion, Wright injured his ankle and missed 5, Kelly was out for 1 and of course they were already without Mackay. On the night of the Ipswich clash, promoter Graham signed Newcastle's unsettled Brian Havelock in a masterstroke to offset the predicted long-term absence of Mackay. Following the success over Ipswich, Owen only rode in 4 of the next 20 matches, due to a broken arm sustained at Ellesmere Port. He came back for 6 matches, then was injured once more and, like fellow first season campaigner Mackay, was destined never to ride for the Comets again.

Sansom managed to reach mid-July before breaking his collarbone at Berwick in the Bordernapolis, and then jarring it in a comeback at Teesside, putting him out of action for a total of two months. In his absence the Comets lost their way in the league and suffered a narrow 4-point aggregate defeat by Boston in the Knockout Cup quarterfinal, despite missing Owen and Sansom for both legs. Injuries also deprived them of any chance of glory in the inaugural Fours finals held at Kings Lynn, having won all four qualifying rounds to get there. The injured Sansom did, however, act as team manager, standing in for Alan Middleton, who was believed to be suffering from a viral infection, for the Inter-League Cup quarter final tie against Kings Lynn at Derwent Park. Yet again the Comets defeated First Division opposition 40-38 in another classic encounter, which once again went down to the final heat. This time it was a last-lap engine failure for Kings Lynn's Terry Betts that gifted the Comets the points they needed for victory. However, the dreaded injury jinx was about to strike once more. Steve Lawson, who had ridden superbly all season and contributed more than anyone towards Comets on-track success that year, broke his arm in a second-half crash at Belle Vue. Lawson was without doubt the most improved rider in the New National League and remarkably had raised his average by more than 5 points per match from the previous season.

A weakened Comets side had an unkind Inter-League Cup semi-final draw, away at Hull, and not surprisingly exited the competition, 54-23, racing the semi-final with only five riders and double rider-replacement for Lawson and Owen. At the end of the season, third position in the league can be considered miraculous bearing in mind their injury problems, and their Inter-League Cup exploits simply astounding.

Following an incredible season it became a winter of discontent at Derwent Park. Sansom wanted to try his hand in the First Division on a full-time basis with Birmingham, having made several useful appearances for the Brummies during 1976. Mackay had retired to Australia and Owen demanded a transfer, signing for Newcastle, where he raced in only 3 official matches before retiring. The departure of the three longest serving Comets of all time in one fell swoop signalled the end of an era for the Derwent Park fans. To many people Lou, Mal and Taffy were the Comets, and, in being such loyal servants to the club, the public had become so accustomed to their presence that they were reluctant to accept anyone else in quite the same way.

Once again promoter George Graham had to delve into the transfer market, buying Barrow domiciled Ian Hindle from Coventry and once again bringing crowd favourite Mick Newton from Stoke. In addition, he hoped that one or more of juniors Bevan, Dickinson and Wilson would do a Lawson-like improvement.

Mick Newton was always a crowd favourite at Derwent Park, returning for his second spell in 1977.

The season opened with a benefit meeting against a Newcastle Select, in aid of the Comets 1976 team manager Alan Middleton, who had developed multiple sclerosis, which, sadly, later claimed his life. This was followed by a string of home victories and impressive away performances that, by mid-June, saw the Comets third in the table after a dozen matches. However, by only the third home match of the season promoter George Graham had been calling for increased attendances and launched a fighting fund, as crowds had fallen alarmingly to 1,000.

The first major injury victim of the season was Mick Newton, who picked up a leg injury in a spectacular crash with Jiri Svoboda of the Red Star Prague touring side during an international challenge at Derwent Park, which the Comets won 40-38. This kept Newton out of action for two months just when he had been showing the best form of his career. Newton's injury gave an opportunity for sixteen-year-old Mark Dickinson from South Cumbria to gain valuable experience, while several other juniors were tried throughout the year but without much success.

The Comets were bundled out of the Inter-League Cup by Hull for the second successive year, this time going down 28-50 at home. They did, however, manage an away league success at Mildenhall, albeit in controversial circumstances. Steve Lawson was excluded for a tapes offence and Workington threatened to withdraw from the meeting unless he was reinstated. After a substantial delay he was, and the Comets went on to record a 41-37 victory. For this action Workington were given a fine of £300 but the result was allowed to stand.

During this time crowd levels continued to worry the promotion, and the Comets lost their first home league match in mid-July in a very bad-tempered meeting with Eastbourne, where arguments centred around the legality of Mike Sampson's silencer. From mid-August onwards they never won another league match, home or away, as the apathy on the terraces spread to the team.

By the end of the season the Comets had slipped to sixteenth out of nineteen, in a campaign that could not end soon enough. New signing Hindle was the only ever-present, while Havelock, Newton and Wright were each injured for a quarter of the season. Colin Goad had several very bad crashes, which led to his retirement at the end of the season, and the enigmatic Terry Kelly had been transferred to Berwick mid-term. Steve Lawson, who set a new Derwent Park track record of 69.8 seconds, was sold to Belle Vue during the season and then publicly stated that he would not ride for Workington in 1978. Following the final meeting, promoter George Graham put the club up for sale.

The close season saw the club sold to two local men, financial consultant Ron Cooper and garage owner Eddy Thornborrow. Their first action was to install former Comet Geoff Penniket as team manager, albeit with virtually no team. Local star Steve Lawson had joined Glasgow (on loan from Belle Vue), along with Mick Newton (who did return to Workington in October after a very unhappy spell in Scotland), Roger Wright signed for Berwick and Colin Goad had retired. Reserves Andy Reid and Chris Bevan both joined newcomers Barrow, so only Havelock and Hindle remained out of the previous season's eight regular team members.

Dave Baugh was signed from Scunthorpe and Chris Robins from Weymouth, two new Australian riders were recruited, Andy Margarson from Kings Lynn and Dave Coles

Far left: *Former Barrow rider Ian Hindle was an ever-present for Workington in 1977. (R. Spencer Oliver)*

Left: *Alan Emerson, from Appleby in East Cumbria, joined the 'Comets' in 1979. Alan had been a junior at Derwent Park back in 1973, but he opted to join Teesside at the time. (R. Spencer Oliver)*

on loan from Leicester, and completing the squad was promising seventeen-year-old local rider Mark Dickinson and the impressive late 1977 second-halfer Trevor Oldham.

Following 6 early season challenge matches Hindle was out with a dislocated shoulder, having been fenced by the man the Workington fans loved to hate, Berwick's Jack Millen. Oldham had a leg injury and Robins was dropped, never to reappear. The start of the league campaign saw veteran Tony Childs join the club but, after five very disappointing performances, he was sacked for failing to appear in 2 Knockout Cup matches. Hindle returned from injury for the third league match, which also saw Dave Baugh break his arm and effectively end his career. After 6 league matches and only one victory the writing was on the wall, so the new promoters made a double swoop, bringing in Belle Vue loanee Rob Maxfield from Newcastle and 1973 Second Division Riders Champion Arthur Price, on loan from Cradley Heath. Those two signings stemmed the tide and from then on home wins were the norm and away trips were at least respectable. Trevor Oldham came back from his leg injury but then broke his arm, which, as with Baugh, finished his career. Then a disastrous trip to Eastbourne ended with a compound fracture of the left leg for Dickinson and internal injuries for Coles, keeping them out of the saddle for two months and three weeks respectively.

Mid-season behind-the-scenes wrangles, brought to a head by the reinstatement of Tony Childs for a challenge match, saw Penniket leave the promotion at the end of July. Crowds had improved slightly on the previous year and the Comets climbed to fourteenth out of twenty in the league table, winning only one away league fixture, 40-38 at Boston. Considering the scale of rebuilding that had taken place it was not a disastrous position to be in, but there was still a lot of room for improvement.

A relatively quiet close season by Workington standards saw the departure of Price to Scunthorpe and Maxfield recalled by parent track Belle Vue. Meanwhile late 1978 season loanee Mick Newton retired. The only new arrival was Alan Emerson from First Division Birmingham. Emerson, who lived at Appleby in East Cumbria, had contested many second-half races at Derwent Park in 1973 at the age of sixteen, before signing for Teesside. Additionally, behind the scenes, Cooper and Thornborrow recruited the experienced Neil Macfarlane as team manager.

An eve-of-season contract dispute with Ian Hindle was resolved, but then, after the opening 2 challenge matches, Aussie Dave Coles quit the club. A succession of riders were given an opportunity to hold onto a reserve berth before extended runs were given to Birmingham loanee Mick Blaynee and Neil Collins (who had been discarded by Nottingham after 2 matches). After a run of disappointing scores Collins was dropped, then in a cup tie at Middlesbrough, Margarson crashed and broke his arm, which sidelined him for two months, before an aborted comeback saw him out for good. Neil Collins was recalled and, after five poor displays, he suddenly clicked in the away match at Weymouth, scoring paid 11. From then on Collins was a revelation, being paid for double figures in half of the season's remaining fixtures.

Emerson picked up a leg injury in the Grand National round at Middlesbrough and was out of action for a month. In an attempt to shore up the side, the unsettled veteran Arnie Haley was taken on loan from Belle Vue. However, after four impressive meetings his scores tailed off, before an injury at Scunthorpe put him out for the season. Minor injuries also saw Havelock and Dickinson out of action for 4 and 8 matches respectively towards the end of the campaign. Meanwhile, Havelock tabled a transfer request at the end of August following a dispute with the promotion, although he agreed to see out the season with the club.

By the end of the season it was a very ragged and battle-scarred squad that finished in fifteenth position (out of nineteen) in the league, and for the first time since speedway opened at Derwent Park they picked up no league points away from home. However, without injuries to key riders they would surely have had success at Milton Keynes, Weymouth, Scunthorpe and also at Newcastle, where they lost 38-40, with only two tape exclusions for the otherwise unbeaten Ian Hindle costing them a certain victory. Meanwhile, at Derwent Park crowds had again dipped alarmingly, giving rise to heavy losses at the turnstiles.

The close season saw Ron Cooper quit the promotion, so leaving local garage owner Eddy Thornborrow in sole control. At a pre-season supporters' meeting at Derwent Park an emotional Thornborrow explained that the club had no money to sign riders and would have to struggle on with what they had, on the basis that any speedway was better than no speedway at all. As a consequence this was without doubt the weakest team ever to take to the track in British speedway's modern era.

Gone from the previous season were Emerson (to Glasgow), Havelock (to Middlesbrough), Haley (to Exeter), Collins (to Edinburgh) and Blaynee (to Milton Keynes). The experienced Chris Roynon was tempted out of retirement and the promising duo of seventeen-year-old Wayne Jackson and twenty-year-old Kevin Clapham were signed from non-league Castleford. Only Hindle, Dickinson and Wilson remained from the 1979 regulars, plus several of the local juniors.

*Des Wilson, another of the local riders who had
worked their way up through the second half
races. (R. Spencer Oliver)*

Predictably, the entire season was a disaster. With a young and inexperienced side, and no recognised heat leaders, all away matches were lost by large margins, including a record 65-12 defeat at Crayford. Only at Canterbury did they score over 30 points and on twelve occasions, out of nineteen, they failed to reach 20 points on their travels. Their home form was little better, winning only 2 matches all season. They defeated Canterbury 40-37 and Milton Keynes 40-38, whereas the visit of high-flying Newcastle set a club record 20-58 home defeat. Hindle, Wilson and Dickinson were all injured during the season, missing 17, 5 and 7 matches respectively. Chris Roynon retired after 11 matches, while Andy Margarson returned to the club, rode 7 matches, and then he too retired. Indeed, by the end of the season the Comets had tracked twenty-six different riders in official fixtures with some hopelessly outclassed, but others such as Wayne Jackson, and the late season arrival from Leicester, Steve Regeling, showed great promise. Ian Robertson, making a comeback from a broken leg sustained the previous season, was taken on loan from Stoke at the end of May and former Derwent Park hero Terry Kelly made a comeback in July, both riders adding vital experience to an otherwise youthful squad.

Against all odds the Comets managed to fulfil all of their official fixtures, clearly losing money in the process. They received a great deal of criticism from rival promoters but, unfortunately, very little help, and it really looked like the end of the road for the Comets.

When promoter Eddy Thornborrow put the club up for sale during the winter, even he was amazed to find a buyer. Initial speculation was that Sheffield promoter Ray Glover would purchase the club, having expressed an interest during the 1980 season. However, the whole of speedway was surprised when the buyer was found to be ex-rider and former Ipswich and Mildenhall team manager Ron Bagley.

Bagley sold up his Colchester-based photographic business and moved up to Workington, insisting he knew the size of the task that lay ahead. Upon taking control of the Comets, Bagley inherited Hindle, Kelly, Jackson, Clapham, Dickinson and Wilson. The expected transfer of Ian Robertson failed to materialise and he reverted to Stoke, meanwhile Leicester loanee Steve Regeling opted to join Boston in order to reduce his travelling. An attempt was made to coax the locally based former star Mitch Graham out of retirement but he eventually declined the invitation. Clearly Bagley had to enter the transfer market. His first target was Nicky Allott who, following a practice and photo session at Derwent Park, chose to remain at Scunthorpe, again due to the travelling involved. Bagley then made two disastrous signings; firstly he tempted Mike Hiftle out of retirement, and then he paid out a club record fee for ex-England international Chris Pusey from Weymouth, supplying him with a brand new bike as part of the deal.

In an unfortunate start to the season, Hiftle broke his leg in the first league match and was never seen again. Meanwhile Pusey was hopelessly out of touch and, after several behind-the-scenes arguments, he was sacked after 3 league matches. In an act of defiance, Pusey took the bike Workington had bought for him, only for it to be 'retrieved' in a clandestine operation! The Comets were now weaker than in the previous season and when the stylish Ian Hindle broke his ankle in only the third meeting – an injury that was to rule him out for the rest of the season – the alarm bells were ringing loud and clear. Ex-favourite Mick Newton was tempted back after a two-season retirement but, after only 6 matches, he quit the sport for good. Then local second string Des Wilson picked up an injury and spent eight weeks on the sidelines. Leicester loanee David Blackburn and Keighley-born West Australian Guy Wilson (on

Kevin Clapham in conversation with Maurice Stobbart, the Derwent Park machine examiner. Maurice had been one of the top riders at Workington in the 1930s. (R. Spencer Oliver)

Wayne Jackson, a promising teenager who joined the 'Comets' from non-league Castleford. (Tony Jackson)

David Blackburn came to Workington on loan from Leicester and held on to his team place for the remainder of the season. (R. Spencer Oliver)

loan from Halifax), were both given chances, holding on to their team places for the remainder of the season, although Guy's season was interrupted by a broken arm. Several juniors were used to plug the many gaps (including future World finalist Paul Thorp) but, by the end of June, the Comets had only two victories from 16 league matches.

Following more behind-the-scenes arguments, the talented Mark Dickinson left the club (and the sport) for good. Mark became very disillusioned with the way Workington Speedway was being run and was also convinced that his bike was sabotaged on more than one occasion. During the season he had wrecked three engines. After one such incident, his father found shale in the bottom of his tank and on another, water had been added to his fuel, causing his engine to run weak and hole the piston. In the end, Mark simply had enough and walked out. Kevin Clapham also handed in a transfer request and drifted away from the scene while Sheffield loanee John Frankland and Mancunian Howard Jackson joined the side for the latter part of the season.

The Comets finished next to the bottom of the league, with only six wins and a draw from their 18 home matches, and on only two occasions did the Comets score over 30 points on their travels. However, things would have been much worse without the magnificent never-say-die attitude of Terry Kelly and the rapidly emerging talent of Wayne Jackson. Guy Wilson was a real crowd-pleaser and showed plenty of promise. The Comets used twenty riders to struggle through the season but bad luck with injuries, particularly to Ian Hindle, contributed to many of the home defeats. The lack of an out and out number one cost them dearly and, while the signing of Pusey was the greatest mistake, the loss of Mark Dickinson was a major waste of a natural talent.

Terry Kelly added vital experience to the team in 1981 and his never-say-die style of riding was one of the highlights of an otherwise depressing season. (Tony Jackson)

Understandably, crowds dropped again (after an initial increase due to the new promotion), and Workington Speedway lost a lot of money. Despite these losses, Bagley was willing to try once more in 1982. However, in mid-February the League Management Committee and the Speedway Control Board ultimately gave him four days to clear all the club's debts (said to be around £5,000), and also lodge a £5,000 bond with the BSPA. This he could not do, although £7,000 was raised with £2,000 of this coming from the supporters. Bagley applied for more time but was refused, and so Workington were denied entry into the 1982 National League. The promised appeal did not materialise and the track remained closed, ending twelve continuous seasons of Second Division racing.

Programme from the 1985 non-league season. A total of twelve meetings were run under the watchful eye of Dave Younghusband.

In 1985, ex-rider Dave Younghusband was given the go-ahead to stage a series of open licence junior events at Derwent Park. The first of these was an individual event for the Jim Bowen Trophy and included former Comets mascot and future world champion Gary Havelock in the line-up. This opening meeting drew a crowd of around 1,000, but extremely wet weather not only hit the attendance but caused the meeting to be abandoned after heat twelve with Garry Clegg declared the winner. A total of twelve meetings were held and, although attendances were insufficient to justify a return to league racing in 1986, they did encourage Younghusband to apply to run a further season of open meetings at a junior level. However, a short-sighted decision saw this application refused, so denying juniors further organised opportunities for training and practice at an amateur level.

The sport did return to Derwent Park in 1987, albeit as a stop-gap base for the Glasgow Tigers while their new base was made ready. However, after a very encouraging first meeting attendance of just under 2,000 speedway starved supporters, the logistical problems of the venture soon became apparent. The Glasgow promotion only came to the track on race day, which did nothing to help track preparation, the temporary track lighting was woefully inadequate and coupled with a weak team that the local supporters could not identify with, it was a recipe for disaster. In mid-season, when it became obvious that they would be based at Derwent Park all year, the team name was changed to the Workington Tigers. But it was too little too late, the initial support had been lost. By then the Tigers were adrift at the bottom of the league and way behind in their fixtures. In fact, the whole operation was a shambles.

Eventually, in mid-September, in an unprecedented move of sheer frustration by the National League management committee, they were expelled from the league. The Tigers' final meeting at Derwent Park took place on Sunday 13 September and resulted in a 37-41 home defeat at the hands of Wimbledon. The only two Glasgow riders to shine during this whole unhappy episode were Gordon Whitaker and the Tigers' Workington-born skipper Steve Lawson, as the club managed just three wins and a draw from the 25 official fixtures they fulfilled prior to their expulsion. But, for the Workington public, the harm done by this venture made a full-time return to league speedway by a Workington side seem even further away than at any time since the end of 1981.

It was almost eleven years later, on 5 June 1998, that the front page of *The West Cumberland Times & Star* announced the possibility of the sport's return to Workington and that experienced promoter Tony Mole was the man behind the proposal. After a lot of negotiations over the following months, the Comets were back in business, with Mole installing former promoter Ian Thomas as general manager and the club being accepted into the Premier League.

The return of the Workington Comets was, without question, the success story of British Speedway in 1999. By the end of their comeback season, they had become one of the best supported clubs in Britain, won their first ever national speedway trophy and had a rider qualify for the Grand Prix series for the year 2000.

Promoters Tony Mole and Ian Thomas assembled a side from scratch while at the same time reconstructing the Derwent Park circuit, which included the introduction of

banking to turns three and four. Opening night saw well over 4,000 fans turn out as a Del Boy look-alike, complete with Reliant Robin, officially reopened Workington Speedway with the Comets defeating Newcastle, 47-41 in a challenge match.

Within a week Peter Scully became the first of several Comets on the injured list, suffering concussion in a high-speed crash at Edinburgh. Soon there were more injury worries as they lost the services of Geoff Powell and Brent Werner, both being innocent victims of incidents at Berwick and Newcastle respectively. Powell was ruled out for ten weeks with a broken hand, while Werner suffered concussion.

It was a depleted Comets side that faced Berwick in the opening home league fixture of the season. The Comets tracked David Walsh as a guest in place of skipper Carl Stonehewer, who was forced to take part in the rearranged British semi-final at Wolverhampton. Indeed, Stoney had offered to forsake his World Championship ambitions to help the injury ravaged Comets, but, after initially being granted dispensation to miss the semi-final, he was compelled to compete by the powers that be. Little could anyone have imagined the ultimate consequences of that decision!

When James Birkinshaw became the next injury victim with severe friction burns, Ian Thomas brought Wayne Broadhurst into the side as his replacement. Barry Campbell then arrived at Workington, having begun the season with Belle Vue, and Australian Darren Groves came on loan from Kings Lynn. Meanwhile Stonehewer, having qualified for the British Final, progressed to the Overseas Final where he finished an excellent equal fourth to go forward to the Inter-Continental Final at Poole. From there he qualified as reserve for the Grand Prix Challenge, following a hard-earned eighth place. But, with Hans Nielsen's impending retirement, Stonehewer was elevated into the meeting proper.

Opposite: *The 1999 Workington 'Comets'. Left to right: Brent Werner, Mark Blackwell, Geoff Powell, Carl Stonehewer (on bike), Jamie Birkinshaw, Peter Scully & Grant MacDonald. (Tony Jackson)*

Right: *Brent Werner and Carl Stonehewer – 1999 Premier League Best Pairs Champions. (Tony Jackson)*

The turning point of the season was undoubtedly the arrival of Swede Peter I. Karlsson in July. At the same time Stonehewer challenged Sheffield's Sean Wilson for the Silver Helmet match race title, claiming a comfortable victory and going on to retain the Silver Helmet for the remainder of the season, making thirteen successful defences. Then success, as the Comets duo of Stonehewer and Werner were crowned Premier League Best Pairs Champions at Newport, the Comets' first ever national trophy.

Geoff Powell did return to the side but August brought its share of problems with Barrow-born Grant MacDonald suffering a knee injury at Derwent Park before badly dislocating an ankle during the Comets visit to Arena Essex. Peter Karlsson also suffered severe bruising to his back in a further spill at Arena Essex. Then, the next day, Werner was injured following a tangle with Will Beveridge during the home meeting with Glasgow.

Thankfully, the popular Karlsson was soon back in the saddle, while Scully was recalled to the side to replace MacDonald. Amazingly, within three weeks, MacDonald declared himself fit to ride and Powell became the unfortunate one to make way, having clearly struggled to recapture anything like his early season form since his return from injury. Then Campbell became the last injury victim of the season, breaking his collarbone, so giving Powell some more outings in a Comets' race-jacket as the Comets ended an injury-ravaged comeback season in eleventh place. Finally, Carl Stonehewer capped a remarkable season by finishing third in the Grand Prix Challenge at Lonigo, earning a place in the 2000 Grand Prix series.

The new Millennium saw the Comets installed as clear favourites for the Premier League title. However, come the end of the season the Comets title-hopes lay in ruins

Carl Stonehewer capped a magnificent 1999 season by qualifying for the 2000 Grand Prix series. (Tony Jackson)

as they just missed out in what was one of the closest and most exciting league championship races in the history of the Premier League. The fact that the Comets went so close in all the major competitions, despite their severe injury problems, simply underlines why they were such red-hot pre-season favourites.

Before the season began a sponsorship deal was signed with a local company, Kirkland Carpets, who became the team's first ever team sponsor. Then, once the tapes rose on the new season, the Comets fully justified their pre-season favourite tag by winning 13 of their first 15 official matches. But, those victories came at a cost.

In only their third official meeting of the season, away at Sheffield in the Premier Trophy, the popular and promising Australian reserve Darren Groves crashed and suffered serious neck injuries. Then, five weeks later, the Comets lost Barry Campbell with an almost identical injury after he reared and crashed at Derwent Park in his opening ride of the Comets first Premier League match of the season. Those injuries meant that the Comets effectively raced their entire Premier League campaign with only five regular riders, which almost certainly cost them the league title.

Local veteran Geoff Powell was recalled to the side to replace Groves, while a series of reserve guests were utilised to cover for Campbell, with Adrian Newman and James Mann being those used most regularly. Mid-June saw the Comets drop their only home league point with a draw against Glasgow when racing without the much-improved Peter Karlsson, and an engine failure by guest replacement Simon Stead, when in a scoring position, ultimately proved to be costly.

Peter Karlsson, the stylish Swedish rider who improved rapidly during the 2000 season. (Author's collection)

Early July saw the Comets experience heartbreak with league defeats on successive nights, by 2 points at Swindon and by 1 point at Arena Essex, ultimately proving crucial. However, the next night saw the Comets successfully retain their Premier League Best Pairs title, which was won by Carl Stonehewer and testimonial man Mick Powell in a curtailed meeting at a rain-lashed Derwent Park. But, the Comets' hopes of adding the Premier League Fours to the Pairs were dashed following a disappointing semi-final performance that saw them fail to reach the final of the Peterborough-staged event.

They reached the semi-final stages of both the Premier Trophy and the Knockout Cup, agonisingly going out in both to Exeter and Hull respectively, with their Knockout Cup defeat being by a mere 2 points on aggregate. Then the injury jinx struck again, with both Geoff Powell and Lee Smethills ruled out for the remainder of the season within the space of eight days at the end of August, effectively reducing the Comets to a four-man team with 13 official fixtures still to fulfil. Amazingly, the Comets then went to Reading and the Isle of Wight and won. But, defeat at Berwick, in a match that featured lone Comet Mick Powell, five guests and a rider replacement and should never have been allowed to go ahead, and a 1-point defeat at Hull, ended the Comets' title hopes. They eventually finished fifth, but a mere 2 points behind champions Exeter, who also saw off the Comets in the semi-final of the Young Shield Play-offs with a 4-point aggregate victory.

Success did come to the Junior Comets team as they became the first ever winners of the Northern British Youth Development League, introducing Phil Bragg, Chris Hunter and Craig Branney to the speedway scene.

Away from the team front, skipper Carl Stonehewer completed his inaugural year on the Grand Prix circuit in eighteenth place and second place in the Grand Prix Challenge ensured his participation in 2001. Nearer home he finally annexed the Premier League Riders Championship with victory at Sheffield, which received good coverage from Channel 5 television. They produced an hour-long documentary on the fortunes of the Comets throughout the 2000 season, which was screened nationwide.

The 2001 season saw the Comets line-up minus Brent Werner, who elected to join Elite League Eastbourne, and Geoff Powell, who had retired at the end of the previous season. Meanwhile, broken-neck victim Darren Groves was still not fit enough to return to the sport.

But the top three of Carl Stonehewer, Peter Karlsson and Mick Powell were augmented by Lee Smethills and Barry Campbell, who were both returning from injury, and new-signings James Mann and newly crowned Australian Under-21 Champion Rusty Harrison.

The season started off brightly enough for the Comets, now sponsored by Harper & Hebson Audi of Carlisle, as they won 9 of their first 11 fixtures, all of them in the Premier Trophy and cruised into the semi-finals for the second successive year. In addition, in one of their two defeats – away at Sheffield – they featured in the first Premier League-level fixture to be broadcast live on Sky Sports. But, even before the season was a month old, their starting septet was minus Barry Campbell following a horrific accident at Derwent Park that almost cost him his life. He suffered a badly broken arm and serious internal injuries and was ruled out for the rest of the season.

After initially using local junior Craig Branney, David McAllan was signed on loan from Edinburgh for the remainder of the campaign to fill the void. Then, a hand injury for

Opposite left: *Workington-based Geoff Powell retired at the end of the 2000 season. Over the years he has ridden for Glasgow, Linlithgow, Mildenhall and, of course, his home town side, Workington. (Tony Jackson)*

Opposite right: *Rusty Harrison, the Australian Under-21 Champion in 2000 and a great prospect for the future. (Tony Jackson)*

Right: *Neil Collins made an unexpected return to Derwent Park in 2001, twenty-two years after his last ride for the 'Comets'. (Tony Jackson)*

Mann saw Justin Elkins added to the side for a six-match period without achieving any success, but before Mann was even restored to the side the Comets suffered another injury blow. Heat leader Mick Powell crashed at Derwent Park, in almost the same place as Campbell, in only the third league meeting of the season, suffering a broken pelvis that ended his racing for 2001.

The Comets management then moved to bring crowd favourite Neil Collins to Derwent Park for the remainder of the season as cover for Powell, for what was to be his second spell with the club. His first had been twenty-two years earlier.

One of Collins' first opponents was his club from the previous season, Swindon, who recorded a second aggregate success of the season against Workington with a 6-point victory in the Knockout Cup, having earlier comfortably defeated the Comets in the semi-final of the Premier Trophy.

However, success did come to Workington in July when the Comets staged the Premier League Best Pairs for the second time and won the title for a record third successive season, with Carl Stonehewer and Peter Karlsson claiming top spot. Less than a month later the Comets had their finest hour when they lifted a team trophy for the first time in their history – the Premier League Fours at Peterborough.

But even then they did it the hard way, with Stonehewer having to defeat Edinburgh's Peter Carr in a run-off to reach the final. In the final itself they came from behind to take the title in the very last race of the event, which was also shown live on Sky Sports. Stonehewer made it a hat-trick of national trophies by retaining the Premier League Riders Championship at Coventry, becoming the first rider ever to do so.

Workington fans got their first taste of sidecar speedway on 23 September 2001 when the track hosted the North of England Open Championship. Fittingly, the only local driver in the field, Paul Bickley from Workington and his passenger Paul Silvera from Coventry, took top honours, but they had luck on their side in the final. Two of their rivals went out with engine failure and their own engine expired just as they crossed the finishing line. Paul Bickley once had ambitions to be a solo speedway rider and rode in second halves at Workington in 1981, but he gave up after breaking his leg at Berwick.

At the end of the 2001 season the Comets finished in sixth place and, including the Premier Trophy, had the best away record in the league. However, three home defeats – including their first league match of the season against Glasgow – and the injuries to Powell and Campbell, stopped an assault on the league title.

They did, nevertheless, qualify for the Young Shield Play-offs, and, after disposing of Hull, were eliminated at the semi-final stage by Edinburgh, while on an individual front Stonehewer ended the season as number twelve in the world and, by virtue of the Grand Prix Challenge, qualified for his third successive Grand Prix series.

Workington 'Comets' – the 2001 Premier League 4TT Champions. Left to right, back row: Rusty Harrison, Lee Smethills, Neil Collins. Front row: Carl Stonehewer, Ian Thomas (manager) and Peter Karlsson. (Dave Payne)

Above: *Paul Bickley and Paul Silvera, winners of the North of England Open Sidecar Championship at Derwent Park. (Author's collection)*

Right: *Carl Stonehewer, the first rider to win the Premier League Riders Championship two years in succession. (Author's collection)*

Following what was arguably their most successful season to date, trophy-wise, hopes were high that the Comets could build on that success in 2002.

Newcomers to the side were twenty-two-year-old Finnish prospect Kauko Nieminen and seventeen-year-old Aussie starlet Scott James. The final team spot was handed to Welsh junior Tom Brown after an impressive display at the club's press and practise day. Moving on from the previous year's side were fit Mick Powell, who was loaned to his former club Glasgow, and loanees Lee Smethills and Neil Collins, who linked up with Hull and Somerset respectively. Meanwhile, Barry Campbell was still some way from fitness following his spill in early 2001.

With three riders starting the season on 3-point averages, the team had a top-heavy look about it. But, once Nieminen attained a real average after completing 12 official fixtures, as opposed to the assessed 9-point figure he started the season with, there would be scope to introduce a new face to strengthen the middle-order while remaining within the points-limit.

However, once again the Comets' injury jinx struck in the cruellest way with Nieminen tangling with Edinburgh's Dalle Andersson in the Comets' opening Premier Trophy fixture at Edinburgh. This resulted in a badly dislocated shoulder for the Finn, who was forced to spend seven weeks on the sidelines, keeping him out of 12 Comets' matches. Consequently, it was mid-July until he attained a real average, by which time the Comets' season lay in ruins. And, for the second successive season, Comets' boss Ian Thomas turned to a member of the Collin's family to plug the gap, with the club-less Les Collins being introduced as cover for Nieminen.

As in 2001, the Comets lost their opening home league fixture, this time to the Isle of Wight, but there was worse to come. Nieminen's injury was only the start of a catalogue of misfortune to befall the side. Next to be hit was reserve Scott James, who had made a promising start to his British career. He tangled with Stokes Lee Hodgson at Loomer Road and ended up with a broken scaphoid, which kept him out of action for two months.

Then, following a string of poor scores, Tom Brown was dropped in favour of Chris Collins, while Les Collins made way for the returning Nieminen and a succession of

The 2002 Workington 'Comets'. Left to right: Peter Karlsson (on bike), Scott James, James Mann (kneeling), Kauko Nieminen (on bike), Tom Brown, Rusty Harrison (kneeling) and Carl Stonehewer (on bike). (Author's collection)

The spectacular style of Finnish international Kauko Nieminen. (Author's collection)

juniors were used as cover for Scott James, with only limited success. But one junior who did have a good night was Workington-born Phil Bragg, whose 7 paid 9 from the reserve berth proved to be a match-winning performance in the home clash against Exeter. However, a coming together of Exeter's Bobby Eldridge and Comet James Mann saw Mann suffer a dislocated shoulder, which effectively ended his season.

Next to be hit by the injury-jinx was Chris Collins, who, following a fine display at Glasgow where the Comets achieved their only away league success of the season, broke his collarbone when riding for Buxton. In his place came Reading asset Shane Colvin, who was a disappointment. Meanwhile, it was the turn of the Swede, Peter Karlsson, to be injured. He was ruled out for a month with concussion following a spectacular pile up in a Swedish league fixture.

Before Karlsson was fit to resume racing, the final hammer-blow came with the loss of inspirational skipper Carl Stonehewer. As an innocent victim of a first-bend pile-up in Gothenburg's Scandinavian Grand Prix at the end of August, it not only ended his Grand Prix adventure but also his 2002 campaign.

Meanwhile, long-time transfer target Blair Scott finally joined the side late in the season as the Comets finished their injury-ravaged year without a trophy for the first time since their return to the sport, ending a league season to forget in a disappointing fifteenth place out of seventeen.

16

BRAYTON DOMAIN SPEEDWAY, ASPATRIA

When speedway came to Derwent Park in 1970, it seemed like the whole of West Cumberland had gone speedway mad! Maurice Stobbart, the Workington Speedway rider from the pre-war days, had a bright idea and started his own speedway evening classes at the Workington Town Boys' Club on Bolton Street. Every Wednesday, as many as fifty budding speedway riders would turn up for Maurice's 'Bessemer Speedway Club'.

Part of the course was the manufacture of a complete speedway racing machine. The pupils prepared all of their own jigs and made all but a few minor components. Even the engine was built from scratch. Between September 1970 and July 1971, the club turned out four complete Bessemer speedway machines. The project was so successful that the club was honoured with a Gold Award from the Association of Northern Clubs.

Once the bikes were ready, it was time to start the practical lessons. At first Maurice took his pupils onto the beach at Allonby, and later the club was allowed to use the track at Derwent Park for practice laps after the main meeting had finished. Maurice's star pupils were Steve Watson, who broke into the Comets' side in 1971, and Ian Hindle from Dalton-in-Furness, who was signed by Belle Vue. Other pupils from the first year included John Carter, Mick Harper, David Moore, Curly Langley, William and Dennis Farish, and Alan and Ian Johnston.

When the new term opened on 1 September 1971, Maurice had his pupils building new jigs to produce a new frame based on the Czechoslovakian Jawa. He also revealed plans to build a training track near his home at Aspatria. Two weeks later, the Forestry Commission agreed to let Maurice build a track on the site of the old No.4 Coal Mine, just off the road to Carlisle. The track would be known as Brayton Domain Speedway.

Maurice and a band of local enthusiasts set about levelling the pit bank and soon the Brayton Domain track was finished. Every Saturday morning volunteers would turn up to prepare the track for the Sunday training sessions. It was quite common to find a couple of the Workington team on hand to offer advice. Ken Vale, Bernie Hornby and Lou Sansom all helped out at Brayton Domain while Maurice recorded the sessions on cine film.

Being a training circuit, no racing was allowed and riders could only go out for practice laps one at a time. To give them some racing experience, Maurice chose four of his most promising pupils and put them into a special race at Derwent Park. If any

Above: *Steve Watson, another protégé from the Bessemer Speedway Club. Steve is seen here practising at Derwent Park in 1971. (Mr Miller)*

Right: *Darrell Stobbart, son of pre-war rider Maurice Stobbart. Darrell was one of the more successful products of his father's training track at Aspatria. (Wright Wood)*

of them showed promise, they were offered regular rides in the second half of the Workington meetings. One rider to benefit was Maurice's own son Darrell. When Dave Kumeta retired towards the end of the 1972 season, Darrell was drafted into the Comets team as his replacement. Current Workington starting marshal, Kenny Fearon, started his riding career at Brayton Domain too and went on to become joint winner of the 350cc Scottish Grass-Track Championships in 1972. Kenny still rides in classic scrambles today. Another Brayton Domain protégé was David Gate (now owner of Gates Tyres). Tony Jackson's excellent *History of Workington Speedway* video has a scene where David crashes at an Eric Boocock training school in 1972 and then gets interviewed for television.

Former Workington and Glasgow star Steve Lawson had just started out in 1973 and in his 1988 testimonial brochure he says that, 'the local training track at Aspatria closed up about then and I only rode there a couple of times'. As so often happens, the initial enthusiasm had started to cool off and the number of pupils at Brayton Domain went into a sharp decline. The track wasn't used much after 1973 and the site is now covered by a small industrial estate.

17

NORTHSIDE SPEEDWAY TRAINING TRACK

One thing you can't fault about the people of West Cumbria is their enthusiasm for speedway racing. When speedway returned to Workington's Derwent Park in 1999, it was inevitable that local youngsters would want to try it for themselves. Derwent Park is not always available and apart from the beach at Allonby, there wasn't anywhere else to practice.

Bernard O'Neill and a hardcore of enthusiasts came up with the idea of an independent training facility. The result is a unique facility in the UK, the Northside Speedway Training Track, at Oldside, Workington.

Built on the site of a former caravan park, Northside took two and half years to complete and cost around £20,000. Local individuals and companies chipped helped with the funding and the club also received £5,000 from the Workington Regeneration Partnership 'Community Chest' towards safety fencing and equipment.

The track was built to Speedway Control Board specifications and each bend has been designed to be a different shape. Some 900 tons of crushed slag and hardcore were laid and rolled to form the base and a further 600 tons of shale has been used for the top dressing. The official length of the circuit is 138m. The straights are 13m wide

The Northside pits – better than some at established league tracks! (Tony Jackson)

One of the juniors making the most of the specially designed bends at Northside. (Tony Jackson)

and the bends extend to 20m at their widest point. The chain-link safety fence is 2m high with tyres to cushion the uprights. The track also boasts a purpose-built covered pits area, which can accommodate twenty bikes.

In July 2002, Colin Meredith, the SCB Track Inspector, gave it his full approval. The necessary track licence was obtained and on the evening of Tuesday 6 August 2002, twelve youngsters christened the circuit. The Northside track was officially opened by Workington captain Carl Stonehewer, who took a spin on the track himself and described it as 'perfect – just the right size and shape'. Four times World Speedway Champion Barry Briggs was also in attendance and gave the track his full approval, commenting that Northside was better than some of the tracks he had ridden during his long and distinguished career.

Being a truly amateur club, racing is not allowed. Bernard's idea was to see young riders take their first tentative rides on a speedway bike at Northside before progressing to the Conference or Premier League (preferably with Workington). Louis Carr and Les and Peter Collins have also visited the circuit and it is hoped that more established speedway riders will come along and run training schools in the future.

Riders who have benefited from the Northside facility so far include Matty Swales (the son of Derwent Park track curator Tony Swales), Craig and John Branney, Kris Irving (the nephew of former Comets 'Jacko' and Des Irving), David Haigh, Keith Langley, Phil Bragg, Jonathan Bethell (a reformed moto-crosser from Kendal) and eight-year-old Sam Irving of Siddick.

Northside speedway is the future of speedway in Cumbria. Long may it continue.

18

ON A DIFFERENT TRACK

There simply aren't enough pages in this book to give you the full story of grass-track racing in Cumbria and Lancashire, so all I can do is give you a few highlights along the way and introduce you to some of the region's great characters and champions.

Immediately after the First World War, there was a tremendous amount of motorcycle-racing activity in the north-west, but the popularity of grass-track and beach racing really began to take off after the ACU banned motorcycle racing on public roads in April 1925. The decision was taken after a number of spectators had been injured (and even killed, in one instance).

Beach races made motorcycle racing accessible to everyone, and sand was one of the safest track surfaces to race on. Events ranged from simple half-mile sprints to twenty-mile, fifty-mile or even one hundred-mile circuit races. Due to the peculiarities of the surface, sand racers had to develop unusual cornering techniques; some of the more spectacular riders 'skidded' their bikes around the corners, a style that was soon adopted on the grass tracks, too. The coastline around Morecambe Bay and along the Solway Firth has been the breeding ground for some very famous riders over the years. A teenage Bill Kitchen had his very first competitive ride at Middleton Sands, as a

Opposite: *Harold Jackson and J.W. Hackett held the sidecar track record at Bolton speedway and also raced at Belle Vue and White City in Manchester. This picture was taken during a sand race at Ernse Bay, Walney Island.*

Right: *Programme from a sand race meeting at Skinburness, 30 June 1928. (Author's collection)*

passenger in Len Slater's sidecar. They actually won their first race together, and Bill became Slater's regular passenger whenever he raced in the north-west.

During the summer season, Blackpool & Fylde Motor Club held speed trials on a half-mile stretch of sand near the old Victoria Pier. In June 1928, over 20,000 spectators lined the promenade in the pouring rain to see Ernie Aspden, 'Dank' McKeowan and George Brough hurl their machines down the beach in treacherous conditions. The summer of 1928 must have been a really wet one, because it was still raining on 28 July when the Lancaster & Morecambe Motor Club held a big sand race meeting at Middleton Sands.

M. Davenport was easily the outstanding rider in the sprint events, but he found himself at a distinct disadvantage during the long-distance races when he could not master his cornering technique on the wet sands. Peter Blundell and Frank Charles were victorious in the two-lap races, whilst R. Sumner and Clarrie Wood ignored the high winds and driving rain to take the honours in the twenty-mile solo championships.

A little further up the coast, Lune Valley Motor Club held sand race meetings on the beach at Hest Bank, near Carnforth. Norman Houlding of Bolton-le-Sands was a prolific trophy winner there between 1925 and 1927. On the opposite side of the bay a young lad named Frank Charles was the undisputed king of the sands around the Furness peninsula, where the Furness Motor Sports Club had been holding speed trials since 1924. Moving further north, Silloth and District Motor Club and the Cumberland County Motor Cycle Club used the wide open sands at the rear of the Skinburness Hotel for their sand race events. Roland Stobbart, Harry Meageen and scrambling legend Billy Tiffen all raced on Skinburness' sands during their formative years.

Sand races and speed trials continued to attract huge crowds throughout the 1930s, but grass-track racing was a branch of motorcycle sport that had yet to capture the imagination of the public. Many of the region's clubs had organised grass-track meetings, but they were usually held as part of a gymkhana or other fund-raising event.

The South Manchester Motor Club were amongst the first to promote grass-track racing as a stand alone sport and had been holding grass-track races at Kingsway since 1926. Many northern folk would also argue that the South Manchester club staged the very first dirt-track meeting in the UK, long before the Ilford club staged their famous meeting at High Beech. The South Manchester meeting was held at Dodds Farm in Droylsden on 25 June 1927. For the first time, a properly constructed cinder track was used and the racing was held in the Australian speedway style: anti-clockwise. Prior to this, it is alleged that the club had organised motorcycle races on a half-mile trotting track at Audenshaw, but these races were held in a clockwise direction and spectators were allowed to bet on the outcome of each race, just like the horse races. Tommy Hatch and Aubrey Todd were amongst the riders who are supposed to have ridden at Audenshaw before it officially opened in March 1928.

At the same time, the equally ambitious North Manchester Motor Club were also organising grass-track races. In atrocious conditions, over 6,000 spectators turned out to see Oliver Langton win the main event at their first meeting in October 1927. Four months later, the club held a grass-track meeting in Belle Vue Gardens, on the same site that would later become the famous Belle Vue speedway track.

Inspired by the success of the Manchester meetings, grass-track racing became more and more popular in the north-west. Cumberland County MCC tried to organise

Cecil O'Loughlin leads a race at Kendal Rugby Field in 1930. (Margaret Duff collection)

Grass-track racing at Levens Hall, 1930. Left to right: Cuthbert Whiteside, Ted Tuer (AJS) and Bill Kitchen (Rudge). The starting marshal is Freddie Brennand. (Margaret Duff collection)

meetings in Carlisle in 1928, but had their thunder stolen by the owners of the Harraby Park Stadium (see the chapter on Carlisle earlier in this book). The Kendal-based Westmorland Motor Club were more successful with their plans and organised grass-track meetings on Kendal Rugby Field, at Mints Feet (now the site of the Lakeland Laundry) and even in the grounds of Levens Hall.

The East Lancashire MCC were behind the races that were held in the field behind the Commercial Inn at Gisburn on every Easter Monday. Joe Abbott, Frank Cotton, Les Martin and Oliver Hart were amongst their most successful competitors. Nelson Gypsy MCC was another very active club in East Lancashire. They held a grass-track meeting at Crow Wood Farm, near Burnley, on 16 June 1929. J.M. Hoyle won both the 350cc and 500cc finals but he lost out to Frank Cotton in the six-lap 'all-comers' race. Four weeks later Nelson Gypsy held another meeting at Nelson itself, where a crowd of around 3,000 saw H. Boys of Blacko win the ten-lap 500cc final on a Rex Acme.

Following the closure of the Highfield Road and St Anne's Road dirt tracks, the Blackpool Motor Cycle & Light Car Club held grass-track meetings at Bennett's Field in Poulton-le-Fylde and at Squires Gate on South Shore (now the site of Blackpool Airport). The Squires Gate events were very popular and regularly attracted crowds of 2,000 or more. Stars from the dirt tracks were invited to appear in match races at Squires Gate, but very often the visitors had to concede defeat to local heroes like Bill Kitchen, Frank Burgess, 'Dank' McKeowan and Joe Abbott. Throughout the early 1930s, Squires Gate was something of a breeding ground for the northern speedway tracks. Jack and Norman Hargreaves were both winning trophies at Squires Gate in the

Blackpool Motor Cycle and Light Car Club Ltd.

(Affiliated to the Auto-Cycle Union, through the North-Western Centre)

GRASS TRACK RACES

Under the General Competition Rules of the A.C.U.

The Stadium, Squires Gate, Blackpool

ON

SUNDAY, AUGUST 18th, 1935,

Commencing 2-30 p.m.   Price 1d.

OFFICIALS OF THE MEETING:

CLERK OF THE COURSE AND SECRETARY OF MEETING	- C. LAW
TIMEKEEPER AND RESULT STEWARD -	- L. S. CONSTABLE
TREASURER - - - - -	- W. T. DEWHURST
COMPETITORS' STEWARD - - -	- G. MORRISON
A.C.U. STEWARD - - - -	- A. TAYLOR

Left: *Programme from Squires Gate, Blackpool, 18 August 1935.*

Opposite: *Lionel Cordingley, star of the 'spiked tyre' class at Scale Hall Speedway, Lancaster. (Stan Cordingley)*

mid-1930s, as were Ernie and Tommy Price, Charlie Oates, Albert 'Aussie' Rosenfeld, Stan, Ron and Oliver Hart, Jack Gordon and Alex Grant. On 4 August 1935, the Blackpool club staged an inter-county team match at Squires Gate, with Lancashire beating their Yorkshire rivals 14-10.

In the summer of 1930, the St Michaels-on-Wyre Sporting Motor Club opened their first ever season with a grass-track meeting at Garstang. The two senior finals turned into a battle between Peter Blundell and Frank Burgess, both from the village of Galgate. Blundell took the honours in the 500cc final with Burgess getting his revenge in the handicap final.

Probably the biggest and best known meetings in the region during the 1930s were held by the Lancaster & Morecambe Bay MC. Their track was at Scale Hall Farm, on the outskirts of Lancaster. Locally known as the Scale Hall Speedway, the track was actually a very bumpy 500-yard grass-track oval, but it was a regular pilgrimage for riders and fans alike.

Lionel Cordingley was one of the star men in the 'spiked tyre' class at Scale Hall and also held the 500cc track record during 1931. Frank Burgess and Bill Kitchen usually dominated the 350cc and 500cc events during the early 1930s and both won the annual Scale Hall Golden Helmet. Maurice Stobbart recalled one meeting in 1930 where his elder brother Roland was inadvertently entered into a race with the spiked tyre brigade. Roland was on his dirt-track Rudge fitted with normal grass-track tyres, but by holding the inside line and gently sliding his back wheel he beat all of them. Spiked tyres and other 'anti-skid devices' were banned by the ACU in 1931 when they decided it was time to introduce special regulations for grass-track racing.

Maurice also recalls his very first grass-track meeting at Scale Hall; he was only fifteen. The organisers got Roland and Maurice mixed up, leaving Maurice with all the hard races! Even so, he managed to reach the final only to be beaten by his elder brother. In his second meeting at Scale Hall, Maurice actually beat Bill Kitchen, his first notable scalp! The fields at Scale Hall Farm have long since vanished beneath a vast housing estate and a school, but the original farmhouse still survives and is now a public house.

The Lancaster & Morecambe club also organised grass-track meetings at the annual Garstang Agricultural Show. In 1931, the 350cc event was won by local champion Bill Kitchen, with Jim Quarmby taking the honours in the 500cc class. Bill Kitchen continued to dominate the Garstang races, winning the senior final in 1933 and the Grade 'A' final in 1935.

The outbreak of the Second World War brought a complete halt to grass-track and sand-racing in the north-west. The Belle Vue track in Manchester continued to hold speedway meetings throughout the war, but fans had to wait until 1946 for the return of any grass-track or beach racing in Cumberland, Westmorland or Lancashire.

The years immediately after the war were some of the best for grass-track racing in Lancashire. Crowds of over 5,000 were commonplace, even at the smallest events, and whilst the 1950s saw the popularity of grass-track racing decline in many regions, it remained very popular in the North-Western Centre.

Ken Mellor, from Leeds, was a regular competitor at Lancashire grass-track meetings and recalls how the sport developed alongside horse races at the agricultural shows. Pony harness racing has always been popular in the Dales and local farmers were always keen to make a few extra pennies by running an unofficial book. The organisers realised that motorcycle races would not only give the farmers more scope for wagers, but also keep the beer tent busy too! The Ribble Valley MCC were one of the first clubs to get in on the act. Their first meeting was at Poolford Farm, Blackburn, on 15 August 1947. Grass-track races were also held at the Giggleswick Agricultural show, near Settle and at the Great Eccleston Agricultural Show, near Garstang.

Three of the biggest meetings in the Dales were at Kilnsey in Wharfedale, Low Row in Swaledale and Bainbridge in Wensleydale. The Bainbridge meetings were held at Lamberts Field, just outside of Hawes. Many competitors considered this to be the 'Daddy' of all the northern grass tracks and it had a reputation for being a fast track, too. Speeds of over 75mph were possible on the straights. The pony galloping and trotting races would start around lunch time and the bike races would get going about 5 p.m. The track was a 500-yard oval with long straights and sweeping bends. If the conditions were right and the horses had cut the track up sufficiently, the circuit would be more like a speedway track than a grass track.

A typical sand racing bike from the 1940s. This particular 500cc BSA was raced by Jim Scott. (John Fisher)

Next Sunday Afternoon, August 17th, 1947, at 2-30 p.m.
Grass Track Speedway Races
at CLIFTON ROAD, (behind Co-op Bakery), BLACKPOOL.
ORGANISED BY BLACKPOOL MOTOR CYCLE & CAR CLUB.   Have a ride to Blackpool and see some Good Racing.

Above: *Advertisement for 'Grass-Track Speedway' at Blackpool in 1947.*

Right: *Programme from Helsington Laithes, Kendal. (Author's collection)*

WESTMORLAND   MOTOR   CLUB

THE   HANDLEY   TROPHY

GRASS TRACK RACES

A Restricted Competition to be held under the
General Competition Rules of the Auto-Cycle Union.
AT
HELSINGTON, NEAR KENDAL
ON
THURSDAY, JUNE 28th, 1951
at 7-0 p.m.

Northern Centre Restricted Permit No.   (applied for)

OFFICIAL PROGRAMME - - Price 6d.
Judge, J. H. LAFONE.
A.C.U. Steward : T. Burrow.   Starter : B. A. Crabtree.
Competitors' Marshal : R. Cannon.   Paddock Marshal, L. M. Gorton.
Timekeepers :
L. Pickthall, J. Woodburn, B. Dixon, J. F. Gillham, Doug. Mallinson.
Chief Course Marshal : T. W. Hodgson.
Course Marshals : Members of W.M.C.
Programme Steward and Hon. Treasurer of Meeting : G. W. Dodds.
Sportscasting : W. Aspinwall, Windermere.

WESTMORLAND MOTOR CLUB
Hon. Trials Secretary : T. W. HODGSON, The Laurels, Spital Park, Kendal.
Hon. Secretary, L. M. GORTON, 14, Calgarth Road, Windermere.
Hon. Treasurer : G. W. DODDS, 22, Kendal Green, Kendal.

NOTICE !   WARNING TO THE PUBLIC ! !
Motor Racing is DANGEROUS, and Spectators attending this Track do so entirely
at their own risk. " It is a condition of admission that all persons having any connection
with the promotion and/or organisation and/or conduct of the meeting, including the owners
of the land and the Drivers and owners of vehicles and passengers in the vehicles, are
absolved from any liability arising out of accidents causing damage or personal injury to
Spectators or Ticket Holders."
This Course is on private land, and the Westmorland Motor Club is indebted to the
owner and tenant.
Spectators are requested not to break down fences or otherwise damage any property
MANY   THANKS

Westmorland Gazette Ltd., Printers, Kendal.

Not all grass-track meetings were held at agricultural shows, though. The Blackpool Motor Cycle and Car Club held grass-track meetings on the football ground at Pilling, a venue that was also used extensively by the Fleetwood Motor Cycle and Car Club. John Ogden recalls a meeting on the Rugby Field at Lea in June 1951, organised by the Preston and District MCC. There was a real 'Battle of the Roses' between Lancashire's Jim Baybutt and Yorkshire butcher, Eric Carr. Baybutt had narrowly beaten Carr in the 500cc final only for Carr to get his revenge in the unlimited final. The stage was all set for a big show down in the final race of the day, but it turned into a bit of an anti-climax. Carr fell on the first lap and Baybutt's engine packed up on the second lap, leaving Naaman Baldwin to win the race ahead of another local hero, Jack Barrowclough.

The post-war years had seen real progress in the Northern Centre of the ACU, too. The old established clubs in Westmorland and Cumberland had reformed and two new clubs arrived on the scene in Whitehaven and Penrith. Apart from organising social runs, trials and hill climbs, the Westmorland Motor Club had been offered the use of farmland at Helsington Laithes for scrambles and grass-track racing. The land was just off the old A6 main road and was owned by the Martin family, who just happened to be club members. Helsington was a regular venue for grass-track meetings right through the 1950s and only stopped when the new Kendal by-pass was constructed in the early 1960s.

Racing at Helsington Laithes. Amongst the riders in this picture are Billy Milburn, Alan Thornton and John Airey. (Margaret Duff collection)

Furness and District Motor Club were great supporters of grass-track racing and organised meetings on the Strawberry Ground, near the junction of Abbey Road and Strawberry Lane in Barrow-in-Furness. A record 5,000 crowd saw Robin Clinch win the Harold Jackson Cup there on 21 May 1952. Barrow & District MCC also held regular meetings on the field at the rear of the Crown Hotel at North Scale on Walney Island. Amongst the competitors were veterans Hugh Tatham and Tommy Simpson, who had both ridden at the Barrow Speedway before the war. The Wigton Motor Club held a couple of grass-track meetings in the early 1950s, too, on the site of an old airfield near to the Wigton to Thursby road.

The Whitehaven Motor Club started in 1947 and originally organised scrambles meetings in Overend Quarry at Hensingham, but by 1952 they were also holding grass-track races high above the town on Harras Moor. The track, at Standing Stones Farm, was a spectacular venue with views of the Lake District Fells in one direction and the Irish Sea in the other. On 15 August 1954, the Whitehaven Motor Club had the honour of organising the first Northern Centre Championship at Church House Farm, Calderbridge. F. Hetherington of Brough & District MCC won the 250cc class, Angus Tyson of Barrow & District MCC won the 251-350cc class and Billy Milburn of the Westmorland Motor Club took the top honours in the unlimited class.

Without a doubt, the club that did most for grass-track racing in the region during the post-war years was the North Lancashire Motor Club. Formed in the late 1930s, the club originally held social runs and reliability trials. The club reformed in 1946, and throughout the 1950s, organised scrambles and grass-track meetings at Warton, near Carnforth. The track was just west of the Carnforth to Barrow railway line and near to the unmanned level crossing. The track had several fairly large humps in it and included the face of a small hillock on one straight.

Right: *Grass-track racers from the Whitehaven Motor Club. Left to right: Joe Wood, Tom McLaughlin, Tom Wightman and Eddie Thornborrow. (Glenn Hinde)*

Below: *Racing at Harras Moor, Whitehaven, 1952. (Glenn Hinde)*

Top: *Gilbert 'Smoky' Dawson of Far Sawrey, near Coniston. Smoky was one of the top scrambles men in the Northern Centre, but never really managed to repeat his success on the grass. (Glenn Hinde)*

Below: *Tommy Butler of Ulverston. (Glenn Hinde)*

Top: *Doug Chapman of Bentham, near Lancaster. A classic 'leg-trailer' in action at Warton. (David Alderson)*

Below: *An unidentified rider at Warton in June 1951. (David Alderson)*

Jim Baybutt was one of the top riders at Warton and used the same white painted Rudge/JAP for solo and sidecar races. To enable the sidecar to be removed or refitted quickly, Jim had all the nuts and bolts colour coded! His wife, Millie, was his sidecar passenger and his eldest son, David, rode a miniature bike around the circuit during the interval. He wore his father's helmet with a handkerchief stuffed inside to make it fit. Another successful competitor at Warton was Gilbert Walker, who lived in the village itself. Gilbert used to turn up on race day with his 500cc Velocette propped up on the back of an ancient stake truck.

The 1951 North-Western Centre Championship was held at Warton on 16 September, the final being won by Naaman Baldwin, a real crowd favourite from Blackpool and one of the few Jewish riders to have ridden grass-track or speedway. Naaman rode the 'Golden Eagle', a 350cc JAP-engined special with Norton front forks and painted in a metallic bronze colour. He also wore nut-brown leathers and a helmet painted to match his bike. In second place was Ted Ogden from Heywood. Ted was also a top scrambler and represented Great Britain in the Motocross Des Nations during the same year. Ted rode a 'works' Featherbed Norton, developed from Geoff Dukes' famous road-racing machine. Eric Carr finished third and Jack Barrowclough was fourth. Andy Courtney and A.R. Eastwood failed to finish in the muddy conditions.

North-Western Centre Championships at Warton, 16 September 1952. First place – Naaman Baldwin (10), second place – Ted Ogden. (David Alderson)

Naaman Baldwin had also tried his hand at speedway, starting in second-half races at Fleetwood in 1948 and somehow ending up as team manager a couple of years later! When Fleetwood closed down in 1952, Naaman had the starting gate removed to Warton. By the end of the 1950s, the Warton site was no longer available for grass tracks and the club moved to a new venue at Quay Meadows in Lancaster. The track was behind some buildings on St Georges Quay and the pits were right up against the arches of the railway viaduct. The circuit itself was a perfect 350-yard oval and meetings were usually held once a month on Saturday evenings.

Ken Mellor has vivid memories of the 1958 North Lancashire Championship meeting at Quay Meadows, where he maintains he was robbed of victory! Ken had gained maximum points in all of his qualifying races, but, in the final, he was left at the start when his nearest rival, Eric Carr, 'anticipated' the flag and got off to a flyer. Ken finally finished second, but he still insists that the flag marshal was at fault for not restarting the race and that he was 'too gentlemanly in remaining on the line until the flag actually fell'!

By the mid-1960s the popularity of grass-track racing was in decline. In fact, motorcycle sport as a whole was going through a tough time. Cars were becoming more affordable and the 'Mods and Rockers' scene had tarnished the image of the genuine motorcycle enthusiast. Quite a few motorcycle clubs had folded through a lack of numbers, and those that survived tended to concentrate on scrambles or trials. Some even changed their emphasis to car events. Nevertheless, a few die-hard enthusiasts were determined not to let grass-track racing fade away completely.

Despite losing their best track at Helsington, the Westmorland Motor Club continued to promote grass-track meetings at Levens and Heversham right through the 1960s, but they were not alone. A new club was formed in 1962, specifically to promote grass-track racing in Lancashire. The Lancashire Grass-Track Riders Club was the brainchild of Harry Draper, an all-round motorcyclist from Chorley. Amongst the founding members were Cliff Walmsley, a veteran from the Ribble Valley MCC, Jim Meadows, another all rounder from Pilling and Jim Baybutt, the star rider from the North Lancashire meetings at Warton and Quay Meadows.

Jim Baybutt was a larger than life character, who had been riding motorcycles since he was a boy. After the war he took up car and bike racing, even racing in the Isle of Man TT, but his greatest passion was grass-track racing, a passion that he passed down to his sons, David and Chris.

David made his grass-track debut in the first meeting of the Lancashire Grass-Track Riders Club when he was only fifteen. Riding a 250cc Greeves scrambler, he finished third in the 250cc class. David also rode in a meeting at Bainbridge in 1962, where he reached the 250cc final again. When Mrs Lambert, wife of the landowner, remarked that he must have come to collect his father's prize, David replied 'Oh no, this ones mine!'. By mid-1964, David had won his first final and was almost unbeatable in the LGTRC 250cc class.

Dave Baybutt went on to become one of the UK's greatest grass-track riders, winning the British 350cc and 500cc titles in 1966, but his career very nearly came to a premature end in October of that year. David had taken up speedway and joined the

Sidecar racing at Warton. Left to right: Jim and Millie Baybutt, Tom Parkinson of Lancaster and Roy Cunliffe. The starting marshal is Alan Smith. (Margaret Duff collection)

Belle Vue team. He made a promising start, scoring 7 points in his first 3 matches, but on his final outing, David laid his bike down to avoid the fallen Taffy Owen. As he got to his feet, another rider ploughed into him, leaving David with a badly injured left arm. After eighteen months out of the saddle, David made a quiet comeback in an LGTRC meeting at Accrington and by the end of the season he was riding better than ever. Despite the fact that his left arm was now virtually useless and he was suffering with asthma, he won the 1968 LGTRC 250cc championship and finished third in the 350cc class. He went on to win the British 250cc Championships on four occasions: 1969, 1973, 1979 and 1981, his final year on the grass.

Like his elder brother, Chris Baybutt also made an underage debut, riding at Accrington under the pseudonym of Fred Dean. Chris was another 'chip off the old block', winning numerous LGTRC and British Championships, and becoming the first ever European Grass-Track Champion in 1978. Chris also tried his hand at speedway, having a few rides for Nelson in 1969. He was rumoured to be joining Barrow in 1972, but once he had passed his surveying degree he opted against a career on the shale.

Over the years the Lancashire Grass-Track Riders Club reads like a 'who's who' of track racing. 1976 World Speedway Champion Peter Collins is probably the most famous, but who could forget the spectacular Chris Pusey and his younger brothers, Geoff and Steve from Maghull. Then there was former Ellesmere Port speedway rider Paul Tyrer, who was named as the club's 'Most Improved Rider' in 1969. Tom Owen, the 1970 and 1971 Northern Centre Champion and his younger brother Joey from

Ormskirk, and last but not least, Derek and Keith Evans from Rochdale, who both won North-West Centre Championships in 1971.

All good things must come to an end, however, and the Lancashire club eventually folded, but not before a junior off-shoot of the club was formed, 'to give the kids something better to do other than trying to eliminate each other with air rifles'!

Charlie Newsham, Bob Jones, Jack Carr, Dave Harrison and Tony Clarke were all involved in the early stages of the Lancashire Grass-Track Junior Riders Club (LGTJRC) and the very first meeting took place on bonfire night 1971, at a place called Croston, near Leyland. About twenty riders turned up with a variety of machines, ranging from BSA Bantams to 250cc C15s. David Harrison remembers the evening well, 'it rained in bucket loads!' A big bonfire had been lit before the racing had started, but some dads were still dragging bikes out of the mud long after the fire had gone out.

The club really got going in 1972 and prospered during the 1970s and '80s. At one point, the club had attracted so many members from neighbouring counties that they had to split the club into three sections covering Lancashire, Yorkshire and Cheshire. Eventually, the Yorkshire section went their own way and the LGTJRC started to run adult classes too, a decision that still raises eyebrows in certain quarters.

Some of the best grass-track and speedway riders in the country have passed through the ranks of the LGTJRC: Les Phil, Neil and Stephen Collins (their sister Ann had a few outings too), Louis and Peter Carr from Preston, 1990 World Speedway Champion Gary

Chris Baybutt from Wrightington, near Wigan on his 500cc Elstar.

215

Top: *Brian Havelock on the outside of Graham Isherwood at the Kendal Long Track meeting in 1972. (Margaret Duff collection)*

Below: *Chris Pusey leads eventual winner, Peter Collins at Kendal, 23 April 1972. (Margaret Duff collection)*

Havelock, England internationals Joe Screen and Andy Smith, Workington Speedway captain Carl Stonehewer and current LGTJRC chairman, Graham Lowe.

The Westmorland Motor Club introduced long-track racing to the north-west on 23 April 1972. A huge crowd gathered for a superb meeting, eventually won by Peter Collins after a terrific tussle with the spectacular Chris Pusey.

Percy Duff was the club secretary at the time and can remember approaching the local show committee about the possibility of staging a motorcycle race on the Westmorland County Showground trotting track. After an initially cool response, the committee eventually agreed. From a racing point of view, the meeting was a complete success and Percy will freely admit that 'it was probably the most exciting event ever held by the club', but the bikes completely destroyed the track. The half-mile circuit was made up of crushed hardcore and most of it ended up spread all over the arena. The show committee were horrified at the damage and stated there and then that motorcycles would never be allowed onto the track again. The Westmorland County Showground was eventually sold for redevelopment and a Morrisons supermarket now stands on the site.

Full results from the meeting were as follows:

Qualifying scores after thirty heats:
Peter Collins (Hagon/JAP) 15pts; Cyril Jones (Elstar/JAP) 13; David Baybutt (Cole/Elstar) 12; Doug Brankley (Hagon/JAP), Chris Pusey (CPS) and Brian Havelock (Maxmade/Jawa) 11; Mike Fishwick (Jawa), Graham Peel (Hagon) and Ken Raw (Comet) 10; Mike Beaumont (Comet) and Tom Owen (Hagon) 9; Maurice Wilson (Frog) and Geoff Pusey (CPS) 7.

1st Semi-Final	D. Baybutt; D. Brankley; M. Fishwick.
2nd Semi-Final	P. Collins; C. Pusey; M. Beaumont.
Final	1st Peter Collins; 2nd Chris Pusey; 3rd Dave Baybutt; 4th Mike Fishwick; 5th Mike Beaumont. (Doug Brankley did not finish)

The Fleetwood & District Motorcycle Club were behind another long-track meeting on Saturday 19 August 1972. The venue was Fluke Hall, near Pilling, and the circuit was laid out on Preesall Sands. Tom Owen was the star of the show, scoring maximum points in his heats and winning the race for the President's Trophy. The meeting also featured his younger brother Joe, Maurice Wilson from Kendal, and Brian Havelock, the Teesside speedway rider.

Following the relaunch of Speedway at Holker Street Stadium in 1972, the Barrow & District MCC made an attempt to reintroduce grass-track racing to the area with a meeting at Peasholme Farm, Rampside. Keith Evans of the LGTRC cleaned up in the 250cc class and Alan Wilkinson, the Belle Vue speedway rider from nearby Ulverston, won the 500cc final on a bike he'd borrowed from Ian Hindle. Tom Owen had been the outstanding rider of the day, but he sheared a back sprocket in his last qualifying heat and could only in finish fourth place in the 500cc final, also riding a borrowed bike.

In July 1972 Cliff Hindle organised a sand race on the shore at Askam-in-Furness as part of a gala day for the Duddon Inshore Rescue Team. Tom Owen and Alan Wilkinson took part in the demonstration races, as did Cliff's son, Ian. Cliff also used the beach at Askam to train youngsters from his Barrow Speedway track. Probably his most famous pupil was Mark Courtney, who lived in Workington at the time. Further up the coast, the beach at Allonby has long been a favourite venue for riders to practice too. Steve Watson, Andy Reid, Des Wilson, Jacko Irving, Darrel Stobbart and Geoff Powell have all trained there at some point. In recent years, Craig and John Branney have ridden there, too. In January 1988 Steve Lawson organised an unofficial team match on the beach behind his farm at Allonby. The match between Lawson's Louts and Courtney's Crusaders ended with a 41-37 win for the 'home' side, which also included Geoff Powell and Shaun Bickley. A return match was held in the north-east on 7 February.

Speedway returned to Workington in 1970 and three young grass trackers, Maurice Wilson, Tony Sharpe and Alan Bradley, were amongst the trialists. Maurice was actually picked to ride for the team in their opening-night challenge against Berwick, scoring 2 points for the Comets. Maurice was also behind the formation of another new grass-track club in the Northern Centre, the Lakes Grass-Track Racing Club, and with the help of his brother Graham, they have ensured that grass-track racing has continued to prosper in Cumbria.

Maurice's son Ian followed in his father's tyre tracks during the 1980s, while Graham's son, Scott, is the only member of the famous Lakeland family still racing, although in April 2002 it looked like his career had come to a premature end. Scott's

Scott Wilson, the only member of the famous Lakeland family still racing competitively. (Author's collection)

John Pepper is one of the most successful riders to have emerged from the Lakes grass-track scene. (Author's collection)

van was broken into and two engines, all of his racing gear and another engine belonging to Stuart Dent were stolen. Luckily, a sponsor has come forward with a new engine, his father has offered him the use of his old leathers and his family has bought him a new helmet. Scott started the 2003 season in sparkling form. He was unbeaten in seven races at Congleton in June and was chosen to represent Great Britain in 2003 European Grass-Track Championships.

Probably the two most successful grass-track riders to have emerged from the Lake's club in recent years are John Pepper and Jason Handley. John started out in motocross (read 'scrambles', if you are over forty!) before progressing to sand-racing in 1984. John missed out on the 1984 British Sand-Racing championship by a single point, but made amends by winning the event in 1985, 1986, 1987, 1989 and 1990. He had to miss out on the 1988 championship after sustaining an injury racing grass track.

John had taken up grass-track racing in 1984 and won the Northern Centre 250cc championship in 1985, the last year that motocross and grass-track bikes were allowed to compete side by side. In 1986 he bought his first proper grass-track machine and two years later he purchased the first official Nu-Trak frame from Dave Lord in Farnworth. The Nu-Trak took him to victory in the 1990 and 1991 250cc Northern Centre Championships and with a new 250cc Kawasaki engine, supplied by Mick Barker, he won the championship again in 1992 and 1993. Mounted on a 500cc Nu-Trak Jawa, John won the Northern Riders Championship in 2000 and 2001.

Like John, Jason Handley progressed to grass-track from motocross. His first grass-track meeting was at Pickering in 1991, where he won a special race for motocross machines. Maurice Wilson saw him at that meeting and offered him the use of his own 350cc machine for a Lake's club meeting. Jason turned down the offer, but bought his own 500cc Antig/Weslake grass-track bike before his next outing at Pickering. He won his very first race, but was then excluded from the final when an official noticed he was wearing motocross gear. John Pepper came forward with a spare pair of leathers and after a quick change Jason promptly went out and won the novice race.

With the purpose of getting more rides, Jason bought a 350cc bike too, a move that paid dividends when he won the 1996 British 350cc title at Minsterley in Shropshire and qualified for the European Championships. Jason missed out on the entire 1997 season after an accident at the family haulage business. He fell from the back of a lorry onto the concrete floor, breaking his pelvis in three places. After five agonising weeks in hospital, the doctors informed Jason that he would never be able to race motorcycles again, but he proved them all wrong by coming back stronger than ever.

That comeback was on 5 April 1998 at a Cheshire Club meeting. Even though Jason had to be lifted on and off his bike, he managed to win two races, beating Tony Atkin (the Cheshire champion) in the process and ended the season by taking his second British 350cc title. Jason now has four 350cc titles to his name, winning the title again in 2001 and 2002. He has never really considered speedway as a career even though he has ridden after the meeting at Middlesborough and also ridden one of Roy Young's bikes on the beach at Allonby. In his own words, 'speedway tracks are just too slick!'

Representing the ACU Northern Centre, Scott Wilson, John Pepper and Jason Handley entered the 1998 British Team Championships as rank outsiders and won every heat to become champions. Despite all of his individual successes, John rates this as his most satisfying result, not only because the Lake's trio had been written off before the meeting, but because it was a real team effort.

The talented Jason Handley, four times British 350cc champion, in full flight at Heversham. (Author's collection)

Paul Bickley and Paul Silvera in action at Southfields Farm, Appleby. (Author's collection)

The 'Rivington Barnstormers' were born in 1998, with the intention of organising one big grass-track meeting every year in the Wigan area. With Dave Baybutt, Tony Clarke and former LGTJRC champion Geoff Warwick on the committee, plus the added bonus of some excellent prize money, they should have had a winning formula. But to date, events have conspired against them and only two meetings have ever been staged. 1998 was one of the wettest summers on record and the proposed track became so waterlogged that they had to postpone their plans for twelve months. The 1999 meeting, held on 26 September at Haigh, nearly went the same way when a torrential downpour hit the track just before the start. After a short delay, the track was declared fit for racing and Cheshire champion Tony Atkin took top honours in the 500cc final. Ricky Scarboro beat fifteen-year-old James Mann in the 350cc final and the Jim Baybutt Memorial Trophy was awarded to James Complin, for being the 'lap scorer's rider of the day'.

A second meeting was held at the same circuit on 24 September 2000, but any chance of running a third meeting in 2001 was scuppered by the Foot and Mouth epidemic and a lack of available riders put paid to a meeting in 2002.

The Lake's GTRC has had a tough time over the past few years. Following changes on the committee, only one meeting was held in 2000, at Southfields Farm, Appleby, on 1 October. As usual, Jason Handley dominated the 350cc and 500cc solo classes, with Rod Winterburn of Colne winning the sidecar class ahead of Egremont's Paul Bickley. The Foot and Mouth epidemic put paid to any Lake's meetings in 2001 and, despite promises of a big comeback, only one meeting was held in 2002 with Jason Handley winning the 500cc and unlimited events and Dave Norris taking the honours in the 350cc and 2-valve classes.

Some of the Lake's riders have been travelling up to Scotland, where there has been a recent resurgence in grass-track racing. Stephen Morris came out of semi-retirement to win the Scottish Open Championship on 13 July 2002 with compatriot Scott Wilson taking the honours in the 500cc class. Another Lakelander, Stuart Dent, won the Pre-75 Championships.

The LGTJRC continues to go from strength to strength and in June 2003 they had the honour of staging the British 250cc/350cc and 500cc Sidecar Championships, the first time the meeting has been held in the north. Pre-meeting favourite Jason Handley missed out on a fifth 350cc crown and could only finish in third place. The class was won by Paul Cooper with Adam Shipp taking the honours in the 250cc event. The club holds meetings on a regular basis, using tracks at Hambleton, Much Hoole and Wythenshawe Park in Manchester. The club introduced an adult 'novice class' in 1998, which has proved quite popular. Andrew Constantine from Morecambe won the inaugural title, and Bill Brown from Whitehaven won the title in 2001. Bill found it frustrating sitting in the pits while his young son Robert was out riding, so he got himself a grass bike and just went out to enjoy himself. Another notable name from the past making a spirited 'comeback' in the LGTJRC 'novice' races is former Nelson and Barrow Speedway rider, Sid Sheldrick.

The Lancashire club have introduced classes for pre-75 and motocross machines now, and even run an amateur speedway class at the Buxton track in Derbyshire. The club's latest 'discoveries' include Lee Hodgson, who has ridden speedway for Sheffield,

Jack Hargreaves (22) leads Joshua Auty (8) at Much Hoole, near Preston. Jack was the LGTJRC Intermediate champion in 2002.

John Pepper leads Cheshire's Daniel Winterton at Southfields Farm, Appleby. (Author's collection)

Stoke and Workington, and brothers Lee and James Complin. Lee was one of the most naturally gifted young riders to emerge from the youth grass-track scene in recent years, but he sensationally quit racing at the start of 2003, citing personal reasons for his decision. Let's hope we haven't seen the last of him.

The next generation of youngsters is already beginning to make an impression. Robert Brown (the son of Bill Brown) has been producing some impressive performances after some coaching sessions from Andy Smith and multi-World Champion Barry Briggs. Adam Roynon, the son of former Barrow rider and promoter Chris Roynon, is incredibly keen and has been seen putting in practice laps the length and breadth of the country. Adam underlined his exceptional talent when he finished second to Jack Hargreaves in the youth event at Hollands Exloo indoor speedway in January 2003 and has since ridden for the England under-16s Speedway team. Another Cumbrian youngster who made his grass-track debut in 2001 was Martin Emerson, the son of former Workington and Middlesborough speedway rider, Alan Emerson. With dedication, enthusiasm and talent abound, the future of track racing in Cumbria and Lancashire looks to be in safe hands.

Other Speedway Titles Available from Tempus

07524-3225-7	Breaking the Limits: Sam Ermolenko Story	Brian Burford & Sam Ermolenko	£14.99
07524-2231-6	Bristol Bulldogs	Dave Woods & Geoff Rose	£10.99
07524-2865-9	Bristol Bulldogs Speedway (50 Greats)	Robert Bamford & Glynn Shailes	£10.99
07524-2727-X	Clay Country Speedway	Robert Bamford & Dave Stallworthy	£14.99
07524-2406-8	The Story of Grass-Track Racing	Robert Bamford	£12.99
07524-2838-1	Grass Track Racing 1950–1965	Robert Bamford & Dave Stallworthy	£14.99
07524-2737-7	Hackney Speedway: Friday at Eight	Chris Fenn	£14.99
07524-2438-6	Hammerin' Round: Speedway in the East End	Brain Belton	£12.99
07524-2738-5	Heathens: Cradley Heath Speedway 1977–96	Peter Foster	£14.99
07524-2704-0	Heathens: Cradley Heath Speedway 1947–76	Peter Foster	£14.99
07524-2210-3	Homes of British Speedway	Robert Bamford & John Jarvis	£17.99
07524-3200-1	Hull Speedway 1930–81	Roger Hulbert	£16.99
07524-2424-6	The Moran Brothers	Brian Burford	£14.99
07524-3152-8	Norwich Speedway	Norman Jacobs & Mike Kemp	£12.99
07524-2856-X	Peter Craven: Wizard of Balance	Brian Burford	£14.99
07524-2433-5	Southampton Speedway	Paul Eustace	£10.99
07524-1882-3	Speedway in East Anglia	Norman Jacobs	£14.99
07524-2221-9	Speedway in London	Norman Jacobs	£14.99
07524-3000-9	Speedway in Manchester 1927–1945	T. James	£14.99
07524-3192-7	Speedway in the North-West	Adrian Pavey	£14.99
07524-2229-4	Speedway in Scotland	Jim Henry	£14.99
07524-2725-3	Speedway in the South-East	Norman Jacobs	£14.99
07524-2915-9	Speedway in the South West	Tony Lethbridge	£14.99
07524-2408-4	Speedway in the Thames Valley	Robert Bamford & Glynn Shailes	£16.99
07524-2701-6	Speedway in Wales	Andrew Weltch	£12.99
07524-2749-0	Speedway the Pre-War Years	Robert Bamford & Dave Stallworthy	£14.99
07524-2596-X	Speedway Through the Lens of Mike Patrick	Mike Patrick	£17.99
07524-2748-2	Swindon Speedway (50 Greats)	Robert Bamford & Glynn Shailes	£12.99
07524-2955-8	Tempus Speedway Yearbook 2004	Robert Bamford (Ed)	£17.99
07524-2873-X	White Ghost: The Ken Le Breton Story	Jon Jon White	£12.99
07524-2402-5	World Speedway Chamionship: A History of the World Speedway Chamionship	Robert Bamford & Glynn Shailes	£14.99

If you are interested in purchasing other books published by Tempus,
or in case you have difficulty finding any Tempus books in your local bookshop,
you can also place orders directly through our website

www.tempus-publishing.com

or from

BOOKPOST, Freepost, PO Box 29, Douglas, Isle of Man IM99 1BQ
Tel 01624 836000 email bookshop@enterprise.net